Twenty Plays of the Nō Theatre

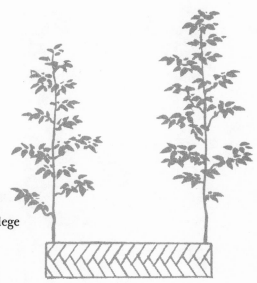

Prepared for the Columbia College
Program of Translations from
the Oriental Classics
Wm. Theodore de Bary, Editor

NUMBER LXXXV OF THE *Records of Civilization:
Sources and Studies* EDITED UNDER THE AUSPICES OF THE
DEPARTMENT OF HISTORY, COLUMBIA UNIVERSITY

Twenty Plays

of the Nō Theatre

EDITED BY DONALD KEENE

WITH THE ASSISTANCE OF ROYALL TYLER

Illustrated with drawings by Fukami Tanrō
and from the Hōshō Texts

COLUMBIA UNIVERSITY PRESS

NEW YORK

Donald Keene is Professor of Japanese at Columbia University and is the translator of *Major Plays of Chikamatsu* and *Essays in Idleness*.

UNESCO COLLECTION OF REPRESENTATIVE WORKS
JAPANESE SERIES
This book
has been accepted
in the Japanese Series
of the Translations Collection
of the United Nations
Educational, Scientific and Cultural Organization
(UNESCO)

Portions of this work were prepared under a contract with the U.S. Office of Education for the production of texts to be used in undergraduate education. The draft translations so produced have been used in the Columbia College Oriental Humanities program and have subsequently been revised and expanded for publication in the present form.

Records of Civilization: Sources and Studies

Edited under the auspices of the Department of History, Columbia University

GENERAL EDITOR

W. T. H. Jackson, *Professor of German and History*

PAST EDITORS

1915–1926 James T. Shotwell, *Bryce Professor Emeritus of the History of International Relations*
1926–1953 Austin P. Evans, *Professor of History*
1953–1962 Jacques Barzun, *Seth Low Professor of History*

EDITOR: ORIENTAL RECORDS

Wm. Theodore de Bary, *Horace Walpole Carpentier Professor of Oriental Studies*

CONSULTING EDITORS: ORIENTAL RECORDS

Ainslie T. Embree, *Professor of History, Duke University*
Chih-tsing Hsia, *Associate Professor of Chinese*
Donald Keene, *Professor of Japanese*
Ivan Morris, *Professor of Japanese*
Burton Watson, *Associate Professor of Chinese*
C. Martin Wilbur, *Professor of Chinese History*

EDITOR: EUROPEAN RECORDS

W. T. H. Jackson, *Professor of German and History*

CONSULTING EDITORS: EUROPEAN RECORDS

Gerson D. Cohen, *Associate Professor of History*
Gilbert Highet, *Anthon Professor of the Latin Language and Literature*
Gerhart B. Ladner, *Professor of History, University of California, Los Angeles*
Paul O. Kristeller, *Professor of Philosophy*
John H. Mundy, *Professor of History on the Mathews Foundation*
Jacob W. Smit, *Queen Wilhelmina Lecturer and Associate Professor of Germanic Languages*

DEDICATED TO THE MEMORY OF
Etienne Dolet

BURNT AT THE STAKE IN 1546
FOR A MISTRANSLATION

FOREWORD

Twenty Plays of the Nō Theatre is one of the Translations from
the Oriental Classics by which the Committee on Oriental Studies
has sought to transmit to Western readers representative works of
the major Asian traditions in thought and literature. Our intention is to provide translations based on scholarly study but written
for the general reader rather than primarily for other specialists.

The addition of twenty Nō plays to the number available in
English translation is a considerable fact in itself. What makes it
doubly significant is the nature of the project which has produced
them. For several years this series has benefited from support by
the U.S. Office of Education, encouraging the production of texts
and translations for use in American college education. At the
same time the NDEA fellowship program administered by that
office has supported the training of a new generation of scholars
in foreign area studies. Many of the young scholars whose work is
represented in this volume have benefited from that support, as
well as from the guidance of Professor Keene, who has edited
their translations and is making them available to a wider public.
It is gratifying to see the results of that language training bear
fruit in works that will contribute further to the educational
aims of the National Defense Education Act.

WM. THEODORE DE BARY

ix

PREFACE

Western scholarship on Japanese drama is at last reaching the level of maturity. The first popular books about the Japanese theatre have been succeeded by more specialized works, and the way is open for studies that will illuminate not only the Japanese but also the Western dramatic arts. The chief obstacle to general appreciation of the Japanese drama is the insufficiency of translations that are both reliable and readable. In the case of the Nō plays, the glory of the entire Japanese theatre, it is still necessary to depend for the most part on translations made fifty years ago, before modern Japanese scholarship had made possible a real understanding of the texts.

Translation of any Japanese work is likely to involve problems rarely encountered in the translation of European literature. The Nō plays in particular pose almost insuperable difficulties. The texts are extremely hard to understand, even for an educated Japanese. But decipherment of the surface meanings is usually only the first hurdle. The poetic parts of the play are riddled with complex currents of imagery and language: plays on words, "related words" (*engo*) that run through long passages unifying them, phrases that must be read with different meanings depending on what precedes and follows, a large repertory of allusions to unfamiliar literature, poetry that is often magnificent but also includes exclamations like, "Oh, how vexing!" Anyone translating a Nō play is likely to despair.

At the same time, there can hardly be another form of translation so satisfying to the translator. It demands the utmost, but the great plays are so overpowering that no translator can doubt that the necessary labors are justified. The would-be translator must be able to decipher the involuted texts, track down the allusions, reproduce somehow the intricacies of style without being unintelligible, and, at the same time, write effective English poetry. For this reason translations can be improved almost indefinitely. The present versions were originally made by students of mine. They were revised by myself, re-revised by the students, in most cases read by two poets (Carolyn Kizer and Andrew Glaze), edited by Royall Tyler, then revised once more by myself. This process could have been repeated many times, as long as we had time and patience enough. The goal—achieving in English the glory of the Nō plays—is unattainable, but I hope that the present translations will at least reveal the high seriousness of our efforts.

The plays were chosen from among the 240 works in the active repertory, in part because most had never before been translated into English, in part to illustrate with representative works the main developments in Nō from the time it achieved maturity in the late fourteenth century until it began to merge in its tone with the popular drama of the late sixteenth century. The chief dramatists—Kan'ami, Zeami, and Zenchiku—are of course represented, but other works are of unknown authorship. The attributions are sometimes tentative and open to dispute, but the plays should suggest the characteristic styles of the masters whose names they bear.

The traditional manner of classifying the plays was into five categories: god plays, warrior plays, woman plays, realistic (or mad!) plays, and demon plays. Some translators have published collections that give equal representation to each of the five categories, usually one of each, but such representation is in fact unequal, for the Nō repertory includes only 16 warrior plays as against 94 realistic plays, an indication not only of audience preferences but also of the importance the dramatists attached to the different categories. The present collection leans heavily toward plays of the third and fourth categories, in general the best works of the repertory. I have also included, however, a complete "program" of five plays, one from each category, in the traditional manner. The particular examples were chosen to suggest in somewhat extreme form the stately grandeur of the god plays, the ferocity of the warrior plays, the poetic immobility of the woman plays, the familiar realism of the realistic plays, and the intensity of the demon plays.

In these translations the poetry—the sung parts—of the originals has almost always been rendered into English verse. The nature of this verse has depended somewhat on the translator, but it has been attempted throughout to incorporate every allusion and wordplay, even those dismissed by Japanese commentators as being "mere decoration." If the effect is sometimes not altogether normal English expression, this may have the desired effect of slowing the reader's pace. It should not be forgotten that a play less than ten pages in translation may require two hours to perform, and that every syllable is pronounced with the utmost deliberation. Nō is a theatre of perfection, certainly not caviar to the general, but of such abiding value that it has withstood change for 500 years and is now more popular than ever.

Thanks are due to Monumenta Nipponica, in which the translations of *Kanehira* and *Obasute* first appeared; to Malahat Review for *Yōkihi;* and to Drama Survey for *Nishikigi.* The stage drawings for the plays, made by Fukami Tanrō, are reproduced from *Yōkyoku Taikan,* published by Meiji Shoin. The line drawings that illustrate most of the plays are taken from the singing texts (*utaibon*) of the Hōshō School, and are reproduced by kind permission of Mr. Ejima Ihei, whose company Wanya Shoten publishes these texts. Two plays, *Komachi at Sekidera* and *The Deserted Crone,* are considered to be of such great "dignity" that they have not been illustrated.

New York   DONALD KEENE
March 1970

CONTENTS

xiii

A PROGRAM OF FIVE PLAYS

Twenty Plays of the Nō Theatre

Glossary of the Names of Roles

SHITE	the "doer," the principal role
MAE-JITE	the *shite* of the first part of a play
NOCHI-JITE	the *shite* of the second part of a play
TSURE	the "companion" of the *shite*
MAE-ZURE	the *tsure* of the first part of a play
NOCHI-ZURE	the *tsure* of the second part of a play
WAKI	the person at the "side," generally a priest
WAKIZURE	the "companion" of the *waki*
KOKATA	the role of the "child"
KYŌGEN	generally a comic or menial role

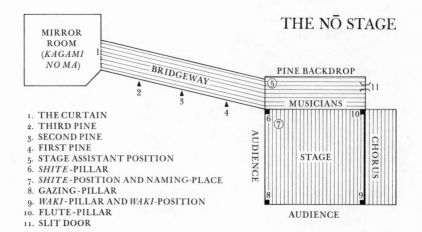

THE NŌ STAGE

MIRROR ROOM (*KAGAMI NO MA*)

BRIDGEWAY

PINE BACKDROP

MUSICIANS

AUDIENCE

STAGE

CHORUS

AUDIENCE

1. THE CURTAIN
2. THIRD PINE
3. SECOND PINE
4. FIRST PINE
5. STAGE ASSISTANT POSITION
6. *SHITE*-PILLAR
7. *SHITE*-POSITION AND NAMING-PLACE
8. GAZING-PILLAR
9. *WAKI*-PILLAR AND *WAKI*-POSITION
10. FLUTE-PILLAR
11. SLIT DOOR

THE CONVENTIONS OF THE NŌ DRAMA

Any form of drama is difficult to describe in words alone. Inevitably, much of its effect depends on physically apprehended sensations—sights or sounds that have struck the ear or eye, or even the mere proximity of other spectators sharing the same experience. The inflection an actor gives to a word or phrase, the hardly perceptible but telling gesture that accompanies an utterance, the length of the interval between the knock on the door and our discovery of who is on the other side—any of these can determine the success of a play in a manner almost impossible to guess from the printed text. Indeed, the tacit assumption in most countries of the West that drama is the highest form of literature ("Who is the Shakespeare of *your* country?") may be based on no more than the accident that since the days of the Greeks many European poets have devoted themselves to the theatre. In other parts of the world, even where drama is highly developed, it has not been considered primarily a literary genre but instead a musical or choreographic entertainment built around a mere framework of plot. Even within our own tradition the emergence of the film as a serious dramatic art, despite its lack of literary value, challenges our long-time assumptions.

It is nonetheless entirely proper to consider European drama as a form of literature, as is testified by innumerable studies of Greek drama by scholars who have never witnessed a performance. By a curious coincidence—one of a number of remarkable coincidences between Japanese and European literatures—it is also possible to consider the different forms of Japanese drama as works of literary interest.

In the case of Nō the appreciation of the texts has usually been overshadowed by the attention given to nonliterary elements in the performance. It might even be said that performances of Nō tend to obscure the literary values. The lines are delivered in so muffled and stylized a manner as to be almost unintelligible unless one already knows the text by heart, and the actors make little differentiation in expression between saying, "I am suffering unbearable agony" and "The cherry trees are in blossom." Every inflection of the actor's voice and every move of his body is prescribed by long traditions that have as their object the revelation of the ultimate meanings of the texts, but these meanings transcend the meaning of any one line, and it is therefore possible for an actor to deliver a line perfectly without understanding it. So heavy is the emphasis placed on the symbolic qualities of the plays that some authorities have suggested that the texts of Nō were intended as no more than necessary preparation for the dances that evoke the "message" of the plays. Yet the experience of the reader is quite otherwise; even if he has never seen the play he is reading, even if the stage directions give only the vaguest clues to the actors' movements, he can be moved by the play's literary qualities hardly less profoundly than if he were in the theatre.

The problems of communicating in translation the beauty of the original texts are daunting. The lines abound in allusions and quotations, some of which still baffle the most diligent scholars; and even if one recognizes their sources it is not always apparent *why* an allusion has been made. This may not trouble the actor or the spectator at the theatre, for the images themselves are beautiful, and even if not fully understood their majestic sounds carry conviction; readers of modern English poetry sometimes have a not dissimilar experience. But the translator must decide what each line means, and act on the assumption that the texts are not wantonly obscure or deliberately intended to mystify. Translation inevitably reduces the complexities of the original texts, either for the sake of clarity or because English is incapable of the same effects. The plays on words that are so prominent a feature of the texts become tedious or strained in translation; this is true even when the translation is into modern Japanese, and for this reason most modern Japanese translations omit altogether the characteristic intricacies of language.

The allusions that are so troublesome to the translator could not have been entirely clear even to the first audiences; they were used by the playwrights to enrich their texts with the overtones of earlier poetry, and the patterns of imagery were not mere displays of virtuosity but conscious attempts to create a unified effect in performance. The imagery is often deeply affecting, and the evocations of emotions have an absolute quality, even in translation, that goes beyond time or country. Kabuki drama is certainly more realistic than Nō, and in many ways it is closer to European drama, but being intimately associated with the particular situation of its age it is less absolute in its depiction of the human condition, and cannot be appreciated by us in the same way as by its original audiences. A Nō play like *Matsukaze*, on the other hand, means almost exactly to us what it must have meant to the Japanese of the fourteenth century. Whether seen in performance or only read, it is an unforgettable experience, even if we cannot fully understand it.

It should be the function of a critic of Nō to analyze the excellence of *Matsukaze* or any other play and describe why it still moves us in this way, five or six centuries after it was first written, living as we do in a society totally unlike that of the court of the Ashikaga shoguns where the plays were performed. But though great care has been devoted to establishing the texts and explaining the allusions, as yet scholars have produced nothing resembling the literary analysis that has been applied in the West to the works of European dramatists.

The difficulties confronting the would-be critic of Nō are enormous. Not a single play is dated, and all we can infer about even the most famous works is the date before which they must have been composed, information perhaps gleaned from a diary entry mentioning a performance. Some plays can be dated only by century, and others seem to have been rewritten so often that the establishment of a single date of composition would be impossible. Even when we know that a play with a certain title was performed, say, in the fifteenth century, it is by no means clear that this is the same work currently performed with that title. *Dōjōji* was formerly attributed to Kan'ami (1333–1384); it has recently been attributed by careful scholars to Nobumitsu (1435–1516); but other authorities are convinced that in its present form it cannot be older than the late sixteenth century.[1] A few texts have been miraculously preserved in Zeami's own handwriting. Some are of plays no longer performed, but those of plays in the current repertory differ so conspicuously from their present versions as to throw doubt on claims by the schools of Nō that they have preserved unaltered the authentic traditions of the past. The dating of the plays is further complicated by the fact that they were written in an artificial poetic language that only inadvertently reflected current speech; this meant that the differences in language separating, say, Shakespeare and Congreve, do not distinguish a Nō play of the fourteenth century from one of the sixteenth.

The authorship of the plays is almost as perplexing as the dating. Before 1940 scholars generally accepted the traditional attributions that gave credit to Zeami for about half the plays in the repertory of some 240 works. The application of more rigorous standards drastically reduced the number of plays attributed to Zeami, and some scholars now hesitate to allow him more than a dozen or so.[2] Zeami undoubtedly borrowed and modified works by his father Kan'ami and other early dramatists to suit the audiences of his own time, and these revised plays were further modified after his death. The main outlines of the plays and much of the poetry might remain essentially unchanged, but innumerable variants cropped up in the prose sections. The five schools of Nō each insist that their own texts are the only authentic ones, and they sometimes have their own traditions about the authorship as well.

Attributions of the plays were formerly based chiefly on various lists prepared in the sixteenth and seventeenth centuries, but these lists are no longer trusted. Too often they credited plays to Zeami, rather than admit that the author was unknown. Today scholars recognize as genuine works by Zeami only those mentioned by name in his critical writings. Zeami quoted extracts from different plays, and we know that he identified by author only works by other men; an extract not followed by the author's name must therefore have been from a play by Zeami himself. However, the insistence on a mention in Zeami's critical works may be imposing too rigorous a criterion. It is possible that he failed to mention all of his plays in his criticism, and some plays may have been written after the critical works relied on for dating. It is difficult otherwise to imagine who else could have written such masterpieces as *The Shrine in the Fields* (*Nonomiya*) or *Yuya*, works now listed merely as "anonymous" by meticulous scholars.[3]

Attributions on the basis of style have also been attempted. It obviously does not make much sense to speak about a dramatist's style if his works were all revised again and again by later men; nevertheless, critics customarily praise Kan'ami's "strength and simplicity," Zeami's *yūgen* (or style of mystery and depth), Moto-masa's pathos, Miyamasu's realism, or Zenchiku's philosophical loftiness. But surely no one reading *Matsukaze,* attributed to Kan'ami, would be struck by its "strength and simplicity"; perhaps his original play was so extensively revised by Zeami and others as to remove any personal imprint. The danger of making attributions on the basis of preconceptions as to a dramatist's distinctive manner is obvious, but some critics feel so sure of their grasp of Zeami's style as to be able to declare, for example, that *The Shrine in the Fields* cannot have been written by Zeami because the last word is a noun (*kataku,* the Burning House) and Zeami always ended his plays with verbs. Certainly the style of a play offers important clues both to the authorship and the date, but as yet it is not possible to do more than suggest with varying degrees of confidence some twenty-five plays that may be by Zeami. Not only do we lack information on the dates of these plays, but we have no way of establishing their relative order. It is as if we were able to decide on the basis of internal and external evidence that both *Romeo and Juliet* and *King Lear* were by Shakespeare, but had no idea which work came earlier in his career or if Shakespeare merely revised the work of a predecessor.

Studies of Nō as a literary form are still in their infancy, though the history of the Nō theatre and the techniques of performance have been investigated with diligence and sometimes with brilliant results.[4] Japanese critics have generally contented themselves with describing the characteristic style of the poetry as a "brocade" consisting of lovely bits and pieces of old poetry. The extensive borrowing from such collections as *Kokinshū* ("Collection of Poems Old and New," 905) and *Wakan Rōei Shū* ("Collection of Japanese and Chinese Poems for Reading Aloud," c. 1010) sometimes does indeed suggest a "brocade" of allusions, but the Nō plays clearly possess a distinctive style of their own. Because drama fell outside the range of interest of traditional scholars of Japanese literature it was left to Yeats to point out the patterns of symbols in the plays, a remark that inspired some Japanese scholars for the first time to examine the recurring imagery that is so characteristic a feature of Zeami's style.[5]

The evolving style of the Nō plays can also be traced in terms of the degree of conformity to the "standard" models. Zeami himself cited his work *Yumi Yawata* as a paradigmatic example of Nō, but hardly another play in the repertory conforms exactly to its formulae.[6] It is nonetheless true that plays of Zeami's time tend to follow a set form. With respect to the division into parts, for example, there is little deviation from the established categories: *shite,* the principal character, the only true "person"; *waki,* or secondary actor, whose arrival on the scene introduces the story and who asks the questions the audience itself might ask; and *tsure,* or companion, who may accompany either the *shite* or *waki,* but rarely rises above being a shadow. Some of the older works of the repertory (like *Shōkun*) seem to have been composed before the standard roles (*shite, waki,* and so on) had been evolved, and the present divisions seem arbitrary and unnecessary. Even Zeami's works do not always follow the paradigms of composition: in *Lady Han (Hanjo),* for example, the *kyōgen* part is vital to the action and not merely a diversion. But such departures from the standard seem minor when compared to those in pre-Zeami or post-Zeami plays. In *Komachi and the Hundred Nights (Kayoi Komachi),* for example, Komachi is the *tsure,* but far from being a mere "companion" to the *shite* is his antagonist. *Hatsuyuki* by Zempō (c. 1474–c. 1520) altogether lacks a *waki* part. The *shite* part in *The Valley Rite (Tanikō)* is so minor the character does not utter a word. In other late works the distinction between *shite* and *waki* is so vague that the nomenclature differs according to the school.

In terms of the roles, then, one can say that before Zeami the distinctions were probably fluid; with Zeami they attained a "classical" definition; but after Zeami the conventions increasingly tended to break down in face of new demands by the audiences. A similar pattern of development can be described with respect to other aspects of Nō. The art gradually reached maturity late in the fourteenth century, largely thanks to the patronage by the shogun's court. Nō had originally developed as a popular theatre, and its repertory consisted mainly of plays on religious themes presented at Buddhist temples and Shinto shrines throughout the country. But when the shogun Ashikaga Yoshimitsu decided in 1374 to extend his patronage to the art, it changed its character. The texts were embellished with quotations from the poetry and prose of the past, no doubt to please members of the shogun's court who had literary pretensions; but this meant that the illiterate commoners who had formerly supported Nō were gradually forgotten by the playwrights who turned their backs on dramatic or didactic themes in favor of aesthetic excellence. Zeami especially delighted in literary display, even when it led to a static dramatic situation. The speech in *Komachi and the Hundred Nights* in which Komachi describes the fruits and nuts she has gathered, giving a poetic allusion for each, contributes nothing to the action, but it helps create a mood that is associated with Zeami, who added this section to the less ornamented text by Kan'ami.

With Zeami Nō attained its classic form and its highest level of literary distinction. Although Zeami also composed some works in a realistic manner, his plays are known especially for their *yūgen,* a haunting poetic quality both in the language and in the overall effects. *Komachi at Sekidera* (*Sekidera Komachi*) is perhaps the supreme example of *yūgen* in Nō. There is almost no plot to the play—some priests take a young disciple to hear from an old woman the secrets of poetry and gradually become aware she is the celebrated poet Komachi—and the *shite* is virtually immobile during the first hour of the performance, but the poetry and the atmosphere it creates make this play incredibly moving.

The *yūgen* style was nobly continued by Zenchiku in such works as *Yōkihi,* and even Nobumitsu, who is more widely known for highly dramatic plays like *Dōjōji,* was capable of the symbolic overtones of *yūgen* in his lovely *The Priest and the Willow* (*Yugyō Yanagi*). But after Nobumitsu, no doubt as the result of the civil disorders that weakened and impoverished the court, the actors were forced to turn again to the general public for support. Spectacular effects or else easily grasped realism displaced Zeami's *yūgen.* A late work like *The Bird-scaring Boat* (*Torioi-bune*) indicates the level of realism that became possible in Nō and anticipates the emergence of a true popular theatre at

the end of the sixteenth century. After the establishment of the
Tokugawa shogunate at the beginning of the seventeenth century
Nō became enshrined—and petrified—as the official court ceremonial music. New plays continued to be written in the traditional form and language, but they were lifeless pastiches, and
Nō had become what it is today, a theatre consecrated to the
performance of a repertory largely established in the fifteenth
century.

The distinctive features of Nō, whether during the classical
period or the long period of change and decline, remained
closely connected with the extraordinary freedom permitted the
dramatist in both the language and the structure of the plays.
Surely no other theatre has disregarded so completely the normal
considerations of time and space.[7] We have only to remember
the desperate expedients to which Corneille was driven in his
attempt to satisfy the demands of the Three Unities to ap-
preciate what the freedom of the Nō plays mean. How Corneille
would have envied a playwright whose theatre permitted him to
change at will the time and place of the action without even a
break in the dialogue! Many Nō plays begin with the *waki* an-
nouncing his intention of making a journey to some distant
place. He takes a few steps on the stage, describing as he does
so his travels, then returns to his original position where he de-
clares he has reached his destination. This freedom—like all the
other freedoms in Nō—is based on a convention. The *waki*'s
journey establishes the scene of his first encounter with the *shite*
and also his identity as a stranger who may properly ask questions about what he sees. The journey is accepted as a convention
by the audience, which is willing to admit that a great distance
has been covered in a few steps and that days of travel have
shrunken into a sentence of description. The freedom extended
even to the convention itself; although the journey usually
serves only the formal requirement that it begin the play, it
could be of dramatic interest itself and embellished with references to the poetic associations of the places passed, or it could
be prolonged (as in the case of *Kanehira*) to fill up the entire
first part of the play.

The freedom which the Nō stage conventions permitted with
respect to time is particularly striking. Generally the only indica-

tion of time is the month of the year in which the action of the play occurs. Japanese audiences, with their sensitivity to nature, insisted that plays be presented only in the appropriate season; performing a play about snow in the summer was unthinkable. Even within a given season, *The Sought-for Grave* (*Motomezuka*) clearly belongs to early spring, when the first sprouts are barely visible, but *Dōjōji* is set much later in the spring, when the cherry trees have blossomed. *Matsukaze* or *The Shrine in the Fields* are autumnal not only in setting but in their prevailing mood and imagery, and a performance should evoke the feeling of autumn even in the musical accompaniment. But despite this attention to the month, the year is normally not indicated, nor even whether the events in the play took place long ago or recently. Sometimes, as in the case of works based on *The Tale of Genji* or *The Tale of the Heike*, events recalled in the course of the play may have occurred at a particular time (fictional or historical), but the central action—the encounter of the *waki* and the *shite*—takes place at some unidentified time many years later when Matsukaze or Miyasudokoro or Kanehira is a ghost, drawn back to this world by unsatisfied longing.

The dramatist can at will in a few lines of verse make a day, a month or years elapse, as in this example from *Komachi and the Hundred Nights*:

At last the final day is here,

(*He goes to the front of the stage.*)

And it has drawn to a close.

A formalized movement by the actor and the simple statement that the day has ended suffices for Nō though a Western dramatist would normally have had to specify a new scene ("Later the same day"). The passage of time can be contracted in this manner, but the dramatist can also prolong the action of a moment almost indefinitely. One or more dances epitomizing the emotions of the dancer occupy the major part of this time, and a dance that takes twenty minutes to perform may be the expression of a flash of nostalgia. Even a work like *The Imperial Visit to Ohara* (*Ohara Gokō*) that lacks any dances is so stylized that actions which would take only a few moments if performed realistically are prolonged in a manner that stretches time out of recognizable shape.

The disregard of ordinary concepts of space and time extends to the usual limitations on what an actor in a part may say. Most lines spoken by the *shite* are in fact utterances of the character, but sometimes he describes his actions as from the point of view of an outsider, and sometimes too the chorus speaks for the *shite* in the first person. In still other instances, speech divided between the *shite* and the *waki* or *tsure* altogether lacks any suggestion of dialogue between two people but suggests instead—thanks to the vagueness of the subject in a Japanese sentence—a single thought shared by two persons.

Other conventions of Nō permit an extraordinarily free use of the materials of the play. Many works are in two scenes separated by an interval. Towards the conclusion of the first scene it has become apparent that the *shite* we have seen as a peasant girl, a boatman, or an anonymous old man is actually the ghost of some celebrated person of the past or the temporary manifestation of a god. The *shite* leaves the stage and a "man of the place" (played by a *kyōgen* actor) enters, to relate in response to the *waki*'s question what he knows about the events that form the background to the play. Such interludes, being in a language much easier to follow than the high-flown poetry of the main parts of the play, may have helped the original audiences to understand the plot, or perhaps the sustained narration afforded the pleasure of rhetorical eloquence. But the effect of the speech by the "man of the place" is now one of mild irritation that the moment for which we are waiting, the reappearance of the *shite* in the full splendor of his past, is so long delayed. The interlude speech is occasionally of interest, but even when it is repetitious and almost devoid of literary or dramatic value it serves legitimate purposes: In terms of the staging it gives the *shite* time to change his costume and sometimes his mask; and in dramatic terms it enables the playwright to reverse time—to show us after the interval, which has interrupted the flow of time, events that occurred long before those depicted in the first part. The *kyōgen* speech by its very flatness and closeness to the world of daily experience accentuates the distance separating us from the world of the dead, the world of the *shite* in his different manifestations. If the interval were simply a blank—twenty minutes when the audience filed out of the theatre into the corridors—the two halves of the play might fall apart, and certainly one would not have so strongly the sensation of the *same* person appearing before us in a different guise.

The delivery of narrations by the *kyōgen* actor during the interval is a practice that goes back at least to Zeami's day, but the texts used today probably are no older than the seventeenth century. No doubt the actors formerly improvised, and perhaps there was more of a comic element in the narrations than at present. (Zeami warned against *kyōgen* actors clowning unnecessarily during the intervals.) In any case, the convention of the narration between the two parts of the play seems to have been considered an essential element and the contrast in mood between the poetic utterances of the *shite* and the prose of the *kyōgen* added to the effect of the whole. Generally the "man of the place" is unidentified and colorless, but as he speaks we know he is there not for his own sake but as preparation for the revelation of the *shite* in his "true" form.

Not only is the *kyōgen* anonymous, but the *waki* is generally identified merely as a traveling priest, and even the *shite* sometimes has no name and scarcely a history, as in *The Deserted Crone (Obasute)*. The *shite* expresses his deepest feelings in a manner not often surpassed in other theatres, but by convention there is little attempt to create a character in a Western sense. The expression of the emotion is so absolute as to border at times on the impersonal. One of the hardest things to translate are the exclamations; "Oh, sad!" (*ara kanashi ya*) tends to become "You make me sad!" in free translation. The intrusion of the personal pronouns is typical of English and of a theatre which insists on individuality of characters. The Nō plays, on the other hand, are distillations of powerful emotions—jealousy, the craving for revenge, unswerving loyalty, or heartbreak over disappointed love—that transcend the particular characters. We may find it easier to analyze *Matsukaze* as a dramatic poem than as a work for the theatre, even though it is hauntingly moving on the stage. The great plays produce an unforgettable effect, but are self-contained. We are not tempted to probe the texts for further clues as to the characters, as we might in the case of Shakespeare. Details even of the physical appearance of Hamlet have been deduced from mentions of a beard or the expression "fat and scant of breath." But it makes no sense whatsoever to imagine Matsukaze's height or coloring, or even to ask if Yukihira was equally in love with both sisters or favored Matsukaze over Murasame. Such matters are not mentioned in the play and therefore, almost by definition, they are irrelevant. Everything to be known about the characters is stated, but the efforts of the dramatist were directed towards the creation of an atmosphere rather than a personality.

We accept as another convention that a fisherwoman or peasant girl can possess the exquisite sensibilities she reveals in the poetry she speaks (as we accept the convention in Shakespeare that a rough soldier like Enobarbus can speak magnificent poetry); indeed, *The Iron Crown* (*Kanawa*) has been criticized because the *shite* fails to show sufficient refinement of diction when venting her jealous fury. Regardless of the emotions that may be assailing the *shite,* an artistic dignity and detachment must be preserved. The stylization of language which results in the fisher girl Matsukaze speaking in much the same manner as the Empress Kenreimon-in inevitably makes the characters less distinct and memorable than those in a European tragedy. Extremely few characters in Nō have an existence apart from the poetry which they speak, though we may, of course, discover more about the historical personages on whom the characters are based. Kenreimon-in in *The Imperial Visit to Ohara* is provided with more of the attributes of a true character than most *shite* roles, but this is probably because of what we know about her from the descriptions in *The Tale of the Heike.* Her feelings towards her father, Kiyomori, would be interesting to know and might help to create a more rounded character, but they are not mentioned because they are irrelevant to the central theme of the play, her conviction that she is meaninglessly dragging out a life that should have perished with her son's.

We tend to remember the plays in terms of one prevailing emotion: the bittersweet longing of *The Shrine in the Fields,* the heart-rending loneliness of *Semimaru,* the ethereal nostalgia of *Yōkihi.* Not only is there an absence of characters in the sense that King Lear or Othello is a character, there is often even an absence of action. In extreme cases this means that a play lacks any semblance of conflict (though drama has frequently been defined in terms of conflict) and even of plot. *The Queen Mother of the West (Seiōbo)* creates an appealing atmosphere by its poetry and dances, but it would be impossible to analyze the play in terms of characters or plot. The effect is musical; starting with a slow, undramatic statement of the theme, the play moves into a development section of greater intensity, and finally rises to the climax in the culminating dance.

The musical division of the play into three sections—*jo* (introduction), *ha* (development), and *kyū* (climax)—is basic not only to a performance but to the literary style. The opening sections often describe in a mixture of prose and conventional verse that varies little from play to play the departure of the *waki* on his journey, his arrival, and the questions he asks about some unexpected sight. The first appearance of the *shite* is likely to be subdued rather than dramatic, though there are exceptions, as in works like *Semimaru* in which the *shite* does not appear until the play is well into the development section. The poetry is initially not likely to be deeply emotional in nature; the first speech of Komachi in *Komachi and the Hundred Nights* is a typical example of the deft but not especially dramatic poetry favored by Zeami early in the work. As the musical tempo and the complexity of the plot increase, the poetry also heightens, and gradually rises to the brilliance and power typical of Nō. The final sections of a play usually contain the most moving poetry, whether it consists of a nostalgic evocation of the past (as in *Yōkihi*), a description of brutal combat (as in *Kanehira*), or a relation of the tortures of hell (as in *The Sought-for Grave*).

The development in terms of *jo*, *ha*, and *kyū* of any given play has a parallel in terms of the program of five plays that has traditionally composed a day's entertainment. Such programs existed in the fifteenth century, and the custom of presenting in a fixed order one example from each of five categories—god play, warrior play, woman play, realistic play, and demon play—is still observed vestigially to this day. The effect of seeing a full program of five plays should not only be one of pleasure in diversity, but also a steadily mounting sense of theatrical excitement, with each of the successive plays building to a higher crest in the *kyū* section than the last, until the crest of the fifth and most dynamic play leaves the spectator with a sense of exhilaration. The aesthetic considerations of such programs explain the function of an undramatic work like *The Queen Mother of the West*: it established for the audience coming into the theatre from the confusion of the outside world the special atmosphere of the Nō theatre. Once this was established almost any subject could be treated without any danger of dropping to the level of banal realism or childish fantasy. The material of *The Bird-scaring Boat* easily lends itself to the tritest uses, but the play is saved from sentimentality by its poetry and by being performed in a theatre where the tone is set by nonrealistic works. But it is important too that Nō include such works as *The Bird-scaring Boat*; without them the audience might sense some incompleteness in the program, as if a necessary "human" element were missing. Contrary to the impression sometimes given by admirers of Nō, many plays are realistic in nature and not concerned with ghosts or demons, but their realism is balanced by the stylized techniques of the acting and by the elevation of the poetry.

Even at its most realistic, however, Nō is by the standards of other theatres conspicuously nonrealistic in its presentation. The boat in *The Bird-scaring Boat*, for example, unlike the elaborate props used in Kabuki, is no more than an outline surmounted by a stand for the bird-scaring devices. In *Matsukaze* the hut where the two sisters live is too small for both to fit inside, so Murasame must sit outside the prop, though the audience accepts the convention that she is inside. The crushing of the boy under the stones of the other pilgrims is represented in *The Valley Rite* by covering the boy with a cloak, and his miraculous resurrection is indicated by removing the cloak. Some plays use no props at all, and the scene may shift from a house to a mountainside merely by having a character say this has happened. Convention allows a character to disappear if he withdraws from the playing area of the stage, where he sits immobile until he is required to appear again. By another convention persons may be presumed to be mutually invisible, even though only a few feet apart, if they are not facing each other; this accounts for the master's customary query, "Is anyone here?" even when his servant is almost within touching distance.

Beyond the conventions in the staging are the fundamental conventions of the texts. The patterns of poetry and prose vary from play to play, but they present as a whole a distinctive literary form. The frequent use of quotations is a literary convention, and a text which made few references to the poetry found in the famous anthologies would seem thin and without overtones. Nō is deeply concerned with Japanese poetic traditions. Not only are many poems embedded in the dialogue, but poetry itself is the subject of such plays as *Komachi at Sekidera*, and a principal theme of *The Reed Cutter (Ashikari)*. It would not be normal for characters in a European drama to relate the principles of the art of poetry and give examples of favorite works, but this is precisely what we find in these plays. In the Nō theatre many different arts—poetry, music, dance, and mime—converge, at a level that does justice to all.

The Nō theatre makes maximum demands on the audience. The texts are difficult and the relatively scant mimetic elements contribute more to establishing the inner tensions of the characters than to clarifying the words or actions. Some plays indeed are so exceedingly slow-moving as to lull a sizable part of the audience to sleep. But precisely because it takes this risk Nō succeeds in its unique domain.

The deliberate tempo of a performance of Nō is set by the musicians and actors. It is hoped that readers will not be misled by the contemporary language employed in these translations into perusing too quickly works meant to be savored at the pace of a theatre where the most violent emotions are clothed in ceremony and dignity.

Notes

1. The attribution to Kan'ami may be found, for example in Sanari, *Yōkyoku Taikan;* Yokomichi and Omote credit the work to Nobumitsu; but Konishi Jin'ichi believes that Nobumitsu's play on the theme of *Dōjōji* was the play *Kanemaki* still performed in the countryside, and that the present *Dōjōji* was written much later.

2. Even the same scholar may change his opinion within a short space of time on which plays can be attributed with confidence to Zeami. Attributions in this book have generally been based on Yokomichi and Omote, but where they are silent other sources have been used.

3. Professor Konishi Jin'ichi has suggested that Zeami's second son Motoyoshi, who is not otherwise credited with any plays, may have written some of the important works of uncertain authorship.

4. Keene, *Nō, the Classical Theatre of Japan* covers in some detail the history and techniques of Nō. Rather than repeat the same information here, I refer readers to this earlier book. *Le Nô* by Noël Peri contains an even more detailed description of the formal elements in a Nō drama.

5. Yeats' remarks, first published in *Certain Noble Plays of Japan,* were quoted by me in my book *Japanese Literature* (New York, Grove Press, 1953) and subsequently taken up by Konishi Jin'ichi and other scholars. The unifying imagery they discovered distinguishes Zeami's works from, say, those of his son Motomasa, who was nearly as skillful a dramatist.

6. See Keene, *Nō* and Peri, *Le Nô* for a description of these formulae.

7. But see the interesting article by Armando Martins, "The Japanese Classic Theatre and the Theatre of Gil Vicente," in the periodical *Comparative Literature (Hikaku Bungaku)* (1966). Martins points out similarities between Nō and the works of the Portuguese dramatist Gil Vicente (1465–1536).

Matsukaze

BY KANZE KIYOTSUGU KAN'AMI/TRANSLATED BY ROYALL TYLER

INTRODUCTION

Matsukaze is a play of the third category. The original text was by Kan'ami, but it was considerably reworked by Zeami. In its present form it is a masterpiece, and its popularity has never faltered.

The word *matsukaze* (wind in the pines) evokes for Japanese a feeling of exquisite solitude and melancholy. Suma Bay, the scene of the play, has similar associations, for it was the place where Genji was exiled. The account of Genji's exile, recounted in the "Exile at Suma" chapter of *The Tale of Genji*, was apparently inspired by the exile of Ariwara no Yukihira (818–893), a famous poet, courtier, and scholar. Yukihira's poem on his exile, found in the *Kokinshū*, is quoted in the play. Another source for the play is a story told in the *Senshūshō*, a thirteenth-century collection of tales: One day, when Yukihira was walking along a beach near Suma he met some men spearing fish. He asked where they lived, and they replied,

> "We who spend our lives
> By the shore where the white waves break
> Are fishermen's sons, and we have
> No home we can call our own."

Yukihira was moved to tears.

Most of *Matsukaze*, however, appears to have been the invention of the playwright. It gives an impression of youthful vigor, but is constructed with care. Matsukaze's "mad scene" is made almost inevitable, and the lack of surprise only heightens the dramatic power. Only at the conclusion of the play does the reader (or, even more so, the spectator) realize how completely he has been gripped by the lyrical and dramatic tension, when he is released from the dream by one of the most effective wordplays in literature: Matsukaze and her sister Murasame (Autumn Rain) withdraw, and suddenly the chorus restores their names to their original meanings. The ghosts dissolve back into nature, leaving us alone, listening only to the wind in the pines. No more beautiful awakening could be imagined.

The play's imagery is built around the sea (salt, brine, the tide, waves, the sea wind), the moon, and pine trees. These, with the mountains looming in the background, compose an archetypal Japanese landscape. The moon, moreover, is a symbol of Buddhist enlightenment. Although it shines alone in the sky, it is reflected in many waters, just as the unified Buddha-nature is manifested in seemingly distinct beings.

Suma, the scene of *Matsukaze*, now lies within the city limits of Kobe. The play is performed by all schools of Nō.

19

PERSONS   AN ITINERANT PRIEST *(waki)*
           A VILLAGER *(kyōgen)*
           MATSUKAZE *(shite)*
           MURASAME *(tsure)*

PLACE   SUMA BAY IN SETTSU PROVINCE

TIME   AUTUMN, THE NINTH MONTH

MATSUKAZE

(The stage assistant places a stand with a pine sapling set into it at the front of the stage. The Priest enters and stands at the naming-place. He carries a rosary.)

PRIEST. I am a priest who travels from province to province. Lately I have been in the Capital. I visited the famous sites and ancient ruins, not missing a one. Now I intend to make a pilgrimage to the western provinces. *(He faces forward.)* I have hurried, and here I am already at the Bay of Suma in Settsu Province. *(His attention is caught by pine tree.)* How strange! That pine on the beach has a curious look. There must be a story connected with it. I'll ask someone in the neighborhood. *(He faces the bridgeway.)* Do you live in Suma?

> *(The Villager comes down the bridgeway to the first pine. He wears a short sword.)*

VILLAGER. Perhaps I am from Suma; but first tell me what you want.

PRIEST. I am a priest and I travel through the provinces. Here on the beach I see a solitary pine tree with a wooden tablet fixed to it, and a poem slip hanging from the tablet. Is there a story connected with the tree? Please tell me what you know.

VILLAGER. The pine is linked with the memory of two fisher girls, Matsukaze and Murasame. Please say a prayer for them as you pass.

PRIEST. Thank you. I know nothing about them, but I will stop at the tree and say a prayer for them before I move on.

VILLAGER. If I can be of further service, don't hesitate to ask.

PRIEST. Thank you for your kindness.

VILLAGER. At your command, sir.

> *(The Villager exits. The Priest goes to stage center and turns toward the pine tree.)*

PRIEST. So, this pine tree is linked with the memory of two fisher girls, Matsukaze and Murasame. It is sad! Though their bodies are buried in the ground, their names linger on. This lonely pine tree lingers on also, ever green and untouched

21

by autumn, their only memorial. Ah! While I have been chanting sutras and invoking Amida Buddha for their repose, the sun, as always on autumn days, has quickly set. That village at the foot of the mountain is a long way. Perhaps I can spend the night in this fisherman's salt shed.

(*He kneels at the* waki-*position. The stage assistant brings out the prop, a cart for carrying pails of brine, and sets it by the gazing-pillar. He places a pail on the cart.*

Murasame enters and comes down the bridgeway as far as the first pine. She wears the tsure *mask. Matsukaze follows her and stops at the third pine. She wears the* waka-onna *mask. Each carries a water pail. They face each other.*)

MATSUKAZE AND MURASAME. A brine cart wheeled along the beach
Provides a meager livelihood:
The sad world rolls
Life by quickly and in misery!

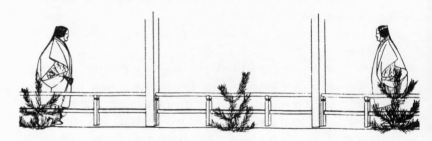

MURASAME. Here at Suma Bay
The waves shatter at our feet,
And even the moonlight wets our sleeves
With its tears of loneliness.
(*Murasame goes to stage center while Matsukaze moves to the* shite-*position.*)
MATSUKAZE. The autumn winds are sad.
When the Middle Counselor Yukihira
Lived here back a little from the sea,
They inspired his poem,
"Salt winds blowing from the mountain pass. . . ."[1]
On the beach, night after night,
Waves thunder at our door;

And on our long walks to the village
We've no companion but the moon.[2]
Our toil, like all of life, is dreary,
But none could be more bleak than ours.
A skiff cannot cross the sea,
Nor we this dream world.
Do we exist, even?
Like foam on the salt sea,
We draw a cart,[3] friendless and alone,
Poor fisher girls whose sleeves are wet
With endless spray, and tears
From our hearts' unanswered longing.

CHORUS. Our life is so hard to bear
That we envy the pure moon[4]
Now rising with the tide.
But come, let us dip brine,
Dip brine from the rising tide!
Our reflections seem to shame us!

   (*They look down as if catching a glimpse of their reflections in the water. The movement of their heads "clouds"
   the expression on their masks, making it seem sad.*)

Yes, they shame us!
Here, where we shrink from men's eyes,
Drawing our timorous cart;
The withdrawing tide
Leaves stranded pools behind.
How long do they remain?
If we were the dew on grassy fields,
We would vanish with the sun.
But we are sea tangle,
Washed up on the shore,
Raked into heaps by the fishermen,
Fated to be discarded, useless,
Withered and rotting,
Like our trailing sleeves,
Like our trailing sleeves.

   (*They look down again.*)

Endlessly familiar, still how lovely
The twilight at Suma![5]

The fishermen call out in muffled voices;
At sea, the small boats loom dimly.
Across the faintly glowing face of the moon
Flights of wild geese streak,
And plovers flock below along the shore.
Fall gales and stiff sea winds:
These are things, in such a place,
That truly belong to autumn.
But oh, the terrible, lonely nights!
　　(They hide their faces.)

MATSUKAZE. Come, dip the brine
MURASAME. Where the seas flood and fall.

　　Let us tie our sleeves back to our shoulders
MATSUKAZE. Think only, "Dip the brine."
MURASAME. We ready ourselves for the task,
MATSUKAZE. But for women, this cart is too hard.
CHORUS. While the rough breakers surge and fall,

　　(Murasame moves upstage to stand beside Matsukaze.)
While the rough breakers surge and fall,
And cranes among the reeds
Fly up with sharp cries.
The four winds add their wailing.
How shall we pass the cold night?
　　(They look up.)
The late moon is so brilliant—
What we dip is its reflection!
Smoke from the salt fires
May cloud the moon—take care!
Are we always to spend only
The sad autumns of fishermen?
At Ojima in Matsushima[6]
　　(Matsukaze half-kneels by the brine cart and mimes dip-
　　ping with her fan.)
The fisherfolk, like us,
Delight less in the moon
Than in the dipping of its reflection;
There they take delight in dipping
Reflections of the moon.
　　(Matsukaze returns to the shite-*position.)*

We haul our brine from afar,
As in far-famed Michinoku[7]
And at the salt kilns of Chika—
Chika, whose name means "close by."

MATSUKAZE. Humble folk hauled wood for salt fires
At the ebb tide on Akogi Shore;[8]

CHORUS. On Ise Bay there's Twice-See Beach—
Oh, could I live my life again![9]

   (Matsukaze looks off into the distance.)

MATSUKAZE. On days when pine groves stand hazy,
And the sea lanes draw back
From the coast at Narumi[10]—

CHORUS. You speak of Narumi; this is Naruo,
Where pines cut off the moonlight
From the reed-thatched roofs of Ashinoya.[11]

MATSUKAZE. Who is to tell of our unhappiness
Dipping brine at Nada?[12]
With boxwood combs set in our hair,[13]
From rushing seas we draw the brine,
Oh look! I have the moon in my pail!

   *(Murasame kneels before the brine cart and places her pail
   on it. Matsukaze, still standing, looks into her pail.)*

MATSUKAZE. In my pail too I hold the moon!

CHORUS. How lovely! A moon here too!

   *(Murasame picks up the rope tied to the cart and gives it
   to Matsukaze, then moves to the* shite-*position. Matsukaze
   looks up.)*

MATSUKAZE. The moon above is one;
Below it has two, no, three reflections
   (She looks into both pails.)
Which shine in the flood tide tonight,
   (She pulls the cart to a spot before the musicians.)
And on our cart we load the moon!
No, life is not all misery
Here by the sea lanes.

   *(She drops the rope. The stage assistant removes the cart.
   Matsukaze sits on a low stool and Murasame kneels beside
   her, a sign that the two women are resting inside their hut.
   The Priest rises.)*

PRIEST. The owner of the salt shed has returned. I shall ask for a night's lodging. *(to Matsukaze and Murasame)* I beg your pardon. Might I come inside?

MURASAME *(standing and coming forward a little)*. Who might you be?

PRIEST. A traveler, overtaken by night on my journey. I should like to ask lodging for the night.

MURASAME. Wait here. I must ask the owner. *(She kneels before Matsukaze.)* A traveler outside asks to come in and spend the night.

MATSUKAZE. That is little enough, but our hut is so wretched we cannot ask him in. Please tell him so.

MURASAME *(standing, to the Priest)*. I have spoken to the owner. She says the house is too wretched to put anyone up.

PRIEST. I understand those feelings perfectly, but poverty makes no difference at all to me. I am only a priest. Please say I beg her to let me spend the night.

MURASAME. No, we really cannot put you up.

MATSUKAZE *(to Murasame)*. Wait!

I see in the moonlight
One who has renounced the world.
He will not mind a fisherman's hut,
With its rough pine pillars and bamboo fence;
I believe it is very cold tonight,
So let him come in and warm himself
At our sad fire of rushes.
You may tell him that.

MURASAME. Please come in.

PRIEST. Thank you very much. Forgive me for intruding.
(He takes a few steps forward and kneels. Murasame goes back beside Matsukaze.)

MATSUKAZE. I wished from the beginning to invite you in, but this place is so poor I felt I must refuse.

PRIEST. You are very kind. I am a priest and a traveler, and never stay anywhere very long. Why prefer one lodging to another? In any case, what sensitive person would not prefer to live

here at Suma, in the quiet solitude. Yukihira wrote,
"If ever anyone
Chances to ask for me,
Say I live alone,
Soaked by the dripping seaweed
On the shore of Suma Bay."[14]
(He looks at the pine tree.) A while ago I asked someone the
meaning of that solitary pine on the beach. I was told it
grows there in memory of two fisher girls, Matsukaze and
Murasame. There is no connection between them and me,
but I went to the pine anyway and said a prayer for them.
(Matsukaze and Murasame weep. The Priest stares at them.)
This is strange! They seem distressed at the mention of
Matsukaze and Murasame. Why?

MATSUKAZE AND MURASAME. Truly, when a grief is hidden,
Still, signs of it will show.
His poem, "If ever anyone
Chances to ask for me,"
Filled us with memories which are far too fond.
Tears of attachment to the world
Wet our sleeves once again.

PRIEST. Tears of attachment to the world? You speak as though
you are no longer of the world. Yukihira's poem overcame
you with memories. More and more bewildering! Please, both
of you, tell me who you are.

MATSUKAZE AND MURASAME. We would tell you our names,
But we are too ashamed!
No one, ever,
Has chanced to ask for us,
Long dead as we are,
And so steeped in longing
For the world by Suma Bay
That pain has taught us nothing.
Ah, the sting of regret!
But having said this,
Why should we hide our names any longer?
At twilight you said a prayer
By a mossy grave under the pine
For two fisher girls,

Matsukaze and Murasame.
We are their ghosts, come to you.
When Yukihira was here he whiled away
Three years of weary exile
Aboard his pleasure boat,
His heart refreshed
By the moon of Suma Bay.
There were, among the fisher girls
Who hauled brine each evening,
Two sisters whom he chose for his favors.
"Names to fit the season!"
He said, calling us
Pine Wind and Autumn Rain.
We had been Suma fisher girls,
Accustomed to the moon,
But he changed our salt makers' clothing
To damask robes,
Burnt with the scent of faint perfumes.[15]

MATSUKAZE. Then, three years later, Yukihira
Returned to the Capital.

MURASAME. Soon, we heard he had died, oh so young!

MATSUKAZE. How we both loved him!
Now the message we pined for
Would never, never come.

CHORUS. Pine Wind and Autumn Rain
Both drenched their sleeves with the tears
Of hopeless love beyond their station,
Fisher girls of Suma.
Our sin is deep, o priest.
Pray for us, we beg of you!
    (They press their palms together in supplication.)
Our love grew rank as wild grasses;
Tears and love ran wild.
It was madness that touched us.
Despite spring purification,
Performed in our old robes,
Despite prayers inscribed on paper streamers,[16]
The gods refused us their help.
We were left to melt away

Like foam on the waves,
And, in misery, we died.
   (Matsukaze looks down, shading her mask.)
Alas! How the past evokes our longing!
Yukihira, the Middle Counselor,
   *(The stage assistant puts a man's cloak and court hat in
   Matsukaze's left hand.)*
Lived three years here by Suma Bay.
Before he returned to the Capital,
He left us these keepsakes of his stay:
A court hat and a hunting cloak.
Each time we see them,
   (She looks at the cloak.)
Our love grows again,
And gathers like dew
On the tip of a leaf
So that there's no forgetting,
Not for an instant.
Oh endless misery!
   (She places the cloak in her lap.)
"This keepsake
Is my enemy now;
For without it
   (She lifts the cloak.)
I might forget."[17]
   (She stares at the cloak.)
The poem says that
And it's true:
My anguish only deepens.
   (She weeps.)
MATSUKAZE. "Each night before I go to sleep,
   I take off the hunting cloak
CHORUS. And hang it up . . ."[18]
   *(The keepsakes in her hand, she stands and, as in a trance,
   takes a few steps toward the gazing-pillar.)*
I hung all my hopes
On living in the same world with him,
But being here makes no sense at all
And these keepsakes are nothing.

(She starts to drop the cloak, only to cradle it in her arms and press it to her.)

I drop it, but I cannot let it lie;
So I take it up again
To see his face before me yet once more.

(She turns to her right and goes toward the naming-place, then stares down the bridgeway as though something were coming after her.)

"Awake or asleep,
From my pillow, from the foot of my bed,
Love rushes in upon me."[19]
Helplessly I sink down,
Weeping in agony.

(She sits at the shite-*position, weeping. The stage assistant helps her take off her outer robe and replace it with the cloak. He also helps tie on the court hat.)*

MATSUKAZE. The River of Three Fords[20]
Has gloomy shallows
Of never-ending tears;
I found, even there,
An abyss of wildest love.
Oh joy! Look! Over there!
Yukihira has returned!

(She rises, staring at the pine tree.)

He calls me by my name, Pine Wind!
I am coming!

(She goes to the tree. Murasame hurriedly rises and follows. She catches Matsukaze's sleeve.)

MURASAME. For shame! For such thoughts as these
You are lost in the sin of passion.
All the delusions that held you in life—
None forgotten!

(Both step back from the tree.)

That is a pine tree.
And Yukihira is not here.

MATSUKAZE. You are talking nonsense!

(She looks at the pine tree.)

This pine *is* Yukihira!
"Though we may part for a time,

If I hear you are pining for me,
I'll hurry back."[21]
Have you forgotten those words he wrote?

MURASAME. Yes, I had forgotten!
He said, "Though we may part for a time,
If you pine, I will return to you."

MATSUKAZE. I have not forgotten.
And I wait for the pine wind
To whisper word of his coming.

MURASAME. If that word should ever come,
My sleeves for a while
Would be wet with autumn rain.

MATSUKAZE. So we await him. He will come,
Constant ever, green as a pine.

MURASAME. Yes, we can trust

MATSUKAZE.   his poem:

CHORUS. "I have gone away
(*Murasame, weeping, kneels before the flute player. Matsukaze goes to the first pine on the bridgeway, then returns
to the stage and dances.*)

MATSUKAZE. Into the mountains of Inaba,
Covered with pines,
But if I hear you pine,
I shall come back at once."[22]
Those are the mountain pines
Of distant Inaba,
(*She looks up the bridgeway.*)
And these are the pines
On the curving Suma shore.
Here our dear prince once lived.
If Yukihira comes again,
I shall go stand under the tree
(*She approaches the tree.*)
Bent by the sea-wind,
And, tenderly, tell him
(*She stands next to the tree.*)
I love him still!
(*She steps back a little and weeps. Then she circles the tree,
her dancing suggesting madness.*)

CHORUS. Madly the gale howls through the pines,
  And breakers crash in Suma Bay;
  Through the frenzied night
  We have come to you
  In a dream of deluded passion.
  Pray for us! Pray for our rest!
    (*At stage center, Matsukaze presses her palms together in
    supplication.*)
  Now we take our leave. The retreating waves
  Hiss far away, and a wind sweeps down
  From the mountain to Suma Bay.
  The cocks are crowing on the barrier road.
  Your dream is over. Day has come.
  Last night you heard the autumn rain;
  This morning all that is left
  Is the wind in the pines,
  The wind in the pines.

Notes

1. From the poem by Yukihira, no. 876 in the *Shinkokinshū*: "The sleeves of the traveler have turned cold; the wind from Suma Bay blows through the pass."

2. A modified quotation from the poem by Hōkyō Chūmei, no. 187 in the *Kin'yōshū*: "Pillow of grass—as I sleep on my journey I realize I have no companion but the moon."

3. The words "salt sea," which can also be translated "brine," lead to mention of the brine cart even though the cart does not logically belong in the context.

4. From the poem by Fujiwara Takamitsu, no. 435 in the *Shūishū*: "In this world which seems difficult to pass through, how I envy the pure moon!"

5. The following description is generally inspired by the "Exile at Suma" chapter of *The Tale of Genji*.

6. Ojima is one of the islands at Matsushima, a place renowned for its scenic beauty. Both names are conventionally associated in poetry with *ama*, fisherwomen.

7. The following passage is a *tsukushi*, or "exhaustive enumeration," of place-names associated with the sea, including allusions and plays on words. This passage was apparently borrowed from an older work, a play called *Tōei* that was set by Ashinoya Bay. Michinoku is a general name for the northern end of the island of Honshu. Chika was another name for Shiogama ("Salt Kiln"), and sounds like the word meaning "near."

8. Akogi is the name of a stretch of shore on Ise Bay. The pulling in of the nets and the hauling of the wood for the salt kilns at Akogi were frequently mentioned in poetry.

9. Futami-ga-ura (Twice-See Beach) is a word evocative of Ise and often used in poetry for the meaning of its name.

10. Narumi was often mentioned in poetry because of its dry flats that appeared at low tide.

11. Ashinoya (modern Ashiya) and Naruo are two places near Suma. Ashinoya means literally "reed house."

12. Derived from the poem in the 87th episode of the *Ise Monogatari*: "At Nada by Ashinoya, I have no respite from boiling brine for salt; I have come without even putting a boxwood comb in my hair."

13. The line recalls the poem quoted in note 12, but it is used because

of the pivot-word *tsuge no,* "of boxwood," and *tsuge,* "to inform."
Similarly, *kushi sashi,* "Setting a comb (in the hair)," leads into *sashi-kuru nami,* "in-rushing waves."

14. Poem no. 962 in the *Kokinshū.*

15. Derived from a poem by Fujiwara Tameuji, no. 361 in the *Shingo-senshū:* "The fishermen of Suma are accustomed to the moon, spending the autumn in clothes wet with waves blown by the salt wind."

16. Literally, "purification on the day of the serpent." The ceremony was performed on the first day of the serpent in the third month. Genji had the ceremony performed while he was at Suma. The streamers were conventional Shinto offerings.

17. A slightly modified quotation of the anonymous poem, no. 746 in the *Kokinshū.* It is also quoted in *Lady Han.*

18. The first part of a poem by Ki no Tomomori, no. 593 in the *Kokinshū.* The last two lines run: "When I wear it there is no instant when I do not long for him."

19. The first part of an anonymous poem, no. 1023 in the *Kokinshū.* The last part runs: "Helpless, I stay in the middle of the bed."

20. The river of the afterworld.

21. A paraphrase of the poem by Yukihira, no. 365 in the *Kokinshū.* Another paraphrase is given in the following speech by Murasame, and the poem is given in its correct form below. In Japanese *matsu* means both "pine tree" and "to wait.'

22. The poem by Yukihira mentioned in note 21.

The Sought-for Grave

(MOTOMEZUKA)

BY KANZE KIYOTSUGU KAN'AMI/TRANSLATED BY BARRY JACKMAN

INTRODUCTION

The Sought-for Grave belongs to the fourth class of plays. Although attributed to Kan'ami it is likely that Zeami revised it extensively. It is one of the gloomiest plays in the repertory. No other work describes hell at such length, and few end on so grim a note. The heroine's punishment is likely to strike us as being unduly harsh for her offense. In the first part there are also some redundant passages that impede the flow of the play, but as a whole it is a highly effective work. A mood of desolation is created by the cold, unnaturally wintry landscape of the first scene. By the calendar it is already the season for picking the spring shoots, and the village women are dutifully doing so, but spring is late this year and there is little to gather. Spring may have come to the Capital, but not to isolated Ikuta. Gradually we are introduced to the story of Unai. Her ghost appears; we suffer with her in hell; and we are finally left, despite the Priest's prayers, in the darkness of her tomb. In this context the recurrent pun on the name Ikuta, which can mean "field of life," is painfully ironic.

Several poems in the *Manyōshū* describe the occasion of the poet's passing by Unai's tomb. (See *Manyōshū*, book 9, nos. 1801-3 and 1809-11; and book 19, nos. 4211-2.) But the immediate source for the play must have been the account in episode 147 of the poem-tale *Yamato Monogatari*, which differs in story only in minor details from the play.

The play was formerly known as *Otome-zuka*, "The Maiden's Grave," as in the source, *Yamato Monogatari*. The present title *Motome-zuka* was perhaps a corruption of the original title, but the searching for the grave mound mentioned in the text may have inspired the change. Some scholars have also suggested that the word *motome* refers to the acts of courtship that occasioned the tragedy; in that case the title might be rendered something like "The Courtship Grave."

The play was traditionally performed only by the Hōshō and Kita schools, but in recent years the Kanze school has also adopted it into its repertory.

PERSONS A PRIEST FROM THE WESTERN PROVINCES *(waki)*
TWO COMPANIONS TO THE PRIEST *(wakizure)*
MAIDEN *(mae-jite)*
THE GHOST OF UNAI *(nochi-jite)*
TWO VILLAGE GIRLS *(tsure)*

PLACE THE VILLAGE OF IKUTA IN SETTSU PROVINCE

TIME THE REIGN OF THE EMPEROR GO-HORIKAWA
(1221–1232) ; EARLY SPRING, THE SECOND MONTH

THE SOUGHT-FOR GRAVE
(MOTOMEZUKA)

(The stage assistant places a prop representing a grave mound near the front of the stage.

The Priest and his two fellow priests enter and face each other near the waki-pillar.)

PRIEST AND COMPANIONS. In traveler's clothes we have come a long way
From a far-off country;
In traveler's clothes we have come a long way
From a far-off country.
Let us hurry on to the Capital.

(The Priest faces front.)

PRIEST. I am a priest from the western provinces. I have never seen Kyoto, the city of flowers, so I have decided to travel there.

(He faces his Companions.)

PRIEST AND COMPANIONS. In traveler's clothes, by the shore of the ocean,
Skirting the many-fold waves we follow the shore,
Making our way. We travel by ship as well.
Now by sea, now through the mountains,
On and on we go. Day and night
We journey on. At last we reach
The village of Ikuta in Settsu,
Known to us only by name;
We have arrived in Ikuta.

(During the last few lines of this passage the Priest takes a few steps forward. He returns to his place at the close of the passage and faces front, thus indicating the journey and his arrival at Ikuta.

The Priest looks round him.)

PRIEST. I have heard of this village. I see many people in that field over there. They have come to gather the young shoots

39

of the spring herbs. I shall wait here for those women coming this way and ask them about the famous places nearby.
(The Priest goes to the waki-*position and sits. His Companions sit behind him.*

*A village Maiden, in reality the ghost of Unai, enters,
preceded by two other Village Girls. She wears the* zō *mask.
The three stop on the bridgeway.)*

THE THREE WOMEN. Across the fields of Ikuta,
Here where we pluck tender shoots,
The morning wind blows clear and cold.
See how our sleeves are waving, fluttering!

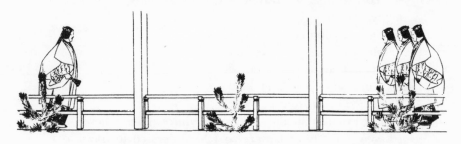

VILLAGE GIRLS. The buds begin to swell upon the branches,
And in the forest, under the lingering snow
Of early spring, the grass lies cold.
(The three women come onto the stage.)
MAIDEN. "Deep in the mountains snow still clings
Even to the pine-tree boughs;
THE THREE WOMEN. But in the Capital,
Surely the season has already come
To pluck tender herbs in the fields."[1]
With what longing we dream of that spring!
VILLAGE GIRLS. Yet here in this remote place
We country folk, cut off from that world,
THE THREE WOMEN. Must spin out our weary lives
By the watercut beach of Ikuta.
And our painful task is to go
Through these fields untouched by spring,
Gathering the tender herbs.[2]
So many villagers have left their tracks
The meadow in places is bare of snow.

But even if snow buried the old roads
We would still know where to pass;
Though the way were invisible
We would still tread a path
To the young shoots in the marshy meadows—
We shall pluck them today!
For, if we waited till the snow melts,
They might grow too old.
The shadows of the trees lie cold
In the forest where the rough wind blows;
Cold too the snow on the fields,
And still there is no spring.
Come, we shall pluck the Seven Herbs[3]
And pull up the young shoots of Ikuta,
And pull up the young shoots of Ikuta.

> *(The Priest stands and faces the Maiden. She stands at stage center, and the Village Girls at the gazing-pillar.)*

PRIEST. I beg your pardon. I have something to ask you. Is this place called Ikuta?

MAIDEN. Yes, certainly. This is Ikuta.

VILLAGE GIRL. Why should you have asked, if you already knew the name Ikuta? Surely you could tell from its appearance that this is the place.

MAIDEN. Ikuta is known for its landmarks. Did you fail to recognize this mist-shrouded woodland? This is Ikuta Forest.

VILLAGE GIRL. And the stream you just crossed was the River Ikuta, a famous river.

MAIDEN. Pale green are its waters,
Like the first, faint green of spring.
Among the lingering snows
We pluck the tender shoots.

VILLAGE GIRL. When you saw this meadow, where little grows,
　　Why did you not know it was Little Field?[4]
THREE WOMEN. The mountain-cherry blossoms
　　Of Yoshino and Shiga,
　　The crimson maple leaves
　　Of Tatsuta and Hatsuse
　　Are known to poets who may never have seen them.
　　But though we live in this famous place,
　　We know nothing of Ikuta Forest—
　　Or perhaps it is called Ikuta Wood?
　　What use is it to question us?[5]
　　(They turn to the Priest and move in his direction.)
PRIEST. Indeed, the scene before me—
　　Forest, sea and river,
　　And mist that swirls across the meadows—
　　All is truly worthy of famed Ikuta.
　　But where is the Sought-for Grave?
VILLAGE GIRL. The Sought-for Grave? The name is familiar, but
　　I really have no idea where it is.
MAIDEN. Please, traveler, do not bother us with such foolish
　　questions. We've no time to spare from picking the spring
　　herbs.
THREE WOMEN. You too had best be on your way.
　　How can you waste so much time here?
　　As the old poem says:

CHORUS. "We pluck spring greens
　　In Little Field at Ikuta,
　　A sight so charming we delay
　　The traveler who stops to watch."[6]
　　Such foolishness, all these questions!
　　"Guardian of the watch fire
　　On Kasuga moor,
　　Come out and look!
　　Guardian of the watch fire,
　　Come out and see!
　　So little time is left
　　Before the tender herbs are plucked."[7]
　　And so little time remains
　　For you too, o traveler,

So few days before you see
The Capital you hurry to.
"For your sake I went out
Into the fields of spring
To pluck the tender shoots."[8]
My sleeves are cold,
The snow lies unmelted,
But we shall gather herbs.
Coated though they may be with sleet,
We shall gather the herbs.

(*The three women mime the action of gathering herbs.*)
In the marsh the ice is thin,
But it lingers on.
Reach down, pull up the watercress
By the long roots
From the blue-green waters.
Pull up the blue-green plants,
Though spring has hardly begun
And they may be few in kind.

MAIDEN. "Spring is here, but this morning
Looking at the snowy meadows
It feels like the old year still."[9]
The new sprouts are so few,
Let us pick the shoots with old leaves too.

CHORUS. Last year's leaves
Are yet the seeds of youth:
Make sure you pick them all
In the fields of spring!

MAIDEN. The poet who came to the fields of spring
To pick violets, he said,
Picked instead the tender shoots
Of the plant we call "young purple."[10]

CHORUS. Yes, purple is known
As the color of affinity,
A bridge that joins lover and beloved;
But now that the bridge has broken

MAIDEN. At Sano the rapeweed stalks[11]
Spring up anew

CHORUS. A brilliant green,

MAIDEN. The famous purseweed of Ch'ang-an,
CHORUS. The Chinese purseweed!
MAIDEN. And the white-root cress
    Merging with the dawn snow
    Is hard to find or pick.
        (The two Village Girls exit via the slit door.)
    The spring is cold and barren,
    The morning wind bleak across the fields,
    While in the forest
    The lower branches of the pines
    Bow with the burden of snow.
    And where is the spring, we wonder.
    Even the breeze is icy
    As it crosses the river's white-flecked waves,
    And our wind-blown sleeves are colder still.
    At last we have gathered all the shoots,
    And we turn back homeward.
    At last we have gathered all the shoots,
    And we turn our steps toward home.
PRIEST. Tell me—the others gathering herbs have all left, but you
    still remain here alone in the field. Why is that?
MAIDEN. You were asking about the Sought-for Grave, were you
    not?
PRIEST. Yes. Do you know where it is?
MAIDEN. If you really wish to see it, follow me.
PRIEST. Excellent! I'll go with you.
        *(The Maiden takes a few steps towards the prop and the
        Priest does likewise, indicating that they are now at the
        grave.)*
MAIDEN. This is the Sought-for Grave.
PRIEST. Why is it called by that name?
MAIDEN. Long ago, a maiden called Unai lived in this village.

    At the same time there were two young men named Sasada
    and Chinu, both of whom loved Unai. On the same day, at
    the very same hour, each sent her a love letter telling of his
    burning passion. If the girl had yielded to one, the other
    would have been jealous and offended. For that reason she
    could give herself to neither. Her parents made the two
    youths compete in various tests of skill, but neither could

outdo the other. Even when they shot their arrows at a
mandarin duck on the Ikuta River, the two shafts pierced
the same wing of the bird. Seeing this, I thought
The tragedy of it!
So deep was the love they vowed,
This deep-green water bird and its mate,
Each cherishing the other's life;
And yet one died because of me!
The pair, alas, is torn apart forever.
"Weary of life,
I will go and cast myself
In the Ikuta River of Settsu—
And Ikuta means Field of Life!"[12]

CHORUS. Those were my dying words,
Those were my dying words
As I sank beneath the waters of the stream.
Then I was lifted out of the waves
And laid to rest here in this earth,
Beneath this very mound.
The pair of youths came then,
Searching for my grave mound.
"Why should we go on living?" they cried,
And, as the evening tide
Swelled the current of Ikuta River,
Each stabbed his rival, and they died.
For this also the guilt is mine.
Please pray for me!
With these words she vanishes into the mound,
She vanishes into the mound.

> *(The Maiden enters the prop. During the ensuing Inter-*
> *lude a Man of the Place tells the story of the Grave in*
> *language almost identical to that of the Maiden herself in*
> *the above passage.*
>   *The same night.)*

PRIEST AND COMPANIONS. Here we spend this night, our voices
Raised in prayer for the repose
Of the lost maiden's soul.
For a moment, short as the space
Between the antlers of a stag,

She emerged from the shadows
Of the grass that hides her tomb.
    *(The Priest presses his palms together and bows towards
    the grave.)*
Namu yūrei jō tōshōgaku
May you attain right understanding
O restless spirit!
Shutsuri shōji tonshō bodai
May you escape the wheel of life and death,
And know sudden enlightenment!
    (Unai's voice is heard from within the mound.)

UNAI. Men seldom find their way
   To this wide and desolate plain.
   Except for my grave, there is nothing here,
   Only wild beasts roaming about
   And quarreling over my bones.
   The wandering ghosts that haunt this tomb
   Fly with the wind over the pines,
   Quick as the lightning flash before the eye,
   And brief as the morning dew.
   "So many ancient tombs
   Are the graves of men who died young."[13]
   Short is our life on this earth,
   And this place mocks its name, Field of Life!

CHORUS. But now, at last, someone has come
   From my old home, the world of men
   Which I fled so long ago,

UNAI. To say a prayer for me.
   I am deeply blessed!
   But oh, how I miss the world!

CHORUS. Each man's soul, they say, suffers
   In a single day or a single night,
   In a single day or a single night,
   Eight hundred million four thousand
   Passions and evil thoughts.[14]
   How many more come to torment me,
   I who died ages ago
   In the time of an ancient emperor?
   Now, long afterwards, in the blessed reign

Of the second Horikawa,
I long to return to the world.
Must I remain forever hidden beneath the moss,
Here in these shadows of the grass?
Then I had rather be buried
Once and for all, in dark oblivion!
Such pains of desire burn my soul!
This is my dwelling, the Burning House,
This is my dwelling, the Burning House![15]

(*Unai sweeps back the covering over the framework of the prop, and appears before the Priest.*)

PRIEST. O painful sight!
But if you abandon this evil obsession,
You surely can escape eternal punishment.
Shuju shoaku gokuki chikushō[16]
This world of manifold and diverse evils,
This earthly hell, these realms
Of hungry ghosts, of brutish monsters,
Shōrō byōshi kui zenshitsu ryōmetsu
The sufferings of life, old age, sickness, and death—
All these in the end shall be destroyed!
May you quickly find salvation!

UNAI. I thank you, priest.
In the midst of my ceaseless agony,
Your words of prayer have reached my ears.
Now, through the smoke of the Hell of Awful Burning,
I see a tiny chink of brightness.
O welcome comfort!
But I am afraid. Who are you there? Are you the phantom
of the young Sasada? And over there—is that the youth
called Chinu?
They seize my left hand and my right,
They cry, "Come with me! Come with me!"
But from this dwelling place, my Burning House,
What strength have I to escape?
And once more—how horrible!—
Their ghosts take flight, and there appears
Before my eyes a mandarin duck,
Now changed to a bird of iron!

Its beak is steel, its claws are daggers,
It tears at my skull and now it will devour
The marrow of my bones!
Is this the punishment for my sins?
How horrible!
Priest, I implore you,
Find a way to free me from this pain!

PRIEST. She shrieks, "My torments have begun!"
　　　Hardly has she spoken than from the mound
　　　A swarm of flickering flames sweeps down.

UNAI. These lights are human souls
　　　Turning into demons!

PRIEST. They brandish their scourges,
　　　They run after her!

UNAI. I try to flee, but the sea is before me!

PRIEST. And behind, an ocean of flames!

UNAI. Now to the left,

PRIEST. Now to the right,

UNAI. Trapped between water and fire,

PRIEST. Hemmed in, nowhere to turn,

UNAI. I am helpless, lost!

PRIEST. In the Burning House

UNAI. Against a roof pillar

CHORUS. She presses and clings fast.
　　　But suddenly the pillar's length
　　　Bursts into flame. Now she embraces
　　　A column of fire.
　　　Alas, I am burning, she cries,
　　　It is unbearable!
　　　Every limb is transformed
　　　To white-hot flame and pitch-black smoke.

UNAI. Then once again I rise up, whole.

CHORUS. She rises up once more.
　　　Hell's demons lash her with their whips,
　　　They drive her off. Away she stumbles,
　　　Destined to suffer again and again
　　　The infinite tortures of the Eight Great Hells.
　　　Behold them now, and repent your sins!
　　　First is the Hell of Ever-renewing Wounds,

Next the Hell of Iron Cords,
The Mountain of Swords, the Hell of Boiling Oil,
The Hell of Hideous Screams, the Hell of Terrible Burning,
The Hell of Unendurable Fire,
And, last, the Bottomless Pit
Where she hurtles head over heels,
To suffer unending torment
For three years and three months.
But then—a brief reprieve in her anguish?—
The demons vanish, the flames die out,
And darkness covers the scene.
"Now I return to the Burning House.
But where is the place I used to live?"
Unai calls as through the black night
She searches here and there.
"Where is the Sought-for Grave, where?"
Uncertainly she gropes her way.
"I have searched it out!" she cries,
And into the shadow of the grass
That hides the Grave of Searching,
She vanishes.
Like the dew on shady meadow grasses,
She vanishes from sight.
The shadow of the dead has disappeared.
The ghost of the dead is gone.
   (Unai stamps to indicate she has disappeared.)

Notes

1. From an anonymous poem, no. 18 in the *Kokinshū*.

2. From the poem by Fujiwara Tamesada in the *Fūgashū* (1344–46): "How many villagers have left their tracks picking young shoots? The fields are now bare of snow in many places."

3. The Seven Herbs were traditionally used for New Year's dishes and were believed to ward off illness.

4. There is a play on words, here rendered by the double use of the word "little."

5. The meaning is that the women, being simple country folk, know less of the poetic associations of the place where they live than poets who may never have visited the spot. The statement is contradicted, however, by their other remarks.

6. From the poem by Minamoto no Moroyori in *Horikawa-in Ontoki Hyakushu Waka* (c. 1100).

7. From the anonymous poem, no. 19 in the *Kokinshū*.

8. From the poem by the Emperor Kōkō, no. 21 in the *Kokinshū*: "For your sake I went out into the spring fields; on the sleeve of the hand with which I pluck the young shoots the snow is falling."

9. From the poem by Taira no Suekata in the *Shūishū*.

10. The poet who went to pick violets was Yamabe no Akahito, one of the great *Manyōshū* poets. The implication is that the poet, who says he spent a night in the field (so enamoured was he of the violets) found a sweetheart, perhaps like the "young Murasaki" of *The Tale of Genji*.

11. The allusion here is to one of the "poems from the Eastland" in the *Manyōshū*.

12. The poem is quoted from *Yamato Monogatari*.

13. A quotation of unknown origin.

14. This statement is derived from the Chinese monk Tao Ch'o 562–645).

15. The Burning House is a familiar Buddhist metaphor for this world, which one should flee as intently as from a burning house.

16. A *gāthā* from the *Lotus Sutra*. These Chinese words, though read in Japanese pronunciations, would have been unintelligible but impressive to the hearers.

Komachi
and the Hundred Nights

(KAYOI KOMACHI)

BY KANZE KIYOTSUGU KAN'AMI/TRANSLATED BY EILEEN KATO

INTRODUCTION

Komachi and the Hundred Nights, a fourth category play, was written by Kan'ami, but like other works attributed to him was probably revised by his son, Zeami. There is evidence especially that the passage in which Komachi describes the fruits and nuts she has gathered, a virtuoso example of the use of allusions, is by Zeami; other passages may even antedate Kan'ami.

According to popular traditions the famous poet and beauty of the ninth century Ono no Komachi was courted by a certain Fukakusa no Shōshō, or Captain Fukakusa, also known as Shii no Shōshō. Komachi promised him that she would yield if he slept one hundred consecutive nights before her house, on a bench used to support the shafts of her carriage: Shōshō came faithfully every night, and each time made a mark on the shaft bench. But the day before the hundredth night his father suddenly died and Shōshō had to forego his visit. Komachi accordingly set him a mocking poem, in which she offered to make the hundredth mark herself.

The play makes use of a variant of this legend and combines it with another story, which concerns Komachi's skull. The col-

52

lection of anecdotes *Kojidan* (c. 1215) relates that when Ariwara no Narihira (825–880, the hero of the poem-tale *Ise Monogatari*) was passing through the province of Mutsu he heard a voice crying:

> Each time the winds of autumn blow,
> The pain! The pain-racked holes that were my eyes!

Looking around, he saw only a skull lying on the ground, with pampas grass (*susuki*) growing through the eye sockets. A companion told Narihira that Komachi had died on this spot, and that this must be her skull. Moved, Narihira completed the verse:

> Ono, my name, is mine no longer;
> Only pampas grass grows here now.

Kan'ami shifted the scene of the play from Mutsu, in the far north, to Ichiwarano near Kyoto.

Of the five plays in the repertory dealing with Komachi, this is the only one in which she appears as a ghost. It is remarkable too for Shōshō's refusal to listen to the priest's teachings. His resistance to salvation is unique in Nō.

The play is performed by all schools of Nō.

53

PERSONS A PRIEST *(waki)*
A YOUNG WOMAN *(mae-zure)*
KOMACHI *(nochi-zure)*
FUKAKUSA NO SHŌSHŌ *(shite)*

PLACE FIRST PART: Yasé in Yamashiro Province
SECOND PART: Ichiwarano, also in Yamashiro

TIME THE NINTH MONTH

KOMACHI AND THE HUNDRED NIGHTS (KAYOI KOMACHI)

(The Priest enters and stands at the naming-place. He carries a rosary.)

PRIEST. I am a priest performing my summer retreat in the mountain village of Yasé. Every day a woman comes—I don't know where she comes from—to bring me fruit and firewood. If she comes again today I'll ask her name and ask her too what manner of person she may be. *(He goes to kneel at the waki-position. The Woman enters. She wears the* tsure *mask and in her left hand she carries a basket of leaves. She stands at the* shite-*position, facing the musicians.)*

WOMAN. The twigs I gather are for firewood,
The twigs I gather are for firewood;
How sad that the incense has left my sleeves![1]
(She faces front.) I am a woman who lives near Ichiwarano. A holy man has come to the mountain village of Yasé, and I always take him fruit and firewood. I intend to go again today. *(She kneels at stage center, indicating she has reached the Priest's hut.)* Forgive me for intruding. I have come again.

PRIEST. Are you the same woman who always comes here? Tell me what fruits you have brought me today.

WOMAN. What are all these fruits and nuts
I have gathered here?
Windfall acorns,
The easy prey of storms
That set them rolling
Like carriage wheels I used to know.[2]

CHORUS *(for Woman).* And what fruits have I to evoke
The houses of the poets?

WOMAN. Persimmons from the hedge,
To recall Hitomaro;[3]
Chestnuts from the hillside,
A memento of Akahito;

CHORUS. Plums from the window

55

WOMAN. And peaches from the garden;
  Pears from Ō-no-ura
  Where cherry-flax grows,
  Named for the cherry blossoms;
  Boughs of burning-oak
  And twigs of fragrant beech,
  Kindlings of the broad-leaved oak;
  Oranges both large and small,
  The mandarin and the cumquat,
  And for sweet, sad remembrance
  Of long-ago loves,
  A flowering spray of orange blossom.

PRIEST. Now I have learned the names of all the fruits and nuts
  you've brought me. But please tell me, what is your name,
  and what kind of person are you?

WOMAN. Oh, no, I am too ashamed!
  Ono, my name, is now

CHORUS. Mine to use no longer.

  (She rises.)

  I am an old woman and I live
  Near the moors of Ichiwara
  Where the wild pampas grass grows.
  Pray for my repose, o priest!
  And suddenly, as if blotted out,
  She disappeared from sight;
  As if dissolved into the air,
  She vanished completely.

  (She retires to the stage assistant's position.)

PRIEST. This is the most extraordinary thing that has ever hap-
  pened to me! When I questioned the woman closely, she said
  her name was no longer hers to use, and that she lives near
  the moors of Ichiwara where the pampas grass grows. And
  then she suddenly vanished. A man once passing through
  Ichiwarano heard a voice cry from a clump of pampas grass:
  Each time the winds of autumn blow,
  The pain! The pain-racked holes that were my eyes!
  Ono, my name, is mine to use no longer;
  Only pampas grass grows here now.

    That was a poem by Ono no Komachi. There can be no

doubt but that the woman I have just seen was the spirit of
Ono no Komachi! I shall go to the moors of Ichiwara and
pray for her repose.

Leaving my straw hut

(He rises and takes a few steps towards the front of the
stage.)

Leaving my straw hut
I journey now
To the long, deep grasses
And the heavy dew
Of Ichiwara moor.

(He kneels.)

I spread my prayer mat
And burn incense for the dead.

(He presses his palms together in prayer.)

Namu yūrei jō tōshōgaku:
May this spirit gain
Perfect understanding;
Shutsuri shōji tonshō bodai:
May she escape rebirth
And know sudden enlightenment![4]

(He rises and goes to sit at the waki-*position. Shōshō comes*
through the curtain onto the bridgeway. He wears the yase-
otoko *mask, but his face is hidden by the cloak he holds*
over his head. At the same time, the Woman, now revealed
as Komachi, stands and leaves the stage assistant's position.
She faces the Priest from the naming-place.)

KOMACHI. Blessèd am I, o priest,
That you should pray for my soul!
Instruct me, if you will,
In the Holy Commandments.

(Shōshō faces the Priest
from the first pine.)

SHŌSHŌ. No, you must not!
If you instruct her in the Law,
I will vent my fury!
Away with you, Priest, and quickly!

KOMACHI. Why should you prevent me?
Now that by rare good fortune

I have encountered the Teaching,
Would you still have me suffer
The tortures of hell?

SHŌSHŌ. Even when we suffered them together
The pains were grievous,
But if you alone attain
The Way of the Buddha
You will add to the weight I bear
Yet another cloak of sorrow,
Piling grief on grief.
If then I sink beneath the burden
Into the River of Three Fords,[5]
All the priest's instructions
Will not save you from my wrath.
Go away, at once, you priest!
(*He lifts the cloak over his head a little, and glares at the
Priest.*)

PRIEST. You are still deluded,
Deluded and confused,
But if the Law's power
Takes hold in you,
You too will surely
Enter the Buddha's Way.
Both of you together
Receive instruction in the Law!

KOMACHI. I cannot speak for him,
But my heart is an unclouded moon;
I came before you, o priest,
Pushing aside the pampas grass
To entreat that you pray for me.
(*She moves to stage center, facing the Priest.*)

SHŌSHŌ. I was concealing myself,
But now I emerge from the grass:
(*He removes the cloak from his head.*)
The plumes of grass are beckoning,
Now I have beckoned too—desist!
(*He makes beckoning gestures to Komachi.*)

KOMACHI. My heart that seeks the light
Is like the mountain deer;

Even if you beckon
You cannot hold it back.

SHŌSHŌ. Then I'll become a hound of passion
(He starts towards the stage.)
You can beat but never drive away.
(He comes onstage.)

KOMACHI. What a horrifying sight!
(He comes up boldly behind Komachi.)

SHŌSHŌ. I'll take your sleeve
and hold you back!
*(He puts his hand
on Komachi's shoulder.)*

KOMACHI. My sleeve in your grip,

SHŌSHŌ. My own that pulls on yours,
(He draws back a little.)

CHORUS. Both are drenched
in a dew of tears.
Now you know me,
Fukakusa, the Captain![6]
(He withdraws to the shite-pillar and faces the Priest.)

PRIEST. Then you really are Ono no Komachi and Shii no Shōshō?
Confess your sins and destroy them!

SHŌSHŌ *(to Komachi).* Then you must tell him how I spent one
hundred nights on the shaft bench of your carriage, and I
will mime my hundred nights of journeying to your door.

KOMACHI. Of course I never suspected
Such delusion lay in his heart.
(She sits near the Priest.)

SHŌSHŌ. That is absurd! She falsely promised her love if for one
hundred nights I visited the shaft bench of her carriage. And
I believed her! Every night before the dawn I set out stealthily
in my carriage, again and again, and made my way to the
shaft bench.
(He turns to Komachi.)

KOMACHI. I bade him draw his carriage blinds,
For fear that prying eyes might see him;
I told him he must come disguised.

SHŌSHŌ. So of course I ceased to use
My palanquin or carriage.

KOMACHI. I wondered when his love would end.

CHORUS. In Yamashiro,

In the town of Kowata,

There were horses to hire,[7]

(He takes a few steps forward and looks off into the distance.)

SHŌSHŌ. But I loved you so much

I walked barefoot all the way.

(He picks up the conical kasa *hat provided by the stage assistant.)*

KOMACHI. And how were you dressed?

SHŌSHŌ. A wicker hat and a straw cloak,

(He holds the hat before him and looks at it.)

KOMACHI. A bamboo staff, full of knots,

Like the skein of human grief.

SHŌSHŌ. On moonlit nights

The way was not too dark;

KOMACHI. And in the snow?

SHŌSHŌ. I brushed it from my sleeves.

(He mimes the action.)

KOMACHI. And on rainy nights?

SHŌSHŌ. I walked in dread of demons

Invisible to the eye

Who might swallow me alive.[8]

KOMACHI. And what of the rare cloudless nights?

SHŌSHŌ. On me alone

(He lifts the hat and looks upward.)

There fell a rain of tears.

Ah, how dark the night is!

(He holds the hat before his face.)

KOMACHI. The twilight hour

Aroused particular longing.

SHŌSHŌ. What are you saying?

(He lowers the hat and stares at Komachi.)

CHORUS. The twilight hour

Aroused particular longings in you?

SHŌSHŌ. It must have been the moon you waited for!

You surely never waited for me!

A lunatic would not believe that lie!

(He thrusts the hat towards Komachi.)

CHORUS *(for Komachi)*. The break of day,
   The break of day
   Brought many, many thoughts of love.
SHŌSHŌ. But when you thought of me, you prayed,
CHORUS. "Let the cocks crow if they will!
   Let the morning bell resound!
   Let the night give way to dawn!"
   Lying alone was no hardship.
      (He sits at the shite-*pillar*
      and lowers his head.)

SHŌSHŌ. Thus did I waste
   And exhaust my heart;
CHORUS. Thus did I waste
   And exhaust my heart.
   But when I tallied up
      (He mimes counting on the fingers of his left hand.)
   The notches on the shaft bench,
   There were ninety-nine nights.
   Only one more now—
   How happy I am!
      (He rises.)
   The longed-for day has come!
SHŌSHŌ. I will hurry to her!
CHORUS. How shall I attire myself?
SHŌSHŌ. This bamboo hat is unsightly—
      (He looks at the hat, then tosses it away.)
CHORUS. I shall wear a folded court hat.
SHŌSHŌ. I cast away my coat of straw,
CHORUS. And in this flower-patterned robe
SHŌSHŌ. Richly I array myself
   In fold on fold of color.
CHORUS. Purple-lined
SHŌSHŌ. My trouser-skirts,
   Wisteria-hued.
CHORUS. I'm sure she must be waiting!
SHŌSHŌ. I can't wait to be with her!
   At last the final day is here,
      (He goes to the front of the stage.)

And it has drawn to a close.
I arrange with elegance
CHORUS. My crimson hunting cloak.
What shall we drink to celebrate?
Though the moon itself
Should be our wedding cup,[9]

(He holds out his fan as though offering wine.)

The Precepts order abstinence,
And I will observe them.
This instant of enlightenment
Obliterates a host of sins:
Ono no Komachi
And Shōshō the Captain
Together have entered
The Way of Buddhahood,
Together have entered
The Way of Buddhahood.

(Shōshō gives a final stamp of the foot, then exits, followed by Komachi and the Priest.)

Notes

1. There is a pun on *taki*, to burn, used in "firewood," and *takimono*, perfume. Komachi regrets that she no longer wears elegant robes with incense burnt into them.

2. A reference to Shōshō's carriage which visited her so often.

3. The following passage contains various allusions to the poetical associations of different fruits. Hitomaro's surname was Kakinomoto, interpreted as meaning "persimmon hedge." This occasioned later legends about connections between Hitomaro and persimmons. Akahito, another great *Manyōshū* poet, had the surname of Yamabe (hillside) and traditionally lived in a place noted for its chestnuts (*sasaguri*).

4. A formula for prayer for the dead, given in Chinese.

5. A river in the afterworld which must be crossed by the dead before they are sent into their future lives.

6. The name Fukakusa means "deep grass"; the association with the words "dew of tears," a natural property of "deep grass," leads to revelation of his name.

7. Quoted from a poem in the *Shūishū* attributed to Hitomaro: "There were horses at Kowata in Yamashina, but I came on foot, for love of you."

8. A reference to a passage in the *Ise Monogatari* in which a woman is abducted on a night of lightning and rain.

9. A wedding ceremony in Japan still involves a ritual drinking of saké. The transition from this line to the next is exceedingly abrupt and the text may well be faulty. But perhaps the passage means that in the instant of envisioning the consummation of his marriage with Komachi, the culmination of his worldly desires, he suddenly remembers the Buddhist prohibition on drink and this sudden recollection enables him to submit to the rest of the Buddhist discipline.

Komachi at Sekidera

(SEKIDERA KOMACHI)

BY KANZE MOTOKIYO ZEAMI/TRANSLATED BY KAREN BRAZELL

INTRODUCTION

Komachi at Sekidera belongs to the third category. It was probably written by Zeami, though some authorities hesitate to make the attribution. The play is considered to be the loftiest and most difficult of the entire Nō repertory. In the past century only a few great actors at the close of their careers have ventured to perform it. It enjoys its high reputation because it celebrates, with the most exquisite simplicity, the bittersweet delight of being alive. Childhood, maturity, extreme old age, the pleasure and pain of life, are immediately communicated. The play conveys a timeless moment in the brief interval between birth and death. Its subject is poetry. Much of the great poetry in Nō lies somewhat outside the main Japanese poetic traditions, but *Komachi at Sekidera* is at once a superb Nō play and a splendid expression of the sources of Japanese poetry. The *shite* role is considered so difficult because there is little an actor can add to the text unless he is supremely gifted. During the first hour of the performance Komachi hardly stirs.

The setting is wonderfully appropriate. The time is the festival of Tanabata, the seventh night of the seventh month: the one night of the year when the Cowherd star can cross the River of Heaven to join the Weaver-girl star. On earth all are celebrating

66

the lovers' brief reunion. Even at Sekidera, a place of quiet renunciation, the priests and child acolytes are about to observe the festival. But while talking about poetry with the aged woman who lives in a hut nearby, the abbot of the temple discovers she is none other than Ono no Komachi.

Komachi, a woman of great beauty and literary gifts, lived at the Heian court during the ninth century. She became a legend in later times, with many apocryphal stories surrounding the few known biographical facts. Five Nō plays about Komachi are in the present repertory; *Komachi and the Hundred Nights* presents another aspect of the Komachi legend, and *Sotoba Komachi* (translated in Keene, *Anthology of Japanese Literature*) ranks nearly on a level with *Komachi at Sekidera*.

The structure of the play is classic, and remarkable for its economy and simplicity. Nothing jars, nothing is wasted. The moment when Komachi admits her identity to the Abbot is particularly touching because so unaffected.

Sekidera ("The Barrier Temple") still exists at Ōtsu, a city east of Kyoto; its modern name is Chōanji.

Komachi at Sekidera is in the repertory of all schools of Nō.

67

KOMACHI AT SEKIDERA
(SEKIDERA KOMACHI)

(The stage assistants bring forward a simple construction repre-
senting a hut with a thatched roof. It is covered with a cloth. The
Old Woman is inside.

As the music begins the Child, the Abbot, and two Priests enter
and face each other onstage. The Abbot and the Priests carry
rosaries.)

THREE PRIESTS. So long awaited, autumn has come at last,

So long awaited, the lovers' autumn meeting!

Now let us begin the Festival of Stars.[1]

(The Abbot faces front.)

ABBOT. I am the chief priest of Sekidera in Ōmi. Today, the
seventh day of the seventh month, we come to celebrate the
Festival of Stars here in the temple garden. People say that
the old woman who has built her hut at the foot of the mountain knows all the secrets of the art of poetry. So, on this
festive day dedicated to poetry, I am going to take the young
people to hear her stories.

(He turns to the Child.)

THREE PRIESTS. Early autumn comes and brings a touch of chill.

We feel it in the wind and in our thinning locks.[2]

Soon, soon the Seventh Night will be on us.

(The Abbot faces front.)

ABBOT. We bring offerings for the festival today,

The music of flutes and strings,

TWO PRIESTS. And many poems

ABBOT. Composed in our native tongue.[3]

(He turns to the Child.)

THREE PRIESTS. Our prayers for skill at poetry are decked

With brightly colored streamers:

Fluttering ribbons, each a token of prayer,

Like silk threads woven into rich brocades

On looms of autumn flowers

And pampas grass pearly with dew.

69

The winds in the pines
> (*The Abbot faces front, takes a few steps, then returns to his former position, indicating he has made a journey.*)

Blend with the strings of the *koto*
To make music for the offerings tonight,[4]
Our offerings for this festive night.
> (*The Abbot and his companions are now at their destination.*)

ABBOT. Here is the hut now. Let us call on the old woman. (*To the Child.*) But first, please sit down.
> (*All kneel. A stage assistant removes the cloth around the hut, revealing the Old Woman seated inside. Paper strips inscribed with poems hang from the crossbars of the hut frame. The Old Woman wears the* uba *mask.*)

OLD WOMAN. Days go by without a single bowl of food;
Whom can I ask for one?
At night my tattered rags fail to cover me,
But there is no way to patch the rents.
Each passing rain
Ages the crimson of the flowers;
The willows are tricked by the wind,
And their green gradually droops.[5]
Man has no second chance at youth;
He grows old. The aged song thrush
Warbles again when spring has come,
But time does not revert to the past.
Oh, how I yearn for the days that are gone!
What would I do to recapture the past!
> (*She weeps. The Abbot and the Child rise, and go to kneel before her.*)

ABBOT. Old woman, we have come to speak with you.

OLD WOMAN. Who are you?

ABBOT. I am a priest from Sekidera. These young people are students of poetry. They have heard of your talent, and I have brought them here to question you about poetry and to learn something of your life.

OLD WOMAN. This is an unexpected visit! The log buried in the earth has been so long forgotten you must not expect it will put forth new sprouts.[6] Just remember this: If you will make your heart the seed and your words the blossoms,[7] if you will steep yourself in the fragrance of the art, you will not fail to accomplish true poetry. But how praiseworthy that mere boys should cherish a love of poetry!

ABBOT. May I ask you about a poem everyone knows, "The Harbor of Naniwa?"[8] Do you agree that it should be used as a first guide?

OLD WOMAN. Indeed I do. Poetry goes back to the Age of the Gods, but the meters were then irregular and the meanings difficult to understand. "The Harbor of Naniwa," however, belongs to the Age of Man. It was composed for the joyous occasion of an emperor's enthronement, and has long been beloved for that reason.[9]

ABBOT. The poem about Mount Asaka, which once soothed the heart of a prince, is also beautifully written.[10]

OLD WOMAN. Truly, you understand the art,
For those two poems are the parents of all poetry.

ABBOT. They serve as models for beginners.

OLD WOMAN. Noblemen and peasantry alike,

ABBOT. City dwellers and country folk,

OLD WOMAN. Even commoners like ourselves

ABBOT. Take pleasure in composing poetry

OLD WOMAN. Following the promptings of our hearts.

CHORUS. Though the sands lapped by the waves
Of the lake in Ōmi should run out,
Though the sands of the shore should melt away,
   (*The Abbot and the Child return to kneel with the Priests.*)
The words of poetry will never fail.[11]
They are enduring as evergreen boughs of pine,
Continuous as trailing branches of willow;
For poetry, whose source and seed is found
In the human heart, is everlasting.
Though ages pass and all things vanish,
As long as words of poetry remain,
Poems will leave their marks behind,
And the traces of poetry will never disappear.

ABBOT. Thank you for your words of explanation. It is true that countless poems survive from the past, but they are rarely by

women. Few women know as much as you about poetry. Tell
me—the poem

"I know my lover
Is coming tonight—
See how the spider
Spins her web:
That is a sure sign!"[12]

Was that not by a woman?

OLD WOMAN. Yes, that poem was written long ago by Princess
Sotōri, the consort of Emperor Ingyō. I tried, if only in form.
to master her style.

ABBOT. Ah! You have studied the style of Princess Sotōri? I have
heard that Ono no Komachi, who's so much talked of these
days, wrote in that style.[13]

"Wretched that I am—
A floating water weed,
Broken from its roots—
If a stream should beckon,
I would follow it, I think."

That poem is by Komachi.

OLD WOMAN. Yes, once my husband, Ōe no Koreaki, took up with
another woman, and I grieved at the fickleness of the world.
Then, Funya no Yasuhide[14] invited me to accompany him to
Mikawa, where he was to be the governor. I wrote that poem
in response to his urging and to his promises that life in the
country would bring solace.

Alas, memories of the past!
So long forgotten, they rise up again
Before me as I talk to you.
Tears well up from my suffering heart.
(She weeps.)

ABBOT. Strange! This old woman says she wrote the poem
"Wretched that I am." And she says she wrote in the Sotōri
style, just as Komachi did. She must be nearly a hundred years
old, and if Komachi were still alive today. . . . And is there
any reason why she couldn't be? It *must* be so! *(to the Old
Woman.)* You are what is left of Ono no Komachi. Do not
deny it.

OLD WOMAN. Ah, I burn with shame to be called Komachi, I who
    wrote
        "With no outward sign
CHORUS. It withers—
        The flower in the human heart."[15]
    How ashamed I am to be seen!
        "Wretched that I am—
        A floating water weed,
        Broken from its roots—
        If a stream should beckon,
        I would follow it, I think."
    How ashamed I am!
        (*She weeps.*)
        "Hide them though I may,
        The tears keep flowing,
        Too many for my sleeves to hold—
        A rain of tears dissolving
        Everything except the past."[16]
    Now that my life has reached its end,
    Like a withered flower,
    Why should there still be tears?
OLD WOMAN. "Longing for him,
        I fell asleep,
        Then he appeared before me . . ."[17]
CHORUS. The joy I felt when I composed those lines
    Is gone forever, but still my life goes on,
    Attending the months and years as they come and go.
    The dews of spring depart, and autumn frosts appear,
    The leaves and grasses turn, and insect voices fade.
OLD WOMAN. My life is over, and now I see
CHORUS. It was like a rose of Sharon that knows
    Only a single day of glory.[18]
        "The living go on dying,
        The dead increase in number;
        Left in this world, ah—
        How long must I go on
        Lamenting for the dead?"[19]
    And how long must I, who wrote that poem,
    Live on, like flowers fallen, like leaves scattered,

With nothing left but life—dewlike, they always said.
Oh, how I long for the past!
My middle years were spent in yearning
For the distant glory of my youth.
Now even those days of wistful recollection
Have become such ancient history
I find myself wishing, if not for youth,
At least for middle age.
Long ago, wherever I spent a single night
My room would be bright with tortoise shell,
Golden flowers hung from the walls,
And in the door were strings of crystal beads.[20]
Brilliant as the Emperor's chair in grand procession
The jewellike gowns I wore, a hundred colors.
I lay on bright brocaded quilts
Within a pillowed bridal chamber.
Look at it now, my mud-daubed hut!
Can this be my resplendent room?

OLD WOMAN. The temple bell of Sekidera
CHORUS. Tolls the vanity of all creation—
To ancient ears a needless lesson.
A mountain wind blows down Ōsaka's slope
To moan the certainty of death;
Its message still eludes me.
Yet, when blossoms scatter and leaves fall,
Still in this hut I find my pleasure:
Grinding ink, I dip my brush and write.
My words are all dry, like seaweed on the shore.
Touching, they once said, but lacking strength[21]—
My poems lacked strength because they were a woman's.
Now when I have grown decrepit
My poems are weaker still. Their life is spent.
How wretched it is to be old!

(*She weeps. The Child turns to the Abbot.*)

CHILD. I'm afraid we'll be late for the Festival of Stars. Let's ask
the old lady to come with us.

(*The Abbot kneels before the Old Woman.*)

ABBOT. Please join us on this Seventh Night, the Festival of Stars.

OLD WOMAN. Alas! An old woman should not intrude on such an
occasion. I cannot go.

(She takes down the paper poem cards.)

ABBOT. What harm could come of it? Please come with us.

(He goes to the hut and helps the Old Woman to stand.)

CHORUS. The Seventh Night—

How many years since first I offered the gods
Bamboo tied with colored streamers?
How long has shriveled old Komachi lived?

*(Assisted by the Abbot and leaning on a staff, the Old
Woman leaves the hut.)*

Has Ono no Komachi reached a hundred years?
Or even more?
I who used to watch the Festival of Stars,
Familiar of the noblest lords and ladies,

(She kneels beside the shite-*pillar. The Abbot goes back beside the others.)*

Now stand in shameful hempen rags!
A sight too painful for eyes to bear!

(The Abbot weeps.)

Still, tonight we hold the Festival of Stars,

*(The Child stands and mimes serving wine to the Old
Woman.)*

Tonight we celebrate the Seventh Night
With multitudes of offerings for the stars.
Prayer streamers hang from bamboo,

*(While the following lines are being sung the Child goes to
the gazing-pillar, moves clockwise around the stage, then
stands at the center preparatory to beginning his dance.)*

Music plays and cups of wine go round.
The young dancer—look how gracefully
He twirls his sleeves, like snow
Swirling in the moonlight.

(The Old Woman, still seated, watches the Child dance.)

We celebrate the Festival of Stars,
Streamers flutter from the bamboos. . . .

OLD WOMAN. May it be celebrated through ages as many
As the joints of the bamboo!

(The Old Woman, hardly aware of what she does, taps the rhythm with her fan.)

CHORUS. We pray for eternal prosperity;

We dance the "Ten Thousand Years."[22]

(The Child completes his dance, then sits as before.)

OLD WOMAN. How gracefully that boy has danced! I remember how, long ago in the Palace, the Gosechi dancing girls swirled their sleeves five times at the Harvest Festival. They say that if a madman runs, even the sane will run after him. But tonight the proverb is reversed! Enticed by the boy's floating sleeves, see how a madwoman prances!

(She stands with the aid of her staff and begins her dance.)

One hundred years—

The dance of the butterfly

Who dreamt he had spent

A hundred years enfolded

Within a flower petal.[23]

CHORUS. How sad it is! It breaks my heart!

A flowering branch on a withered tree!

OLD WOMAN. I have forgotten how to move my hands.

CHORUS. Unsteady feet, uncertain wave of sleeves,

OLD WOMAN. Billow after billow, floating wave on wave.

CHORUS. My dancing sleeves rise up,

But sleeves cannot wave back the past.

(She goes before the hut.)

OLD WOMAN. I miss those vanished days!

(She kneels and weeps.)

CHORUS. But as I dance the early autumn night,

The short night, gives way to dawn.

The temple bell of Sekidera tolls.

OLD WOMAN. A chorus of morning birdsong heralds

CHORUS. The coming dawn, the day's approaching light,

The dawn's fresh light that reveals my shame!

OLD WOMAN. Where is the forest of Hazukashi?[24]

(She stands, propping herself on her staff.)

CHORUS. Where is the forest of Hazukashi?

There is no forest here to hide my shame.
Farewell, I take my leave.
Now, leaning heavily on her stick,
She slowly returns to her straw hut.
   (She enters the hut, sits and weeps.)
The hundred-year-old woman you have spoken to
Is all that remains of famed Komachi,
Is all that is left of Ono no Komachi.

Notes

1. The Tanabata Festival, of Chinese origin, is still celebrated in Japan on the seventh day of the seventh month. Bamboo branches are decorated with five-colored streamers and with slips on which poems have been written commemorating the lovers' meeting of the two stars.

2. From some lines by Po Chü-i included in the *Wakan Rōei Shū*, no. 204: "Who could have arranged things so well? The sighing cool wind and my thinning locks at once announce autumn is here." A parallel is drawn between the coming of autumn in the world and the coming of autumn to the person, evidenced by the thinning locks.

3. Many poets wrote in Chinese, especially on formal occasions, but the Japanese preferred their own language for their intimate feelings.

4. The above three lines are based on a poem by the Consort Itsukino-miya in the *Shūishū*, no. 451.

5. Derived from an anonymous poem in Chinese found in a commentary to the historical work *Hyakurenshō*.

6. Quoted, with slight modifications, from the preface to the *Kokinshū*.

7. Also from the preface to the *Kokinshū*.

8. This is the "Naniwazu" poem: "In Naniwa Harbor/ The flowers have come to the trees;/ They slept through the winter,/ But now it is the spring—/ See how the blossoms have opened!" The preface to the *Kokinshū* characterizes this poem and the one on Asakayama, Mount Asaka, as the "father and mother of poetry." Both poems are given considerable attention in *The Reed Cutter*.

9. The poem was traditionally supposed to have been composed to encourage the future Emperor Nintoku, who reigned in the fourth century A.D., to accept the throne.

10. The poem runs, literally: "Mount Asaka—/ Its reflection appears In the mountain spring/ That is not shallow, and of you/ My thoughts are not shallow either." The Prince of Kazuraki was sent to the distant province of Mutsu where he was badly received by the governor. He was so angry that he refused to eat, but the governor's daughter cheered him by offering saké and reciting this poem.

11. Based on lines from the *Kokinshū* preface: "Though you count up my love you could never come to the end, not even if you could count every grain of sand on the shore of the wild sea."

12. An anonymous poem, no. 1110 in the *Kokinshū*.

13. So stated in the preface to the *Kokinshū*.

14. An early Heian poet, one of the "Six Immortals of Poetry." The explanation of the "Wretched that I am" poem was traditional.

15. From poem no. 757 in the *Kokinshū*, by Komachi.

16. A poem by Abe no Kiyoyuki, no. 556 in the *Kokinshū*.

17. The first part of a poem by Komachi, no. 552 in the *Kokinshū*. The last two lines run: "If I had known it was a dream/ I should never have wakened."

18. These lines are based on verses by Po Chü-i, no. 291 in the *Wakan Rōei Shū*.

19. A poem by Komachi, no. 850 in the *Shinkokinshū*.

20. This description is based on a passage in the *Tamatsukuri Komachi Sōsuisho*, a work in Chinese, apparently by a Buddhist priest of the Heian period, describing Komachi's decline and her eventual salvation.

21. The appraisal of Komachi's poetry given in the preface to the *Kokinshū*.

22. The name of a *gagaku* dance, *Manzairaku*.

23. A reference to a poem by Ōe no Masafusa in the collection *Horikawa-in Ontoki Hyakushu Waka*: "This world where I have dwelt a hundred years lodged in a flower is the dream of a butterfly." The poem in turn refers to a famous passage in Chuang Tzu. See *The Complete Works of Chuang Tzu* (New York, 1968), translated by Burton Watson, p. 49.

24. Hazukashi, the name of a wood near Kyoto, also has the meaning "ashamed."

The Brocade Tree

(NISHIKIGI)

BY KANZE MOTOKIYO ZEAMI/TRANSLATED BY CALVIN FRENCH

INTRODUCTION

The Brocade Tree belongs to the fourth category, and is by Zeami. The *Shūchūshō*, a late twelfth-century work, quotes the following verse:

> My brocade trees
> Number a full thousand;
> Now I shall see within
> Her chamber forbidden to other men.

It goes on to explain *nishikigi*, "brocade trees," as follows: "When an Ebisu man in the interior of Michinoku wishes to propose to a girl, he does not write her a letter. Instead, he decorates a stick about a foot long with different colors, and sets it in the ground before the girl's gate. If the girl wishes to meet him, she immediately takes it into her house. If she is slow to do so, her suitor plants more. By the time he has planted a thousand, the girl sees that he really is sincere, so she takes them in and the two meet. If she does not take them in, her suitor gives up. The poem just quoted is by a man whose thousand brocade trees have brought him success." The Ebisu were a "barbarian," probably non-Japanese, people. Michinoku is the area at the northern end of Honshu.

On *hosonuno*, the "narrow cloth of Kefu," the same source quotes the poem,

> The narrow kefu cloth of Michinoku
> Is so very narrow
> That it will not meet across my breasts;
> Just so is my unrequited love!

The *Mumyōshō,* also of the late twelfth century, says, "Narrow kefu cloth is a cloth made in Michinoku. It is woven of feathers. Since this material is scarce, a narrow loom is used and only short lengths of cloth are made." In the play, *kefu* is used as a place name. No such village exists, however. *Kefu* is simply the name of the cloth.

Some Japanese critics admit that the happy tone of the ending of *The Brocade Tree* comes as rather a surprise, but they do not feel that this detracts from the play's quality. Good though it is, however, the play is not often performed.

Ezra Pound's version of *The Brocade Tree*, based on an unpublished translation by Ernest Fenollosa, is too far from the original to qualify as a translation. The present version is based on the Kanze school text. *The Brocade Tree* is performed by all schools of Nō.

THE BROCADE TREE
(NISHIKIGI)

(The stage assistant brings on a structure representing a grave mound, and places it near the front of the stage. The mound is covered with leaves, and its sides with a cloth. The Priest enters, accompanied by two Companions. He carries a fan and a rosary. The three face one another in the middle of the stage.)

PRIEST AND COMPANIONS. Shinobu-yama, the name alone[1]

Shinobu-yama, the name alone

Stirs longings—let us journey there.

 (The Priest turns to the front of the stage.)

PRIEST. I am a priest, traveling about the various

provinces. I have not yet been to the East,

but I intend now to make a pilgrimage as

far as distant Michinoku.

 (He faces his Companions again.)

PRIEST AND COMPANIONS. We go, our hearts unhindered as the flight

of clouds,

Our hearts unhindered as the flight of clouds

That rise, streamers in the evening sky,

Bank on bank, as days of weary travel mount

On this road to the north, to Michinoku.

 (The Priest takes a few steps toward the front of the stage, and returns to his place as the passage ends.)

To the village of Kefu in Michinoku.

At last we have arrived in the village of Kefu.

 (The Priest's return signifies their arrival in Kefu. The Priest turns to the front of the stage.)

PRIEST. Our journey was swift, and we have come already to the distant northern village of Kefu. Look, here comes a villager now. Let us wait for him a moment and ask him the story of this place.

COMPANIONS. Yes, let us do so.

 (All three kneel at the waki-*position. The Man and the Woman enter. The Man is unmasked and carries a fan and*

85

a brocade tree. The Woman wears the tsure *mask; in her
left hand she carries a white robe which represents a length
of* hosonuno. *She stands at the First Pine, while the Man
stops at the Third Pine. They face each other.)*

MAN AND WOMAN. Well we know this narrow cloth,
　　　　Woven time after time in the village of Kefu;
　　　　Familiar too is the brocade tree.
　　　　　(They turn to the front of the stage.)
MAN. Who is to blame that the pattern pressed
　　　　Into this cloth by the stone of Shinobu
　　　　Has gone awry? It is not my doing.
　　　　　(They face each other.)
MAN AND WOMAN. Amid the seaweed an insect chirps
　　　　My fault, my fault,
　　　　Tearing our hearts with his cries.
　　　　With the yearning grass we sigh—
　　　　When will the tears dry from our sleeves?
　　　　Long nights I spent
　　　　In the dew-drenched forest,
　　　　Wakeful and tormented.
　　　　What joy for me in spring's long rain
　　　　When, sick at heart of self,
　　　　The creature of a moment,
　　　　I live as if there were a reward for waiting?
　　　　I yearn for one who has no thought of me,
　　　　I toss between the truth and fantasy,
　　　　Uncertain if I wake or sleep.
　　　　Perhaps, with love it is always so—
　　　　Vain days, vain thoughts unnumbered,
　　　　And no way to forget.

Quickly time flows, a river of tears,
Swiftly they flow, the months and days,
Swiftly they flow, the months and days.
Between Imo and Se,
The bride and her beloved,
A wild river drives.
Where are the mountains of Yoshino?[2]
Far, far is Michinoku,
Farther still, the distance of the heart.
Faded is the cloth she wove,
And the thousand brocade trees,
In vain were the vigils of a hundred nights.

*(The Man goes to stand
at stage center;
the Woman goes to his
right. The Priest rises
and faces the Man.)*

PRIEST. How strange! At first I
thought these villagers were man
and wife, but I see the woman is carrying a cloth that seems
to be woven of feathers, and the man a stick richly adorned
and beautifully colored. What curious things to offer for sale.
(He addresses them.) What are you carrying?

WOMAN. This is a *hosonuno*, a narrow cloth woven to the breadth
of the loom.

MAN. And this painted and adorned piece of wood is a *nishikigi*,
a brocade tree. Both are noted products of this place. Here,
do buy them, please.

(He takes two steps toward the Priest.)

PRIEST. Indeed, I have often heard of the *nishikigi* and *hosonuno*.
Why are they so famous?

WOMAN. What a cruel thing to ask! Famous as they are, it seems
as though no one outside of this locality has heard of them.

MAN. No, no, it's only natural that he should ask. He has only
come here by chance. Why should he know a thing that has
no connection with his own life?

MAN AND WOMAN. We see now that you are one who has given up
the world. That explains why you do not know of the narrow
cloth and the brocade trees, which are tokens of mortal love.

PRIEST. What a delightful answer! Are these emblems famous, then, because they are mentioned in some love story?

MAN. Yes. Every day for three years the man sets up a brocade tree—"love's thousand wands," they are called in poems.

WOMAN. And the narrow cloth, woven only to the width of the loom, not wide enough even to cover a woman's body, is, in poems, a symbol for hearts that love cannot join,

MAN. A sign of thwarted love,

WOMAN. And the sign too

MAN. Of those who cannot meet—

WOMAN. A subject worthy of songs.

CHORUS. Before the woman's gate,
   The brocade tree,
   Still standing, rots away,

   (The Woman kneels in front
   of the Chorus. The Priest
   kneels as well.)

   Still standing, rots away;
   Too narrow is the cloth of Kefu
   For the lovers' meeting.
   So the poem says.
   Now, more shameful
   Than a body
   Discovered by the narrow cloth,
   I tell my tale.
   I tell my tale, but not completely—
   Mere names and scattered words
   Flung down like needles
   Of the pine trees at Iwashiro.
   The rest must wait.
   The sun casts evening shadows;
   Now, let us retrace our way,
   Let us return home.

   (The Man motions to the Woman,
   who rises.)

PRIEST. Please, tell me the tale of the narrow cloth and the brocade tree.

   (The Man kneels at stage center; the woman kneels once
   more. All three face each other.)

MAN. From ancient times it
   has been the custom
   here for a suitor to
   make brocade trees as
   go-betweens, and to
   stand them before the
   gate of his beloved's

house. Because they are signs of his courtship, he adorns them
beautifully. The woman takes into her house only the brocade trees of the man whom she would have; the others stand
unheeded. And the rejected suitor, though he comes for a
hundred nights or for three years, leaving the celebrated
Thousand Love Charms, comes in vain. In the shade of this
mountain is the grave of such a man. Three years he kept his
vigil, setting out his love charm every night, and in the end
he was buried together with the tokens of his love. They call
his grave the Brocade Mound.

PRIEST. I should like to see this Brocade Mound so that I may tell
   of it when I return home. Please show me the way there.

MAN. I shall be happy to. Please follow me.

WOMAN. Tell him please to come this way.

   (All three rise.)

MAN AND WOMAN. Husband and wife lead the way,

   (The Woman takes a few steps forward.)

   They take the traveler with them.

   (Both turn to the Priest.)

CHORUS. Long hours they make their way,
   Threading the narrow roads of Kefu.
   Where shall they find the Brocade Mound?
   Tell us, reaper on the hill,
   What path shall we take?
   But there is none to answer,
   Only the glittering dew
   Upon the roadside grass.
   Where are the jewels of truth?
   If only I knew where to find them.

MAN. Chill autumn evening,

CHORUS. Storm winds and sudden autumn showers.
   In this lonely mountain shade, forever dark,

We make a hard way through dew-drenched grass.
An owl cries in the pines,
Foxes lie hidden in the asters
And live in the grave-mound grasses.
    (The Man turns toward the grave mound.)
Here is the Brocade Mound,
Dyed bright with crimson maple leaves.
    (He turns to the Priest.)
Here is the tomb, he says,
Then man and wife depart,
Descend into the grave,
Descend into the grave.
    (The Man enters the grave mound. The Woman retires to the stage assistant's position, where by convention she is invisible. The Villager enters and stands at the naming-place.)

VILLAGER. I'm a native of this vicinity. This is a market day and I'm on my way to buy a few things. *(He sees the Priest.)* Well, you're a priest I haven't seen before. Where are you from?

PRIEST. I am a traveling priest on a journey through the provinces. Are you a native of this place?

VILLAGER. Yes indeed, I am.

PRIEST. Step over here then. I have something I want to ask you.

VILLAGER. At your service. *(He kneels at stage center.)* What would you like to know?

PRIEST. I dare say this request will seem unusual. I would like you to tell me everything you know about *nishikigi* and *hoso-nuno*, those famous products of this locality.

VILLAGER. I should say that *is* an unexpected request. I'm afraid I don't know much about them, but I'll tell you all I've heard.

PRIEST. Excellent!

VILLAGER. First of all, they call this the village of Kefu. They sell in the market here that narrow woven cloth you mentioned. Also, they gather charms of brightly painted wood called brocade trees, and they use them as go-betweens for lovers. In ancient times, there was a man who placed them before the gate of his beloved's house. When after three years she still had not taken them inside, he died. Then the woman, hearing that he had died because of her, also died. They were buried together with the love charms that had stood for three years before her door. Their grave is called the Brocade Mound.

Now, about the narrow cloth. Once there was in this place a bird of prey which carried off small children, to the intense grief of everybody. A rumor started that if the children were dressed in cloth woven of feathers, the bird would no longer take them. So the villagers wove the cloth to dress their children. At once, as predicted, the bird stopped seizing the children, and the cloth became much prized as a protective charm. But the cloth was narrow and its edges could not be joined; people wrote poems about lovers whose hearts could no more meet than the narrow cloth of Kefu in Michinoku.

That's what I've heard. Why do you ask about such things? I think it strange that you should want to know.

PRIEST. First, let me thank you for your kindness. I will tell you why I asked. Before you came here a village couple passed by. We spoke, and they were kind enough to tell me of the brocade tree and the narrow cloth. We came along the road together as far as this place, and they pointed out the Brocade Mound. Then—and this is very strange—they entered the grave and disappeared.

VILLAGER. That certainly is strange. I think the two people you saw must be the ghosts of those very lovers whose tale I just told you. You should pray devoutly for their remains.

PRIEST. This has been such a strange event that I shall stay a while and recite the blessed sutras, and pray devoutly for their remains.

VILLAGER. As long as you are here, please let me know if I can help you again in any way.

PRIEST. I rely on you.

VILLAGER. At your service, sir.

(He exits.)

PRIEST AND COMPANIONS. Sleep will not come
Even for so short a space
As that between the horns of a young stag.
Beneath these wind-tossed pines,
I will lie down to spend this night
Reciting prayers to Buddha.

(The Woman comes forward to the shite-*pillar.)*

WOMAN. Oh honored priest, they say such signs
 As sharing the protection of one tree
 Or dipping water from the same river
 Tell of a connection in former lives.
 How closely, then, we must be linked,
 To meet like this at the grassy pillow
 Where you lie. Yet you do not waken
 From your holy, wonderful dream!
 (The Man speaks from inside the grave mound.)

MAN. We thank you for the kindness of your prayers
 That have won us back across the worlds.
 How wonderful to hear calling me,
 From beyond the trammels of my long craving,
 My three vain years of vigil,
 The voice of the Buddha's law!
 Witness my true shape;
 It will appear to you
 In the Brocade Tree.

CHORUS. Three years I passed—
 A dream of long ago . . .

MAN. A dream, and now within a dream,
 Tonight by chance we meet.
 Three years that passed,
 Recovered now by our meeting.

CHORUS. Look! From the shadowy grasses
 Over the grave of their love,
 A vision rises,
 An image from the grave!
 (The Man appears from behind the mound, wearing the
 mikazuki *mask. The stage assistant then removes the cover-*
 ing from the mound. The Woman goes to stand on the
 right side of it.)

MAN. They say in the abyss of hell
 Is no distinction between highborn and low,
 No difference at all.
 How ashamed I am to be seen!
 (He turns to the Priest.)

PRIEST. Strange indeed! This grave seems old,

But all is bright within,
Shining like a human dwelling.
There stands the loom,
And there the pile of love charms,
As once they stood in times gone by.
Is this reality, or a dream?

WOMAN. We who dwell in dark delusions
Leave to you who are alive
The question of reality.

(She goes to stand before the Chorus.)

MAN. Indeed, Narihira too wrote long ago,
"It is for those living in the world
To find out what is real";
It is for you, a traveler,
To know existence from a dream.

PRIEST. Whether this is real or an illusion,
Quickly, quickly revive the ancient days,
Reveal them while the night still lasts.

MAN. I shall show you, then, the past,
Faint as a flower in the moonlight.

(The stage assistant gives him a nishikigi.*)*

WOMAN. Entering my grave
(She kneels inside the grave mound.)
I set up the loom to weave the narrow cloth,
Thin as the heart of autumn.

MAN. Holding in my hand the brocade tree,
I knock at my beloved's gate.

(He goes up to the grave mound and strikes it with his fan.)

WOMAN. No reply from within—
Faint sounds alone.

(The Man backs away a little.)

MAN. The sound of the loom,

WOMAN. The autumn cries of crickets;

MAN. Listen to their night voices—

WOMAN. Kiri

MAN. Hatari

WOMAN. Chō

MAN. Chō

CHORUS. Kiri hatari chō chō

(The Man strikes the brocade tree with his fan.)
Kiri hatari chō chō . . .
Sounds of the loom,
The weaving sounds of crickets,
Grasshoppers crying
Patch patch patch—
Is it for clothing that you weep?
Then do not grieve,
For with threads of the thousand grasses
Of the fields where you live,
We shall weave the narrow cloth.

> *(The Man kneels at stage center, and the Woman in front
> of the Chorus.)*

CHORUS *(for the Priest).* I see. You speak of the custom here,
The custom of far-northern Kefu,
That is to weave a special cloth
Matchless in the world.

MAN. I would say nothing of these things:
They fill me with shame.
But you have asked for this vision of the past,

CHORUS. And, following the priest's command,
We weave the narrow cloth,
We place the brocade tree
A thousand times and a hundred nights,
And still the fires of attachment burn,
And bitterness grows strong;
It will never pass away.

MAN. But blessed now, through you,
By this encounter with the Law,

CHORUS. We come, if only in your dream,
To seek repentance and to pray
For the miraculous power
Of the Lotus of the Wonderful Law.

> *(The Man rises and places his brocade tree before the
> Woman. During the following passage, he dances.)*

CHORUS. Outside, the suitor stands his brocade tree;
Within, the woman weaves her narrow cloth.
Like autumn insects sounds her loom.
Wordless, though they sense their nearness—

Unopened, the grass gates of her fence—
And now, too soon, the dawn and the departure
Of the heartsick lover.
Soon too the brocade trees
Thick-clustered at her gate,
Profuse as thoughts of love,
Turn dry and rot away,
And he must watch their fading silently.
If, like a moss-buried log,
He were unknown to men,
Then might his long love end.
But though he sees its emblems fade,
Tongues are busy and gossip knows
That the lovers do not meet.
Then weeps the lover tears of blood;
In poems they call the brocade tree
"The tree dyed with love."

MAN. "How could I have known
That though I notched a hundred nights
Of vigil on my carriage shaft,
I would still sleep alone?"
So a poet complained;
But I kept vigil
Not a single year, not two,
But three full years in the village of Kefu;
Three years have gone, and now
A thousand brocade trees,
Red as the end of autumn,
Stand outside her gate,

And I stand too, decaying,
Vainly waiting, with tears upon my sleeve.
Why could she not, even once,
By chance, reveal herself?
How could she, for three full years,
Remain so unyielding?
  (He continues dancing.)
CHORUS. My brocade trees
MAN. Number a full thousand;
  Now . . .

CHORUS. . . . I shall see within
　　Her chamber forbidden to other men.
MAN. What joy I know this night!
　　For we have met and pledged our love
　　With the cup of mother-of-pearl.
CHORUS. Let us dance,
　　Our sleeves fluttering like snowflakes.
　　　(The Man performs a haya-mai, *a "quick dance," before the text resumes.)*
MAN. Let us dance,
CHORUS. Let us dance, let us sing,
　　For the brocade tree that is go-between
　　For the lover and his beloved,
MAN. And the narrow cloth that is woven.
CHORUS. In songs and dances
　　The night goes by,
　　Till the day's first light
　　Shines in our wine cup.
　　Now we shy from the dawn,
　　Afraid to stand revealed.
　　We were but people of your dreams
　　While you slept. Now, waking . . .
　　The brocade tree and the narrow cloth
　　Vanish with the dream,
　　And leave the murmur of a wind
　　Drifting through the pines,
　　And in the morning light—
　　A grave among the fields.

　　　(The Man kneels and covers his face with his fan, as though he had entered the grave mound.)

Notes

1. Shinobu is the name of a mountain in northern Japan. The verb *shinobu* was used to describe a lover's "stealing out" to meet his beloved. Shinobu also is the name of a type of printed cloth made in northern Japan. This is not the same as the "narrow cloth of Kefu," but it is alluded to below because of its name and its similar geographical origin.

2. The Yoshino River flows between Imo Hill and Se Hill in the present-day Wakayama Prefecture. The word *imo* meant a younger sister or sweetheart, the word *se* a husband. There are frequent references to these hills, particularly in connection with obstacles dividing lovers (as the river divides the two hills).

Semimaru

BY KANZE MOTOKIYO ZEAMI/TRANSLATED BY SUSAN MATISOFF

INTRODUCTION

Semimaru, a work of the fourth category, was written by Zeami. The story of Semimaru, the blind *biwa* player—the *biwa* is a kind of lute—appears as early as the twelfth-century collection of tales, *Konjaku Monogatari*, but apparently has no historical basis. The *Konjaku Monogatari* version relates that Semimaru lived near the barrier of Ōsaka, between Kyoto and Lake Biwa. Once he had been in the service of a courtier, a famous *biwa* master, and learned to play by listening to his master. Minamoto Hakuga, the son of a prince, heard of Semimaru's skill and wished to bring him to the Capital. Semimaru, however, refused. So eager was he to hear Semimaru's *biwa* that Hakuga journeyed to Mt. Ōsaka, a wild and distant place in those days, though today a half-hour journey from Kyoto.

By the time of the writing of the *Heike Monogatari*, a century later, Semimaru had become known as the fourth son of the Emperor Daigo (r. 897–930). Like the Semimaru of the *Konjaku Monogatari*, he lived by a barrier, but it was the one at Shinomiya Kawara. A man named Hakuga no Sammi was so anxious to hear him play that he visited Semimaru's hut every day, rain or shine, for three years without fail.

Zeami borrowed from various versions of the legend of Semimaru as known in his day, but especially from the *Heike Monogatari*. No previous version of the story, however, mentions Princess Sakagami, who was apparently Zeami's creation. *Semimaru* is one of the rare plays in which the *tsure* (Semimaru) is nearly as important as the *shite* (Sakagami); another such play is *Komachi of the Hundred Nights*.

Semimaru is perhaps the most tragic play of the entire Nō repertory. Unlike *The Sought-for Grave*, in which Unai returns to earth to tell of her endless torments in hell, the tragedy of *Semimaru* takes place in this world, and involves two human beings who are nearly as real and immediate to us as characters in Western drama.

During the height of the fanatical nationalism of the 1930s and 1940s *Semimaru* was banned from the stage for its alleged disrespect to the Imperial Family, but today it is performed by all schools of Nō.

101

PERSONS   PRINCE SEMIMARU (*tsure*)
                   KIYOTSURA, AN IMPERIAL ENVOY (*waki*)
                   TWO PALANQUIN BEARERS (*wakizure*)
                   HAKUGA NO SAMMI (*kyōgen*)
                   PRINCESS SAKAGAMI, SEMIMARU'S SISTER (*shite*)

PLACE   MT. ŌSAKA IN ŌMI PROVINCE

TIME   THE REIGN OF EMPEROR DAIGO; THE EIGHTH MONTH

SEMIMARU

(The stage assistant places a representation of a hut at the waki-*position. Semimaru enters, wearing the* semimaru *mask. He is flanked by two Palanquin Bearers who hold a canopy over him. Kiyotsura follows them.)*

KIYOTSURA. The world is so unsure, unknowable;
    Who knows—our griefs may hold our greatest hopes.
    This nobleman is the Prince Semimaru
    Fourth child of the Emperor Daigo.
KIYOTSURA AND ATTENDANTS. Truly in this uncertain world
    All that befalls us comes our way
    As recompense for what we've done before.
    In his previous existence
    He observed intently the laws of Buddha
    And in this life was born a prince,
    Yet why was it—ever since he lay,
    An infant wrapped in swaddling clothes
    His eyes have both been blind: For him
    The sun and moon in heaven have no light;
    In the black of night his lamp is dark;
    The rain before the dawn never ends.
KIYOTSURA. His nights and days have been spent this way,
    But now what plan has the Emperor conceived?
    He ordered us to escort the Prince in secret,
    To abandon him on Mount Ōsaka
    And to shave his head in priestly tonsure.
    The Emperor's words, once spoken
    Are final—what immense pity I feel!
    Yet, such being the command, I am powerless;
KIYOTSURA AND ATTENDANTS. Like lame-wheeled carriages
    We creep forth reluctantly
    On the journey from the Capital;
    How hard it is to say farewell
103

As dawn clouds streak the east!
Today he first departs the Capital
When again to return? His chances are as fragile
As unraveled threads too thin to intertwine.
Friendless, his destination is unknown.
Even without an affliction
Good fortune is elusive in this world,
Like the floating log the turtle gropes for
Once a century: The path is in darkness
And he, a blind turtle, must follow it.[1]
Now as the clouds of delusion rise
We have reached Mount Ōsaka
We have reached Mount Ōsaka.

> *(Semimaru sits on a stool before the Chorus. Kiyotsura kneels at the* shite-*pillar. The Bearers exit through the slit door.)*

SEMIMARU. Kiyotsura!

KIYOTSURA. I am before you.

> *(From his kneeling position, he bows deeply.)*

SEMIMARU. Are you to leave me on this mountain?

KIYOTSURA. Yes, your highness. So the Emperor has commanded, and I have brought you this far. But I wonder just where I should leave you.

Since the days of the ancient sage kings
Our Emperors have ruled the country wisely,
Looking after its people with compassion—
But what can his Majesty have had in mind?
Nothing could have caught me so unprepared.

SEMIMARU. What a foolish thing to say, Kiyotsura. I was born blind because I was lax in my religious duties in a former life.

That is why the Emperor, my father,
Ordered you to leave me in the wilderness,
Heartless this would seem, but it's his plan
To purge in this world my burden from the past,
And spare me suffering in the world to come.
This is a father's true kindness.
You should not bewail his decree.

KIYOTSURA. Now I shall shave your head.

His Majesty has so commanded.

SEMIMARU. What does this act signify?

KIYOTSURA. It means you have become a priest,

A most joyous event.

(*Semimaru rises. The stage assistant removes his nobleman's outer robe and places a priest's hat on his head.*)

SEMIMARU. Surely Seishi's poem described such a scene:

"I have cut my fragrant scented hair

My head is pillowed half on sandalwood."[2]

KIYOTSURA. Such splendid clothes will summon thieves, I fear.

Allow me to take your robe and give you instead

This cloak of straw they call a *mino*.

(*Semimaru mimes receiving the* mino.)

SEMIMARU. Is this the *mino* mentioned in the lines.

"I went to Tamino Island when it rained"?[3]

KIYOTSURA. And I give you this *kasa* rainhat

To protect you also from the rain and dew.

(*He takes a* kasa *from the stage assistant and hands it to Semimaru.*)

SEMIMARU. Then this must be the *kasa* of the poem

"Samurai—take a *kasa* for your lord."[4]

(*Semimaru puts down the* kasa.)

KIYOTSURA. And this staff will guide you on your way.

Please take it in your hands.

(*He takes a staff from the stage assistant and hands it to Semimaru.*)

SEMIMARU. Is this the staff about which Henjō wrote:

"Since my staff was fashioned by the gods

I can cross the mountain of a thousand years"?[5]

(*Kiyotsura kneels at the* shite-*pillar.*)

KIYOTSURA. His staff brought a thousand prosperous years,[6]

SEMIMARU. But here the place is Mount Ōsaka,

KIYOTSURA. A straw-thatched hut by the barrier;

SEMIMARU. Bamboo pillars and staff, my sole support.

KIYOTSURA. By your father, the Emperor,

SEMIMARU.   Abandoned,

CHORUS. I meet my unsure fate at Mount Ōsaka.

You who know me, you who know me not[7]

Behold—this is how a prince, Daigo's son,
Has reached the last extremity of grief.
  (He lowers his head to give a sad expression to his mask.)
Travelers and men on horses
Riding to and from the Capital,
Many people, dressed for their journeys,
Will drench their sleeves in sudden showers;
How hard it is to abandon him,
To leave him all alone;
How hard it is to abandon him,
To tear ourselves away.
  (Kiyotsura bows to Semimaru.)
But even farewells must have an end;
By the light of the daybreak moon
Stifling tears that have no end, they depart.
  (Weeping, Kiyotsura goes to the bridgeway.)
Semimaru, the Prince, left behind alone,
Takes in his arms his lute, his one possession,
Clutches his staff and falls down weeping.
  (Semimaru picks up the staff and kasa, comes forward, and turns toward the departing Kiyotsura. Kiyotsura stops at the second pine and looks back at him, then exits. Semimaru retreats, kneels, drops his kasa and staff, and weeps. Hakuga no Sammi enters and stands at the naming-place.)

HAKUGA. I am Hakuga no Sammi.[8] I have learned that Prince Semimaru has been abandoned on Mount Ōsaka and it pains me so much to think of him at the mercy of the rain and dew that I have decided to build a straw hut where he may live. *(He opens the door of the hut, then goes to Semimaru at the shite-pillar.)* The hut is ready at last, I shall inform him of this. *(He bows to Semimaru.)* Pardon me, sir; Hakuga is before you. If you stay here in this way, you will be soaked by the rain. I have built you a straw hut and I hope you will live in it. Please, come with me. *(He takes Semimaru's hand and leads him inside the hut, then steps back and bows.)* If ever you need anything, you have only to summon me, Hakuga no Sammi. I shall always be ready to serve you. I take my leave of you for now.
  (He closes the door of the hut, then exits. Sakagami enters

wearing the zō mask. Her robe is folded back from her right shoulder indicating that she is deranged. She stops at the first pine.)

SAKAGAMI. I am the third child of the Emperor Daigo,
The one called Sakagami, Unruly Hair.
Though born a princess, some deed of evil
From my unknown past in former lives
Causes my mind at times to act deranged.
And in my madness I wander distant ways.
My blueblack hair grows skywards;
Though I stroke it, it will not lie flat.
(She smooths down her hair.)
Those children over there—what are they laughing at?
(She looks to the right as if watching passersby.)
What? You find it funny that my hair stands on end? Yes,
I suppose hair that grows upside down is funny.
My hair is disordered, but much less than you—
Imagine, commoners laughing at me!

How extraordinary it is that so much before our eyes is upside down. Flower seeds buried in the ground rise up to grace the branches of a thousand trees. The moon hangs high in the heavens, but its light sinks to the bottom of countless waters.
(She looks up and down.)
I wonder which of all these should be said to go in the proper direction and which is upside down?
I am a princess, yet I have fallen,
And mingle with the mass of common men;
(She proceeds to the stage while chanting.)
My hair, rising upward from my body,
Turns white with the touch of stars and frost:
The natural order or upside down?
How amazing that both should be within me!
(She enters the stage.)
The wind combs even the willows' hair
But neither can the wind untangle,
Nor my hand separate this hair.
(She takes hold of her hair and looks at it.)
Shall I rip it from my head? Throw it away?

I lift my sleeved hands—what is this?
The hair-tearing dance?[9] How demeaning!
(She begins to dance, in a deranged manner.)
CHORUS. As I set forth from the flowery Capital
From the flowery Capital,
At Kamo River what were those mournful cries?[10]
The river ducks? Not knowing where I went
I crossed the river Shirakawa
And when I reached Awataguchi, I wondered,
"Whom shall I meet now at Matsuzaka?"[11]
I thought I had yet to pass the barrier
But soon Mount Otowa fell behind me
How sad it was to leave the Capital!
Pine crickets, bell crickets, grasshoppers,
How they cried in the dusk at Yamashina!
I begged the villagers, "Don't scold me, too!"
I may be mad, but you should know
My heart is a pure rushing stream:
"When in the clear water
At Ōsaka Barrier
It sees its reflection
The tribute horse from Mochizuki
Will surely shy away."[12]
Have my wanderings brought me to the same place?
In the running stream I see my reflection.
Though my own face, it horrifies me:
Hair like tangled briers crowns my head
Eyebrows blackly twist—yes, that is really
Sakagami's reflection in the water.
Water, they say, is a mirror,
But twilight ripples distort my face.

(Sakagami sits at the stage assistant's position, indicating she has arrived at Mount Ōsaka. Semimaru, inside the hut, opens his fan and holds it in his left hand as if playing his lute.)
SEMIMARU. The first string and the second wildly sound[13]—
The autumn wind brushes the pines and falls
With broken notes; the third string and the fourth—
The fourth is myself, Semimaru,
And four are the strings of the lute I play

As sudden strings of rain drive down on me—
How dreadful is this night!
"All things in life
In the end are alike;
Whether in a palace or a hovel
We cannot live forever."[14]

(While Semimaru is speaking Sakagami comes before the shite-pillar. Semimaru inclines his head toward her as she speaks.)

SAKAGAMI. How strange—I hear music from this straw-thatched hut,
The sounds of a *biwa,* elegantly plucked—
To think a hovel holds such melodies!
But why should the notes evoke this sharp nostalgia?
With steps silent, as the rain beating on the thatch
She stealthily approaches, stops and listens.

(She silently comes to stage center. Semimaru folds his fan.)

SEMIMARU. Who is there? Who's making that noise outside my hut?
Hakuga no Sammi, lately you've been coming
From time to time to visit me—is that you?

SAKAGAMI. As I approach and listen carefully—that's the voice of
my brother, the Prince!
It's Sakagami! I'm here!
Semimaru, is that you inside?

SEMIMARU. Can it be my sister, the Princess?
Amazed, he opens the door of his hut.

(Taking his staff he rises and opens the door.)

SAKAGAMI. Oh—how wretched you look!

(She comes up to Semimaru as he emerges from the hut.)

SEMIMARU. They take each other hand in hand
(They place their hands
on each other's shoulders
and kneel.)

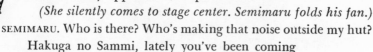

SAKAGAMI. My royal brother,
is that indeed you?

SEMIMARU. My royal sister,
is that indeed you?

CHORUS. They speak each other's names as in one voice.
Birds are also crying, here at Ōsaka,
Barrier of meeting—but no barrier

Holds back the tears that soak each other's sleeves.
(*Both weep. During the following passage Sakagami returns
to the middle of the stage and kneels.*)

CHORUS. They say that sandalwood reveals its fragrance
From the first two leaves[15]—but how much closer still
Are we who sheltered beneath a single tree![16]
The wind rising in the orange blossoms[17]
Awakens memories we shall preserve
We who flowered once on linking branches!
The love between brothers is told abroad:
Jōzō and Jōgen, Sōri and Sokuri;[18]
And nearer at hand, in Japan
The children of Emperor Ōjin,
The princes Naniwa and Uji,[19]
Who yielded the throne, each to the other:
All these were brothers and sisters
Bound in love, like us, like linking branches.

SAKAGAMI. But did I imagine my brother
Would ever live in such a hovel?

CHORUS. Had no music come from that straw-thatched hut
How should I have known? But I was drawn
By the music of those four strings,

SAKAGAMI. Drawn like the water offered to the gods

CHORUS. From deep wells of love and far-reaching ties.

The world may have reached its final phase[20]
But the sun and moon have not dropped to the ground.
Things are still in their accustomed place, I thought,
But how can it be, then, that you and I
Should cast away our royalty and live like this,
Unable even to mingle with common men?
A mad woman, I have come wandering now
Far from the Capital girdled by clouds,
To these rustic scenes, a wretched beggar,
By the roads and forests, my only hope
The charity of rustics and travelers.
To think it was only yesterday you lived
In jeweled pavilions and golden halls;
You walked on polished floors and wore bright robes.
In less time than it takes to wave your sleeve,

Today a hovel is your sleeping-place.
Bamboo posts and bamboo fence, crudely fashioned
Eaves and door: straw your window, straw the roof,
And over your bed, the quilts are mats of straw:
Pretend they are your silken sheets of old.

SEMIMARU. My only visitors—how rarely they come—
Are monkeys on the peak, swinging in the trees;
Their doleful cries soak my sleeve with tears.
I tune my lute to the sound of the showers,
I play for solace, but tears obscure the sounds.
Even rain on the straw roof makes no noise.
Through breaks in the eaves moonlight seeps in.
But in my blindness, the moon and I are strangers.
In this hut I cannot even hear the rain—
How painful to contemplate life in this hut!
　(Both weep.)

SAKAGAMI. Now I must go; however long I stayed
The pain of parting never would diminish.
Farewell, Semimaru.
　(Both rise.)

SEMIMARU. If sheltering under a single tree
Were our only tie, parting would still be sad;
How much sadder to let my sister go!
Imagine what it means to be alone!
　(Sakagami moves toward the shite-*pillar.)*

SAKAGAMI. Truly I pity you; even the pain
Of wandering may provide distraction,
But remaining here—how lonely it will be!
Even as I speak the evening clouds have risen,
I rise and hesitate; I stand in tears.
　(She weeps.)

SEMIMARU. The evening crows call on the barrier road,
Their hearts unsettled

SAKAGAMI. As my raven hair,
My longing unabated, I must go.

SEMIMARU. Barrier of Meeting, don't let her leave!

SAKAGAMI. As I pass by the grove of cedars . . .
　(She goes to the first pine.)

SEMIMARU. Her voice grows distant . . .

SAKAGAMI. By the eaves of the straw hut . . .

SEMIMARU. I stand hesitant.

CHORUS. "Farewell," she calls to him, and he responds,

"Please visit me as often as you can."

(Sakagami goes to the third pine and turns back to look at Semimaru.)

Her voice grows faint but still he listens,

(Sakagami starts to exit. Semimaru takes a few steps forward, stops and listens. His blind eyes gaze in her direction.)

She turns a final time to look at him.

Weeping, weeping they have parted,

Weeping, weeping they have parted.

(Sakagami exits, weeping. Semimaru also weeps.)

Notes

1. In certain Buddhist texts the rarity of meeting a Buddha is compared to the difficulty of a blind sea-turtle's chances of bumping into a log to float on. The turtle emerges to the surface only once a century and tries to clutch the log, but it has a hole and eludes his grasp; this was a simile for the difficulty of obtaining good fortune.

2. The poem referred to is by Li Ho and is actually a description of Hsi-shih (Seishi) rather than a poem by her. The meaning of the original verses was that Seishi's fragrant locks rivaled the perfume of cloves or sandalwood; however, the dramatist here misunderstood the Chinese and interpreted it as meaning she had cut her locks and now would have to rest her head on a hard pillow of sandalwood. (See commentary by Tanaka Makoto in *Yōkyoku Shū,* III, 205 [Nihon Koten Zensho series].)

3. From the poem by Ki no Tsurayuki, no. 918 in the *Kokinshū.*

4. From the anonymous poem, no. 1091 in the *Kokinshū.*

5. From the poem by the priest Henjō, no. 348 in the *Kokinshū.*

6. There is a pivot-word embedded here: *chitose no saka,* the slope of a thousand years; and *saka yuku tsue,* the staff that brings steady prosperity.

7. An allusion to the poem, attributed to Semimaru himself, no. 1091 in the *Gosenshū.* The poem, about the Barrier of Ōsaka, originally had a meaning something like: "This is the Barrier where people come and go exchanging farewells; for friends and strangers alike this is Meeting Barrier."

8. Hakuga no Sammi was in fact the grandson of the Emperor Daigo; and lived from 919 to 980; but here he is demoted to the position of a rustic, in inverse proportion to Semimaru's rise in position from being a menial to being Daigo's son.

9. The *batō* dance is described thus in *The Pillow Book of Sei Shōnagon* (translation by Ivan Morris): "In the Dance of the Pulled Head the dancer's hair is in disorder and he has a fierce look in his eyes; but the music is delightful."

10. The name of the river, *kamo,* meant a species of duck.

11. The name Matsuzaka contains the familiar pivot-word *matsu,* to wait.

12. A poem by Ki no Tsurayuki, no. 118 in the *Shūishū.* The horse referred to was presented as tribute to the moon in a special ceremony

held at the height of autumn on the night of the full moon. The head-note in *Shūishū* attributes this practice to the reign of the Emperor Daigo.

13. An allusion to the poem by Po Chü-i, no. 463 in the *Wakan Rōei Shū*.

14. From the poem attributed to Semimaru, no. 1851 in the *Shinko-kinshū*.

15. An expression used proverbially to indicate that genius can be recognized even in early youth. Here used to mean that a noble person reveals his character spontaneously.

16. Taking shelter beneath the same tree was an illustration of the concept that even casual contact in a previous existence might bring a karmic connection between people in their next incarnation. Because of some connection in a previous life Semimaru and Sakagami were born in this life as brother and sister.

17. The fragrance of orange (*tachibana*) blossoms was believed to summon up remembrance of people one once knew; here the memories are those shared by brother and sister.

18. Jōzō and Jōgen were siblings mentioned in the *Lotus Sutra*. Sōri and Sokuri were the son and daughter of a Brahman king of southern India. They were abandoned by their stepmother. After their death, their father found and recognized their skeletons on the island where they had been abandoned. The story is mentioned in the *Taiheiki* and the *Gempei Seisuiki*.

19. Sons of the Emperor Ōjin. The younger, Prince Uji, had been designated by Ōjin as his heir, but declined, saying the office belonged by rights to his elder brother. Prince Uji died first, and the empire went to Prince Naniwa, known posthumously as Emperor Nintoku.

20. A familiar concept. Believers in the medieval Pure Land Buddhism were convinced that the world had reached the period of the end of the Buddhist Law (*mappō*). According to one method of calculation, this period began about 1000 A.D., and was to continue for another thousand years.

The Deserted Crone

(OBASUTE)

BY KANZE MOTOKIYO ZEAMI/TRANSLATED BY STANLEIGH H. JONES, JR.

INTRODUCTION

The Deserted Crone, a play belonging to the third category, seems unmistakably a work by Zeami. Sanari Kentarō, the editor of the great collection of Nō plays *Yōkyoku Taikan,* summed up the play aptly: "An old woman has been abandoned deep in the mountains. Dressed in white robes, she dances a quiet dance in a landscape brightly lit by the moon. She utters hardly a word of complaint but, resigned to the world, confines herself to expounding the Buddhist teaching of nonattachment. . . . This play surely must be close to the apex of Zeami's *yūgen.*"

The source of the legend of the "deserted crone" may be found in an anonymous poem in the *Kokinshū* (no. 878):

> No solace for my heart at Sarashina
> When I see the moon
> Shining down on Mount Obasute.

The tenth-century poem-tale *Yamato Monogatari,* which gives the same poem, explains that it was written by a man who, at the urging of his wife, had carried his aged aunt into the mountains on a moonlit night and abandoned her there. The next day he regretted his action and brought her back home. The mountain became known as Obasute-yama, the Mountain of the Deserted Crone. However, Fujiwara Toshiyori is reported in the thirteenth-century book of criticism *Mumyōshō* to have said that the poem was composed by the old woman herself, as she gazed at the moon from the place where she was abandoned. Zeami followed the latter version.

Evidence in other sources indicates that at certain times and places old people were indeed taken out into the wilderness and left there, probably in order to conserve the limited food supply of a village. A small body of literature exists on this theme, going down to our time.

The moon is prominently mentioned in many Nō plays, often as a symbol of Buddhist enlightenment, but no other play is as filled with moonlight as *The Deserted Crone*. Sarashina, the site of Mount Obasute, was famous for moon-viewing, and the action of the play takes place on the night when the moon is at its brightest, the "famous moon" of the eighth month. The entire fabric of the play is filled with the atmosphere of a longing melancholy under the "pure full disc of light." The moon descends, and as the play concludes the spirit of the old woman remains behind in the thin glow of dawn, a cold and lonely wraith unable to break away from mortal attachments to the world.

The Deserted Crone is performed by all schools except Komparu.

117

THE DESERTED CRONE
(OBASUTE)

(A Traveler and two Companions from the Capital enter and face each other at stage center. They wear short swords and conical kasa hats made of reeds.)

TOGETHER. Autumn's height,
  The full moon's night is near,
  Soon the full moon's glory.
  Let us go and visit Mount Obasute.
    (The Traveler removes his hat and faces front.)

TRAVELER. I am a man of the Capital. I have yet to see the moon
  of Sarashina and this autumn I have bestirred myself at last.
  I hurry now to Obasute Mountain.
    (He puts his hat back on and faces his Companions.)

TOGETHER. On our journey—
  Fleeting are the dreams at inns along the way,
  Fleeting are the dreams at inns along the way,
  And once again we take our leave;
  Nights and days in lonely hostels
  Bring us here to famed Sarashina,
    *(The Traveler faces front and takes a few steps forward,
    then returns to his place.)*

TOGETHER. We have reached Obasute Mountain,
  Reached Obasute Mountain.
    *(His return indicates that he has arrived. He takes off his
    hat and faces front.)*

TRAVELER. We have traveled so swiftly that we are here already at
  Mount Obasute.

COMPANION. Indeed, that is so.
    (The Companions move to the waki-*position. The Traveler
    goes to stage center.)*

TRAVELER. Now that I am here at Mount Obasute I see that all is
  just as I imagined it—the level crest, the infinite sky, the
  unimpeded thousands of leagues of night flooded by the
  moon so clear. Yes, here I will rest and tonight gaze upon
  the moon.

119

(The Old Woman, wearing the fukai *mask, slowly starts down the bridgeway. The Traveler moves to the* waki-*position.)*

OLD WOMAN. You there, traveler, what is it you were saying?

(Traveler, standing, goes downstage left.)

TRAVELER. I have come from the Capital, and this is my first visit here. But tell me, where do you live?

OLD WOMAN. In this village, Sarashina. Tonight is that mid-autumn night for which all have waited.

> The moon has hurried the dusk of day,
> And now the high plain of heaven
> Glows in mounting brilliance—
> In all directions, the crystalline night.
> How wonderful the moon this evening!

TRAVELER. Oh, are you from Sarashina? Can you tell me then the spot where in ancient days the old woman was left to die?

(The Old Woman has reached the shite-*position.)*

OLD WOMAN. You ask of the fate of the old woman of Obasute?— a thoughtless question. But if you mean the remains of the woman who sang:

> "No solace for my heart at Sarashina
> When I see the moon
> Shining down on Mount Obasute,"

They are here in the shadow of the little laurel tree—the remains of an old woman long ago abandoned.

TRAVELER. Then here beneath this tree lie the woman's remains, the woman who was deserted?

OLD WOMAN. Yes, deep in the loam,

> Buried in obscure grasses
> Cut by the reaper.
> Short-lived, they say, as is this world,
> And already now . . .

TRAVELER. It is an ancient tale,

> Yet perhaps attachments still remain.

OLD WOMAN. Yes, even after death . . . somehow . . .

TRAVELER. The dismal loneliness of this moor,

OLD WOMAN. The penetrating wind,

TRAVELER. The lonely heart of autumn.

CHORUS *(for the Old Woman).* Even now,

> "No solace for my heart at Sarashina,

No solace for my heart at Sarashina."
At dusk of day on Mount Obasute
The green lingers in the trees,
The intermingled pines and laurels,
The autumn leaves so quickly tinged.
Thin mists drift over One-Fold Mountain—
Folds of faintly dyed cloth;
In a cloudless sky a doleful wind.
Lonely mountain vista,
Remote and friendless landscape.

OLD WOMAN. Traveler, from where have you come?

TRAVELER. I am from the Capital, as I told you, but I have long heard of the beauties of the moon at Sarashina, and I come here now for the first time.

OLD WOMAN. Are you indeed from the Capital? If that is so, then I will show myself with the moon tonight and entertain you here.

TRAVELER. Who are you that you should entertain me tonight?

OLD WOMAN. In truth, I am from Sarashina . . .

TRAVELER. But where do you live now?

OLD WOMAN. Where do I live? On this mountain . . .

TRAVELER. This famous mountain that bears the name . . .

OLD WOMAN. Obasute Mountain of the Deserted Crone.

CHORUS *(for the Old Woman).* Even to pronounce the name—
How shameful!
Long ago I was abandoned here.
Alone on this mountainside
I dwell, and every year
In the bright and full mid-autumn moon
I try to clear away
The dark confusion of my heart's attachment.
That is why tonight I have come before you.

CHORUS *(narrating).* Beneath the tree,
In the evening shadows,
She vanished like a phantom,
Like an apparition . . . disappeared . . .
(She exits.)
(The Villager enters and stands at the naming-place. He wears a short sword.)

VILLAGER. I live at the foot of this mountain. Tonight the moon is full, and I think I will climb the mountain and gaze at the moon.

(He sees the Traveler.)

Ah! There's a gentleman I have never seen before. You sir, standing there in the moonlight, where are you from and where are you bound?

TRAVELER. I am from the Capital. I suppose you live in this neighborhood?

VILLAGER. Yes indeed, I do.

TRAVELER. Then come a bit closer. I have something to ask you.

VILLAGER. Certainly.

(He kneels at stage center.)

VILLAGER. You said you had something to ask. What might it be?

TRAVELER. You may be somewhat surprised at what I have to ask, but would you tell me anything you may know about the pleasures of moonviewing at Sarashina and the story of Obasute Mountain?

VILLAGER. That is indeed a surprising request. I do live in this vicinity, it is true, but I have no detailed knowledge of such matters. Yet, would it not appear inhospitable if, the very first time we meet, I should say I know nothing of these things you ask? I will tell you, then, what in general I have heard.

TRAVELER. That is most kind of you.

VILLAGER. Well then, here is the story of Mount Obasute: Long ago there lived at this place a man named Wada no Hikonaga. When he was still a child his parents died and he grew up under the care of an aunt. From the day of his marriage his wife hated his aunt and made many accusations against her. But Hikonaga would not listen to her. At length, however, his wife spoke out so strongly that he forgot his aunt's many years of kindness and bowing to his wife's demands, he said one day to the old woman: "Not far from this mountain is a holy image of the Buddha. Let us go there and make our offerings and prayers." So he brought her to this mountain and in a certain place he abandoned her. Later he looked back at the mountain where now the moon was bright and clear. He wanted to go back and fetch his aunt, but his wife was a crafty woman and she detained him until it was too late. The old woman died and her heart's attachment to this world turned her to stone. Hikonaga later went in search of her, and when he saw the stone he realized the dreadful thing he had done. He became a priest they say. Ever since then the mountain has been called Mount Obasute—Mountain of the Deserted Old Woman. Long ago it seems that the mountain was known as Sarashina Mountain. Well, that is what I know of the story. But why do you ask? It seems such an unusual request.

TRAVELER. How kind of you to tell me this story! I asked you for this reason: As I said a little while ago, I am from the Capital, but I had heard about Sarashina and so I made a special journey here to view the moon. A short while ago, as I was waiting for the moon to rise, an old woman appeared to me from nowhere and recited to me the poem about Obasute Mountain. She promised to entertain me this night of the full moon, and I asked her who she was. Long ago, she told me, her home was in Sarashina, but now she dwelled on Mount Obasute. She had come here this night in order to dispel the dark confusion of her heart's attachment. No sooner had she spoken than here, in the shadows of this tree, she vanished.

VILLAGER. Oh! Amazing! It must be the old woman's spirit, still clinging to this world, who appeared and spoke with you. If so, then stay awhile; recite the holy scriptures and kindly pray for her soul's repose. I believe you will see this strange apparition again.

TRAVELER. I think so too. I will gaze at the moon and cleanse my heart. For somehow I feel certain I shall see this mysterious figure again.

VILLAGER. If you have any further need of me, please call.

TRAVELER. I will.

VILLAGER. I am at your service.

　　(He exits.)

TRAVELER AND COMPANIONS. Evening twilight deepens,
　　And quickens on the moon which sheds
　　Its first light-shadows of the night.
　　How lovely:
　　Ten thousand miles of sky, every corner clear—
　　Autumn is everywhere the same.
　　Serene my heart, this night I shall spend in poetry.

"The color of the moon new-risen—
Remembrances of old friends
Two thousand leagues away."
  (The Ghost of the old woman enters, wearing the uba
  mask. She stands at the shite-*position.)*

GHOST. How strange and wonderful this moment,
  Superb yet strange this moment out of time—
  Is my sadness only for the moon tonight?
  With the dawn
  Half of autumn will have passed,[1]
  And waiting for it seemed so long.
  The brilliant autumn moon of Mount Obasute,
  So matchless, flawless I cannot think
  I have ever looked upon the moon before;
  Unbearably beautiful—
  Surely this is not the moon of long ago.

TRAVELER. Strange,
  In this moonlit night already grown so late
  A woman robed in white appears—
  Do I dream?—Is it reality?

GHOST. Why do you speak of dreams?
  That aged figure who came to you by twilight
  In shame has come again.

TRAVELER. What need have you for apologies?
  This place, as everybody knows is called . . .
  Obasute—

GHOST. Mountain where an old hag dwells.

TRAVELER. The past returns,
  An autumn night . . .

GHOST. Friends had gathered
  To share the moon together . . .
  Grass on the ground was our cushion . . .

TRAVELER. Waking, sleeping, among flowers,
  The dew clinging to our sleeves.

TOGETHER. So many varied friends
  Reveling in the moonlight . . .
  When did we first come together?
  Unreal—like a dream.

CHORUS *(for the Ghost).* Like the lady-flower nipped by time,

The lady-flower past its season,
I wither in robes of grass;
Trying to forget that long ago
I was cast aside, abandoned,
I have come again to Mount Obasute.
How it shames me now to show my face
In Sarashina's moonlight, where all can see!
Ah, well, this world is all a dream—
Best I speak not, think not,
But in these grasses of remembrance
Delight in flowers, steep my heart in the moon.
   (*She gazes upward, then advances a few steps during the
   following passage.*)
CHORUS (*for the Ghost*). "When pleasure moved me, I came;
   The pleasure ended, I returned."[2]
Then, as now tonight, what beauty in the sky!
GHOST. Though many are the famous places
   Where one may gaze upon the moon,
   Transcending all—Sarashina.
CHORUS (*for the Ghost*). A pure full disk of light,
   Round, round, leaves the coastal range,
   Cloudless over Mount Obasute.
GHOST. Even though the vows of the many Buddhas
CHORUS. Cannot be ranked in terms of high or low,
   None can match the light of Amida's Vow,[3]
   Supreme and all-pervading in its mercy.
   (*She dances.*)
   And so it is, they say,
   The westward movement of the sun, the moon, and stars
   Serves but to guide all living things
   Unto the Paradise of the West.
   The moon, that guardian who stands on Amida's right,
   Leads those with special bonds to Buddha:
   Great Seishi,[4] "Power Supreme," he is called,
   For he holds the highest power to lighten heavy crimes.
   Within his heavenly crown a flower shines,
   And its jeweled calyx reveals with countless leaves
   The pure lands of all the other worlds.[5]
   The sounds of the wind in the jeweled tower,

Tones of string and flute,
Variously bewitch the heart.
Trees by the Pond of Treasures,[6]
Where the lotus blooms red and white,
Scatter flowers along their avenues;
On the water's little waves—
A riot of sweet fragrances.

GHOST. The incomparable voices of the birds of paradise—

CHORUS *(for the Ghost)*. Peacocks and parrots call their notes
In harmonies of imitation.
Throughout that realm—unimpeded, all-pervading—
The radiance that gives his name—"Light without limit."[7]
But here the moon through its rift of clouds,
Now full and bright, now dimly seen,
Reveals the inconstancy of this world
Where all is perpetual change.

GHOST. My sleeves move again in dances
Of sweet remembered nights of long ago.
(She continues to dance, her song alternating back and forth between herself and the Chorus.)

CHORUS. "No solace for my heart at Sarashina
When I see the moon
Shining down on Mount Obasute"
When I see the shimmering moon.

GHOST. No stranger to the moon,
I dally among the flowers
For these moments, brief as dew on autumn grasses . . .

CHORUS. Fleeting as the dew indeed . . .
Why should I have come here?
A butterfly at play . . .

GHOST. Fluttering . . .
Dancing sleeves . . .

CHORUS. Over and return, over and . . .

GHOST. . . . Return, return
Autumn of long ago.

CHORUS. My heart is bound by memories,
Unshakable delusions.
In this piercing autumn wind tonight
I ache with longing for the past,

Hunger after the world I knew—
Bitter world,
  Autumn,
    Friends.
But even as I speak,
See how the night already pales,
And daylight whitens into morning.
I shall vanish,
The traveler will return.
  (The Traveler exits.)
GHOST. Now, alone,
  Deserted,
  A moss-grown wintry hag.
  (She watches the Traveler depart, and weeps.)
CHORUS. Abandoned again as long ago.
  And once again all that remains—
  Desolate, forsaken crag,
  Mountain of the Deserted Crone.
  (She spreads her arms and remains immobile at the shite-position.)

Notes

1. Adaptation of a poem by Fujiwara no Teika, no. 621 in the *Shinchokusenshū:* "Is my sadness only for the sinking moon? / With the dawn half of autumn will have passed." The fifteenth day of the eight month was, according to the old Japanese lunar calendar, the midpoint of autumn.

2. Allusion to the words of one Wang Tzu-yu of the Chin Dynasty (A.D. 265–420). On a bright moonlit night Wang had boarded a small boat and gone to visit Tai An-tao. He came up to the gate of Tai's house but then left without seeing him. Asked by a friend the reason for his action, Wang replied: "Moved by pleasure, I came; the pleasure ended, I returned. Why must I see An-tao?"

3. The vow that all living beings would receive salvation.

4. In Sanskrit, Māhāsthama-prāpta, third person in the Buddhist Trinity of Amida (Amitābha), with Kannon (Avalokiteśvara), the bodhisattva of Mercy. Seishi, representative of the Buddha-wisdom, stands on Amida's right.

5. The infinite Buddha paradises of the universe, here as distinct from that of Amida in the West.

6. The pond of the Eight Virtues in Amida's Western Paradise.

7. Muhenkō, another name for Seishi.

Lady Han

(HANJO)

BY KANZE MOTOKIYO ZEAMI/TRANSLATED BY ROYALL TYLER

INTRODUCTION

Lady Han, a play of the fourth category, is one of Zeami's most romantic works. In several Nō plays the *shite* goes mad with grief over the loss of her child, but Hanago is one of only two *shite* in plays of the current repertory who goes mad because of love. Even rarer is the completely happy ending.

No source for *Lady Han* has been found. Hanago's nickname, Hanjo or Lady Han, refers to Han Shōyo (Pan Chieh-yü in Chinese), a poetess of the Early Han dynasty. The lady was a favorite of the Emperor Ch'eng Ti (r. 36–32 B.C.), but was eventually replaced in his affections by an even more celebrated beauty. The discarded favorite wrote a poem comparing herself to a fan in autumn. The round, white fan also resembles the moon, a typical sight of autumn. Zeami alludes to this poem again and again in the course of the play. Other allusions to Chinese poems in the collection *Wakan Rōei Shū* (Collection of Japanese and Chinese Poems for Recitation Aloud) and to Po Chü-i's famous *Everlasting Lament* sustain the Chinese mood of the imagery.

Lady Han begins with a long *kyōgen* passage. This unusual expository device was given special dramatic value by Zeami. The *waki* part is unusual too: Instead of being a priest or a courtier, the *waki* is Hanago's lover, Yoshida. Any suggestion of romantic love was generally avoided on the Nō stage, and the part of one of the lovers would be taken by a child in order to remove erotic overtones, but Yoshida is a full romantic character. Some scholars, however, have suggested that the part of Yoshida may originally have been played by a child, and that the *waki* role was assigned to a traveler or some other character not now in the text, but this remains conjectural.[1]

The play is considered to be about a madwoman, a standard variety of fourth-category plays, but Hanago's madness does not express itself in lunatic behavior. She is obsessed with her memories of the lover who failed to return, so much so that she fails to recognize him when at last she sees him again. Her madness seems to express itself also in an exaggerated form of a typical literary device of Nō, the accidental associations of words. Saying the words *itsu made,* "until when," carries her to *itsumadegusa,* the name of a plant; then to the dew that settles on the plant; then to the time it takes for the dew to evaporate; then (from the shortness of that time) to her main theme, her love and its brevity; then to mention of famous lovers of the past; and finally to what appears to be an attempt to check herself in her rambling, the question as to how we know today what words the lovers of the past exchanged in private. Certainly such chains of associations are not unique to plays describing "madness," but they contribute in *Lady Han* to its atmosphere of distraught love.

Lady Han is performed by all schools of Nō.

LADY HAN (HANJO)

(The Proprietress enters and goes to the shite-*pillar where she stands.)*

PROPRIETRESS. I am the proprietress of the inn at Nogami in Mino province. I provide accommodations here for traveling gentlemen and I keep quite a few women to entertain them. One of them is called Hanago. Last spring a gentleman named Yoshida no Shōshō stopped at my place on his way to the east, and I asked Hanago to wait on him. Before the gentleman went on, he and Hanago exchanged fans. He said that fans had a special meaning, and he gave her the name Lady Han. Ever since then Lady Han has just brooded over her fan, and whenever I've asked her to wait on other guests she has refused. The guests blame me, saying it's my fault. So I've finally decided today that I'm going to get rid of her. *(She faces up the bridgeway.)* Lady Han! Lady Han! I have something to tell you! Come here at once! What are you dawdling over? Come here this minute! *(Hanago enters and kneels at the* shite-*position. She wears the* ko-omote *mask. The Proprietress faces her from the gazing-pillar.)* I simply don't understand you. I've looked after you ever since you were a child. Now you've grown up and everyone in the village knows you. And who do you have to thank for it? You've got *me* to thank for everything! I won't take any back talk about it. I've asked you to wait on other guests, but you absolutely refuse to appear. So they blame me and say it's all my doing. We're not friends any more. I hope you realize that. Do you still have that fan? Give it to me! *(She snatches the fan from Hanago.)* Just looking at this fan is enough to make me seethe with rage! I won't have you in this house another minute! Take your fan *(She throws the fan before Hanago.)* and get out! I don't care where you go, as long as you go. I'm furious! *(She exits. Hanago picks up the fan and weeps.)*

133

HANAGO. The world is an uncertainty
    —How often has that been said!—
    But of all lots a prostitute's,
    Knotted with grief like river bamboo,
    Is surely hardest to bear.
CHORUS. I wander aimlessly,
    My clothes soaked by my tears:
    Now I must leave Nogami Village.
        (She rises.)
    I leave Nogami Village,
    Taking the Ōmi Road,
    But I know I shan't meet him there.[2]
    Ever since that faithless man left me
    The dew on my sleeve has never dried:
    How painful that I must linger on,
    Unable to vanish like the dew.
        (She comes forward a few steps.)
    How painful that I must linger on,
    Unable to vanish like the dew.

        *(She exits, weeping. Yoshida no Shōshō and two Servants
        come onstage and face each other. One Servant carries
        Yoshida's sword. Both Servants wear dirks.)*
THREE MEN. As we start the homeward journey
    We bid Fuji a sad farewell;
    When we return to the Capital
    We shall tell of the snows on its peak.
YOSHIDA. I am Yoshida no Shōshō. Last spring I traveled down to
    the east, but now that autumn has overtaken us I am on my
    way back to the Capital.
        (He faces the Servants.)
THREE MEN. We left the Capital as spring mists rose,
    But hardly had we embarked on the journey
    Than we heard the sound of the autumn wind
    As we reached Shirakawa Barrier.
    At the Barrier we turned in our tracks
    And headed for the province of Mino.
        *(Yoshida turns front, advances a few steps, then returns to
        his original place.)*
    We passed over water and mountains,

And now we have reached Nogami Village,
We have reached Nogami Village.

> *(Yoshida's return to his original place signifies their arrival in Nogami. He turns towards his sword-bearer.)*

YOSHIDA. Where are my servants? *(A man comes forward and kneels.)* We've made good time, and here we are already at the post town of Nogami in Mino province. This is where I once pledged my love to a girl named Hanago. Find out if she's still here.

SERVANT. Yes, sir. *(He faces up the bridgeway.)* Excuse me!

> *(The Proprietress enters and stands at the* kyōgen-*position.)*

PROPRIETRESS. Who is it?

SERVANT. I gather you have a woman here called Lady Han.

PROPRIETRESS. This Lady Han and myself had a fight. She's not here any more.

SERVANT. I'll report that to my master. *(He goes before Yoshida.)* I asked about Hanago and I was told she quarreled with the proprietress. She's not here now.

YOSHIDA. There's no trusting in promises, I see. But I want you to instruct the proprietress that if by some chance Hanago returns, she should send her up to the Capital at the first opportunity.

SERVANT. I'll do that, sir. *(He goes to Proprietress.)* I believe you're the lady I was talking to before. If Lady Han comes back, please send her up to the Capital.

PROPRIETRESS. I'll be glad to. If she returns, I'll tell her.

> *(She exits.)*

YOSHIDA. We've made good time on the way. Here we are in the Capital already. I have a long-standing vow to fulfill, so I'll be going directly to Tadasu.[3] I want you to come with me.

SERVANTS. Yes, sir.

> *(All proceed to the* waki-*position. Yoshida sits on a stool. The Servants sit behind him. Hanago enters and stops at the first pine. Her robe is now off her right shoulder to show she is not in her right mind.)*

HANAGO. "On Kasuga Moor
Sparse is the grass that grows
Breaking through the snow—
As rare as our meetings, my love."[4]

I gave myself to a faithless man,
Now the days weigh on me like robes.
The months go by . . . "I weary of life;
Save for the dismal tidings
Brought by the autumn wind,
No message ever comes for me."⁵
   (She looks around.)
"At the sunset hour
The clouds are massed like banners,
And my thoughts fly beyond."⁶
I wander, dazed and distracted.
Have pity, you gods and Buddhas, on one whose body is but
   the husk of herself!
Grant fulfillment for my love!
The deities of Ashigara,⁷
Hakone, and Tamatsushima,
Of Kibune and Miwa

   (She comes onstage and stops
   at the shite-*position.)*
All have sworn they will protect
The ties of man and woman.
If I address these gods,
   (She kneels and presses her palms together.)
How can they fail to help me?
Twice I bow in supplication.⁸
   (She rises.)
"They say I'm in love,
The rumor is already
In circulation,
CHORUS. Yet when I began to love,
There was not a soul who knew."⁹
   (She dances.)
HANAGO. Ah, I hate him and his faithless heart!
   (She weeps.)

Once someone prayed
"At Mitarashi Brook
I'll love no more."¹⁰
Who said those words? He lied.
An inconstant heart
Is a turbid stream.

Until it clears
The gods reject its prayers,
And rightly so!
Be that as it may,
My love, unknown to others,
Brings forth this dew of tears
CHORUS. That can settle on nothing:
What will become of me?
"Once a man's heart has grown
Attuned to constancy,
Attuned to constancy,
He need pray no more:
The gods will protect him."[11]
Each one of us too
Has a moon of enlightenment
That shines on unclouded
Though we live out our lives
Never suspecting its presence.
A jewel is stitched in our robes,[12]
But the sting of love makes us forget,
And we are all too apt to pray
Not for eternal salvation
But to remain in this world,
The same world with our lovers.
  (A Servant rises and faces Hanago.)
SERVANT. Well, you crazy woman,
why aren't you raving today?
Put on a display of your
antics.
HANAGO. What a cruel thing to say!
Just look there—*(She turns to
her right.)* The branch that
until now seemed motionless is
stirred by the wind, and a
single leaf falls.
  (She faces front.)
My mind for once was clear,
But now you tell me to rave—
You're the one who's mad!

Look how the autumn leaf
Whirls in the wind, whirls like my mind
Driven wild by love—what agony!
I beg you—don't ask me to be mad!
SERVANT. Well then, what happened to Lady Han's fan?
HANAGO. You're driving me out of my senses!
You called me Lady Han!
But I'll pay no attention.
That name too was my cruel lover's gift,
Like this fan I hold in my hand,
A keepsake I cannot put down.
The dew falls on my sleeve,
Tears for old memories.
"In Lady Han's chamber
The bleak color of an autumn fan;
On the terrace of the King of Ch'u
The cold sounds of a lute played at night."[13]
CHORUS. A fan at the end of summer
Or the white dews of autumn[14]—
Which will be first to fall?
Lying down or rising from sleep,
How desolate my solitary bed!
I lie my head on a lonely pillow
And watch the moonlight from my chamber.

(She kneels at stage center. The Servant kneels too.)
"Should the moon be hidden
By the many-folded hills,
I would hold up my fan
To symbolize the moon."[15]
HANAGO. If blossoms scatter on my kerchief
CHORUS. I will gather snow and mourn the spring.[16]
HANAGO. Evening storms and morning clouds—
Which does not evoke remembrances?
It comes back to me now . . .
CHORUS. The lonely tolling bell at dead of night
Would echo on Cockcrow Hill,[17]
Proclaiming the coming of the dawn
And urging us to say goodbye.
HANAGO. If only the moon trickling into my room

—That if nothing else—would linger a while!
But no, it fades from my pillow
And again I am left to lie alone.
　(She looks down in grief.)
The jade-green curtain, the crimson walls,[18]

The bed with twin pillows where we lay
Under familiar coverlets the whole night through,
Dreaming we would rest in one grave—
Everything has vanished without a trace.
Still, as long as we remain alive,
In the same world, I can endure,
I can keep my hopes perpetual.
But how we begrudged even the moment
It takes for a dewdrop to dry
On a spray of forget-me-not.[19]
We promised to fly wing to wing,
To grow together like joining boughs,
—These were the same words they whispered
In the Risan Palace long ago.[20]
But who could have overheard them
And passed on their words to us today?
　(She rises.)
Yes, though my lover promised
He'd come before autumn without fail,
The nights have piled up in vain;
His words were false, like his heart.
He made me trust him and I waited,
Night after night, but he never came.
　(She goes to the gazing-pillar.)
Still I stand at the railing,
　(She looks into the distance.)

I gaze at the sky and think,
"That is where he must be!"
The night winds of the fall,
The storm gusts, the mountain squalls,
And the late autumn gales
All visit the pine trees;
But when will *I* have a visit
From the man for whom I pine?

(She goes upstage and weeps.)
HANAGO. My only comfort is his keepsake,
    This fan I clutch in my hand.
    I stir it, hoping to get wind of him,
    But summer passes, and through my cedar window[21]
    The winds of autumn blow bitter cold.
    My fan is called "Round Snow."[22]
    Its name alone sends chills through me.
    I hate the autumn wind.
    But let it pass—now I realize
    It is true, to meet is to part,
    And since this is the just retribution
    My past lives have earned for me,
    There is no point now to bear a grudge
    Against the world or my lover.
    But still I go on brooding.
    (She goes to the gazing-pillar.)
    I know I am doomed to be unloved.
    How lonely it is for Lady Han
    All by herself in her chamber!
    (She stands before the musicians.)
CHORUS. On my fan is painted . . .
    *(The Chorus pauses while Hanago dances to musical ac-
    companiment. When she concludes she is standing at the
    shite-position.)*
HANAGO. The moon that I hide and carry
    In the breast of my robe,[23]
CHORUS. Triple-fold my fan and my sleeves.[24]
HANAGO. In bright silks I am robed—
CHORUS. He robbed me of his promise!
HANAGO. "I'll come back without fail," he said.
    I waited every evening
    And the days turned into months;
CHORUS. The autumn winds blow, but the reeds
    Never rustle with news of him.[25]
    The belling of stags,
    The insect cries with autumn
    Grow rare and indistinct
    As our ties after long separation.
    There's nothing to hope for!

HANAGO. His keepsake, this fan,

CHORUS. His keepsake, this fan

> Has a front and back, but now I know
> Even more two-faced was his heart.
> He fancied me, he said, but he lied.[26]
> Without him my love only grows stronger,
> Without him my love only grows stronger.
>> (*She kneels at the* shite-*position and weeps. Yoshida, still
>> seated at the* waki-*position, turns towards his servants.*)

YOSHIDA. Where are you?

> (*The sword-bearer bows before him.*)

SERVANT. I am here before you, sir.

YOSHIDA. Tell that crazy woman I want to see her fan.

SERVANT. Yes, sir. (*He stands and faces Hanago.*) Hey, you crazy
> woman! My master—he's the gentleman in the palanquin—
> says he wants to see your fan. Give it to me.

HANAGO. This fan is a keepsake from someone, and I never let it
> from me. Still, I must admit
> "This keepsake
> Now is my enemy:
> Without it,
> There might be a chance to forget."[27]
> But sometimes too, when I feel he's near,
> I can't wait to pick the fan up.
> No, I can't show it to anyone.
>> (*She thrusts the fan into the breast of her robe.*)

CHORUS (*for Yoshida*). I too have a keepsake

> Impossible to forget:
> The words we spoke.
> But if, like azaleas hidden
> In the silent wood of Iwade,[28]
> You do not speak,
> You show nothing in your face,
> How am I to understand?
> One look and I shall know
> Your fan.

HANAGO. One look—what for?

> The evening moon
> Is painted on the fan,
> But why do you importune me so?

CHORUS *(for Yoshida)*. There is no need to explain—
  Have you forgotten the promise I made,
  When I slept on my journey
  Amidst the dew-laden grass of Nogami?
  The promise to return in the autumn?
HANAGO. Did you say Nogami,
  Nogami in Azuma?
  Then you must be the man
  Who went to the end of the Azuma road
  When the waves washed over Pine Hill[29]
  And never returned.
    (She stares at Yoshida.)
CHORUS *(for Yoshida)*. Why should you suppose
  The waves have risen over Pine Hill?
  You have nothing to resent—
  I have kept my promise.
    (He gives his fan to a Servant.)
HANAGO. Then, you too have a keepsake fan?
    (She moves to stage center.)
CHORUS *(for Yoshida)*. I carried this fan next to my skin.
    (The Servant gives it to Hanago.)
HANAGO. From within the palanquin
CHORUS. His hand puts out the fan.
    (She opens the fan. The Chorus now speaks for Hanago.)
  Just now in the twilight
  Dimly, I see moonflowers,
    (She looks at the fan.)
  Painted on your fan.
  What more need I know?
  Have your man hold up the lamp![30]
    (She goes up to Yoshida and gives him her fan.)
  Now you can see the fan
  I have carried.
  Each examines and knows his own:
  He recognizes his fan, snow white,
  The keepsake he gave his beloved,
  And they know the deep affection
  Of husband and wife.
  They know the deep affection
  Of husband and wife.

Notes

1. Yokomichi and Omote, *Yōkyoku Shū*, I, pp. 451–2.

2. The ō of Ōmi is a homophone for the verb "to meet"; hence, the pun.

3. Tadasu is the name of a wood in the northern part of Kyoto where the Shimo-gamo Shrine is situated.

4. A poem by Mibu no Tadamine, no. 478 in the *Kokinshū*.

5. From a poem by Hafuri no Narikage, no. 1244 in the *Shingo-shūishū*. There is a pun on *aki*, which can mean both "autumn" and "weary."

6. Quoted with slight variation from an anonymous poem, no. 484 in the *Kokinshū*.

7. The deities are *myōjin*, Shinto deities who are the incarnations of Buddhist divinities. These gods were all associated with preserving the ties between men and women.

8. This line, *kinjō saihai* in the original, is a formula of invocation.

9. A poem by Mibu no Tadamine, no. 621 in the *Shūishū*.

10. A reference to the anonymous poem, no. 501 in the *Kokinshū*. Mitarashi Brook flows before the Kami-gamo Shrine in Kyoto, and was the site of ritual lustration and the making of vows.

11. A poem traditionally attributed to Sugawara no Michizane.

12. A reference to a story in the *Lotus Sutra*, found in the chapter entitled *The Five Hundred Disciples Receive the Announcement of Their Destiny*: "It is as if there is a man who goes to his friend's house, becomes drunk with wine and falls asleep. Just then the friend must go to attend to his official duties. He sews a priceless jewel into the sleeping man's clothes as a present, then leaves. But the man is lying there drunk, and does not realize what his friend has done. . . ."

13. From the poem by Songyō quoted, no. 380 in the *Wakan Rōei Shū*.

14. From the poem by Mibu no Tadamine, no. 283 in the *Shinko-kinshū*.

15. Quoted from the poem by Chisha Daishi, no. 587 in the *Wakan Rōei Shū*. The meaning is that if the moon of truth is hidden by the mountains of delusion, the speaker will use a round fan as an expedient in representing the moon.

16. The above two lines are apparently a quotation, but their source

is unknown. The word *kinshō*, here interpreted as meaning "on my kerchief," has also been taken to mean "on my lute" or "on the brocade." The fallen blossoms are equated with the snow and give the paradox of gathering snow, a thing belonging to winter, and regretting the passage of spring.

17. Several hills in China were known as Keirō (Chi-lung), called Cockcrow here. This reference is to a poem by Ki no Tadana in the *Honchō Monzui*.

18. There is apparently an allusion to a poem by Ōe no Mochitoki, no. 700 in the *Wakan Rōei Shū*, about Wang Chao-chün (Shōkun in Japanese), the Chinese beauty described in the play *Shōkun*. The scene is Chinese in feeling, especially in the colors mentioned, which would hardly describe a Japanese room.

19. See the Introduction for an analysis of this passage. The plant translated as "forget-me-not" is *itsumadegusa*, literally "plant for all time."

20. The *Everlasting Lament* by Po Chü-i describes this vow made by Yang Kuei-Fei (Yōkihi in Japanese) and the Emperor Hsüan-tsung (Gensō) at the Li-shan Palace. See also the play *Yōkihi*.

21. Mention of cedar (*sugi*) windows may have been inspired by the pun on *sugi* "passes" ("summer passes") above.

22. In the poem in the *Wakan Rōei Shū* (no. 162) by Ōe no Masahira mentioned in the Introduction, Lady Han's fan is referred to as *dansetsu*, "round snow."

23. From a poem by Po Chü-i, no. 199 in the *Wakan Rōei Shū*.

24. The word *miegasane* ("three-layered") refers both to the wearing of three robes and to a kind of fan with end-pieces made of three thin layers of wood.

25. Reference to poem no. 1212 in the *Shinkokinshū* by the Daughter of the Priest Ampō: If this were an ordinary autumn wind at least it should make a noise of rustling the reed-leaves. There is the usual pun on *aki*, meaning both "autumn" and "weary," and the poem, like the passage in the play, reproaches a man for not getting in touch with the speaker.

26. The pun on "fan" and "fancied" here is an attempt to give a rough equivalent of the pun on *ō*, "to meet," and *ōgi*, "a fan."

27. This anonymous poem, no. 746 in the *Kokinshū*, is quoted in various other plays, including *Matsukaze*.

28. The name Iwade is a pun on *iwade*, "not speaking."

29. A reference to the anonymous poem, no. 1093 in the *Kokinshū*: "If I leave you and my heart strays, waves will wash over Pine Hill." Because the speaker is sure that waves will never wash over the hill, the

poem is an assurance that he will never be untrue. It became a pro-
verbial expression of constancy.

30. The mention of moonflowers above is a reference to the *Yūgao*
chapter of *The Tale of Genji;* and at this point the original says, "Have
Koremitsu hold up the lamp," another reference to that chapter. Mention of Koremitsu in the translation does not seem necessary.

The Reed Cutter

(ASHIKARI)

BY KANZE MOTOKIYO ZEAMI/TRANSLATED BY JAMES A. O'BRIEN

INTRODUCTION

The Reed Cutter belongs to the fourth category of plays. It is generally attributed to Zeami, though he may have adapted an older work. The source of the story is the *Shūishū*, an imperial collection of poetry compiled in the late tenth century. Two poems with their prose preface supplied the outlines of the story: "When a certain woman went to Naniwa for a purification ceremony, she met on the way a man who had formerly been her lover. He was now a reed cutter, and presented a most peculiar appearance. Somewhat disconcerted, she remarked that they had not met for a long time. The man replied,

> As I cut reeds without you
> I knew I had been wrong;
> Life here by Naniwa Bay
> Has grown so melancholy.

She answered,

> You did no wrong.
> 'Fare thee well,' we said,
> As our parting words:
> Why should life by Naniwa Bay
> Have grown so melancholy?"

A much fuller account is given in the tenth-century poem-tale *Yamato Monogatari*. A wellborn couple has fallen on hard times. The husband urges the wife to seek employment in the Capital, promising he will join her if his own fortunes improve. The wife succeeds in finding a position in a nobleman's household, and the nobleman eventually marries her when his wife dies. But she continues to worry about her former husband, and goes to Naniwa to look for him. Their old house has vanished, but she finds the husband, attired like a peddler and selling reeds. When she offers to buy his reeds the man recognizes her and, ashamed to be seen in his humble appearance, runs off and hides in a hut. The lady sends a servant after him, but he refuses to come out. Instead he and his wife exchange the poems translated above. She also gives the man her outer cloak before she returns to the Capital alone.

The play modifies the *Yamato Monogatari* story, especially in its ending. It is unusually long, and abounds in plays on words and allusions to old texts. It is notable also for its sympathetic treatment of marital love.

The Reed Cutter is performed by all schools of Nō.

149

PERSONS   THE WIFE OF KUSAKA NO SAEMON *(tsure)*
THE CHIEF ATTENDANT TO THE WIFE *(waki)*
AN ATTENDANT TO THE WIFE *(wakizure)*
A VILLAGER *(kyōgen)*
THE REED CUTTER, KUSAKA NO SAEMON *(shite)*

PLACE   SETTSU PROVINCE, THE SHORE OF NANIWA BAY

TIME   THE THIRD MONTH

THE REED CUTTER (ASHIKARI)

(The stage assistant places the prop, which represents a small hut, on the stage.

The Wife and her two Attendants enter and face each other on the stage. The Wife wears the tsure *mask.ʾ The Chief Attendant carries a short sword.)*

ATTENDANTS. This way lies the ancient Capital,

This way lies the ancient Capital.

Let us visit Naniwa Bay.[1]

(The Wife and the Chief Attendant face front. The other Attendant kneels.)

CHIEF ATTENDANT. I am a servant to a gentleman in the Capital. *(He faces the Wife.)* This lady is the nurse to my master's child. *(He faces front.)* Her home is the village of Kusaka in the province of Settsu, and she has expressed her wish to go there again. We boarded this boat at Yodo,[2] and now we are sailing swiftly towards Naniwa Bay.

(The Attendants face each other.)

ATTENDANTS. Boat on the Yodo!

At dawn the moon lingers

Over the fields of Mizuno,

Over the fields of Mizuno,

And the misty mountain slopes

Merge into Minase River.[3]

We sail past distant Nagisa Wood.

(The Chief Attendant faces front, takes a few steps forward, then returns to his place.)

Already our destination nears;

We pass the Watanabe and Ōe shores.[4]

From inlet to wave-washed inlet,

Villages line the coast.

Now we have entered Naniwa Bay.

CHIEF ATTENDANT *(to the Wife).* We have made such good time

151

that we have already arrived at the village of Kusaka in the province of Settsu. Please wait here a moment. I shall inquire for the residence of Lord Saemon of Kusaka.

(The Wife moves to the waki-*position. The Chief Attendant moves to the* shite-*pillar, and the other Attendant kneels near the Wife.)*

CHIEF ATTENDANT *(looking up the bridgeway)*. Do you live here?

(The Villager enters and stands at the first pine.)

VILLAGER. Who are you?

CHIEF ATTENDANT. Is there anyone called Lord Saemon hereabouts?

VILLAGER. He did live here once, but he fell on hard times and went away.

CHIEF ATTENDANT. How terribly sad. Let me go inform my mistress what has happened. *(He goes to stage center and bows to the Wife.)* I asked for Lord Saemon, but I was told he no longer lives here.

WIFE. Yes, it's just as they say, a poor man has few acquaintances, and even old friends will become strangers when a man goes down in the world. He is not the only one who has suffered that way.
But how humiliating for him! *(She checks her tears.)* Still, I cannot forget the many vows we exchanged. I shall remain here a while and try to discover where he has gone.

CHIEF ATTENDANT. An admirable thought. Please stay here a while and I will try to find him. *(He goes to the Villager.)* Excuse me. I believe I spoke to you before. Do you know of anything interesting to see here? I would like to show the place to my mistress from the Capital.

VILLAGER. Well, let me see. There's a market on the shore of the bay where people buy and sell all kinds of things, and there's a young man who cuts and sells the reeds for which Naniwa is famous. He's an entertaining fellow and tells all kinds of jokes. His reeds are the best quality too, so everybody buys from him. Wait here a while. You'll see him.

CHIEF ATTENDANT. Good! By all means, we'll wait and have a look at this fellow.

(He sits before the Chorus.)

VILLAGER. Hey! Is the reed peddler around? Come out and peddle
your reeds!

> (*He retires to the* kyōgen-*position. Kusaka enters and goes
> up the bridgeway as far as the first pine. He does not wear
> a mask. He carries in his right hand a split bamboo pole
> into which reed-leaves have been inserted, and he wears a
> black lacquered* kasa, *a conical hat woven of reeds.*)

KUSAKA. The mountains are hazy with spring mist.

Across Naniwa Bay
Foaming waves break
On the shores of Awaji.[5]
Truly, in such a famous place
Every scene enchants:
Even the unnamed bays are lovely.
Strings of boats from Naniwa
Float in the light of dawn—
A sight to cleanse the heart!

> (*He comes onstage.*)

Though I go to Mitsu in Naniwa,[6]
No one will ever say he noticed
A humble man like me.
I myself do not know my own face,
I have forgotten it.
In the midst of the market crowd

CHORUS. I shall find a hiding-place.

KUSAKA. Even if in the round of fate
By chance we obtain human form,
A rare gift, seldom given,
How can we know its value
Except in a house of wealth and fame?
But I was born to poverty,
No doubt a punishment for sloth
In serving the Buddha in a former life.
Even now I lack a calling, earn no merit.
Yesterday was wasted;
Today has come to an end;
Tomorrow will surely be the same.
I am merely trying to prolong
A life that counts for no more

Than a grain of sand on a wave-beaten shore;
Here among the stalks wet with soon-vanished dew
I have become a cutter of reeds.

    (He looks at the reeds he carries in his hand.)

CHORUS. I drift without purpose to Naniwa Bay
    Or wander into the village,
    Indifferent to snow and cold;
    And though I am soaked by the salt spray,
    My grief excites no compassion.
    Out along the other bays
    I see the cheerful smoke from evening fires.
    How bitter I feel, how degraded,
    Unable even to support myself.

    I used to watch the cranes in the reeds,
    Quite detached, as if they were remote from me
    As the moon beyond the clouds.
    Now, I myself cut reeds and carry them away.
    I carry also the moon in the dew on my sleeve,
    And my heart feels a gleam of beauty,
    My heart feels a gleam of beauty.

    (He retires to the shite-*position. He removes his hat and gives it to the stage assistant.)*

CHIEF ATTENDANT. You over there. I have something to tell you.

KUSAKA. What could you want with *me*?

CHIEF ATTENDANT. I see peddlers here selling wares of every kind,
    but I am delighted you should be selling Naniwa reeds.[7]

KUSAKA. Yes, most of those who buy and sell here know nothing
    about the associations of their wares. It takes someone from
    the Capital to appreciate Naniwa reeds. How charming to
    have such a visitor!

    Long ago I lived in Naniwa
    The capital famous from poetry,
    A person of some consequence,
    With friends in high places;
    But now I have fallen, dew from a leaf,
    I have withered and faded like a dry reed.
    My reeds have also lost their color,
    But buy them please, the best I have.
    Imagine they are rushes instead.[8]

CHIEF ATTENDANT. That's a surprising suggestion! Are reeds and
rushes the same thing, then?

KUSAKA. Yes. It's true too of the plant we call *susuki*, the pampas
grass. When it goes to ear we call it *obana*, tail-flower.

CHIEF ATTENDANT. Names may even vary from place to place.

KUSAKA. That's right. A man from Ise calls reeds *hamaogi*, but
someone from Naniwa will call them *ashi*.

CHORUS. That's much too complicated!

What would a humble fisherman know
Of reeds and rushes on Naniwa Bay,
Of reeds and rushes on Naniwa Bay?
Only to make a living,
To sustain my fleeting life,
I gather reeds, I take them to market.
Buy my reeds, give me a fair price
For all my weary steps.

> *(Kusaka takes a few steps towards the Chief Attendant. He
> holds forward his bunch of reeds.)*

I cut these reeds at Naniwa,
The dew still on them.

> *(He mimes with his fan the act of cutting reeds.)*

At night I carry the moon too,
Reflected in the drops.
But I begrudge every moment—
Now, before the evening tide floods in,
While the day still lingers, buy my reeds!
Before it grows dark, buy my reeds!

> *(He lays reeds on his fan and takes a few more steps to-
> wards the Chief Attendant. Then the stage assistant relieves
> him of the reeds.)*

CHIEF ATTENDANT. Where is Mitsu Beach, that you mentioned?

KUSAKA *(looking towards the* waki-*pillar).* The noble beach of
Mitsu? Over that way.

CHIEF ATTENDANT. How curious! Why do you describe a beach as
being "noble"?

KUSAKA. You surprise me. Have you really never heard of the
beach of Mitsu? That is where the Emperor Nintoku deigned
to build his palace, by the bay of Naniwa. The name Mitsu
itself means "imperial port." Now you know why I spoke of
it as a noble beach.

CHIEF ATTENDANT. I had no idea! An emperor's palace stood by this
bay! Then it is certainly proper to speak of the "noble beach
of Mitsu."

KUSAKA. His palace was on the
shore where the high waves
break, so even the beacon
fires burning in the fishing
villages seemed like the
sacred torches of the im-
perial court. Everyone here,
from the nobles in the
palace down to the commoners of the humblest ranks shared
then in the gracious blessings of the Emperor. *(He looks off
into the distance, then takes the Chief Attendant's sleeve and
draws him forward a little.)* See over there! A boat is approaching the beach of Mitsu. The crew of netters draw in
their nets to the cadenced cries of *"Eiya, eiya!"*

CHORUS. The famous poem about Naniwa Harbor
Tells us, "The shouts of the fishermen
As they give the netters their cadence
Are heard even here in the palace."[9]
This scene before our eyes—
The fishermen dragging their nets—
Recalls that ancient poem.
Look carefully, gentlemen!
    *(The Chief Attendant returns to his former position before
    the Chorus and sits.)*

KUSAKA. How lovely it is!
"To the man of feeling . . ."[10]

CHORUS. How lovely it is!
"To the man of feeling
I would show the spring in Tsu,
Along the coast of Naniwa."
Boats row in through the haze;
Gulls offshore and plovers on the beach
Go by in pairs, calling to their mates,
Like fishermen shouting, boat to boat.

KUSAKA. I wear in the rain

CHORUS. I wear in the rain
A straw *mino* cloak,[11]

And there is even an island called Tamino;
Why then, when the dew falls so thickly
Should there not be a rain hat called Masuge?
   (Kusaka goes to the shite-*position and opens his fan. The
   stage attendant gives him a* kasa *hat. He dances.)*
Spring at the bay of Naniwa!
KUSAKA. The famous plum trees
   Wear hats of blossoms[12]
CHORUS. Woven, they say, by nightingales;
   And with their wings
KUSAKA. The *kasasagi* birds at dawn
CHORUS. Stretch a halo round the moon—
   The sleeves perhaps
KUSAKA. Of a celestial maiden,
   Or her silken parasol.
CHORUS. Up in the sky a celestial maiden,
KUSAKA. Here below,
CHORUS. A Naniwa girl,
   A Naniwa girl
   Holding over her head
   Her sleeves or her arm,
   Protection from the passing shower.
   The rain-soaked reeds are tangled,
   The tumbling waves roil this way and that,
   Churning and frothing,
   Rattling and pounding,
   Like the wind as it shakes
   An old bamboo blind:

   Too many delights for us ever to weary!
   *(As the passage ends Kusaka tosses his hat away, finishes his
   dance and kneels. The Wife turns to the Chief Attendant.)*
WIFE. Where are you?
CHIEF ATTENDANT. Here I am, Madam.
WIFE. Would you ask the reed seller to bring me one?
CHIEF ATTENDANT. Yes, Madam. *(He rises and turns to Kusaka.)*
   My mistress asks that you take a reed to her carriage.
KUSAKA. Certainly, sir. *(He picks up his hat, places a reed on it, and
   goes up to the Chief Attendant.)* Please take this reed.
CHIEF ATTENDANT. No, you take it, directly to her.

(Kusaka kneels before the Wife. They exchange glances. Suddenly Kusaka drops the reed, rises, and rushes into the hut. He shuts the door and sits inside.)

CHIEF ATTENDANT. How extraordinary! Why should he have done that, I wonder?

WIFE. There's no need to hide any longer. That reed seller was once my husband. . . . But I must be dreaming! What a miserable fate for him! *(She weeps.)*

CHIEF ATTENDANT. This is incredible! But surely there's nothing to prevent you from seeing him. Let me go and bring him here. You mustn't worry.

WIFE. No, wait a while. With all these people about, he would feel humiliated. Let me go by myself, secretly, and tell him I have come for him.

CHIEF ATTENDANT. Of course, that is the right way. Please go to him.

(The Wife goes up to the hut and kneels facing Kusaka.)

WIFE. My husband of long ago—

I have come to you, as I promised
When we pledged that through the years to come
We would remain joined, like beads on a string.
Now our vow has been confirmed.
I live comfortably, as well as another,
And I have come all this distance
Searching for you, but where have you vanished?
Please come out now, quickly!

KUSAKA. Surely this must be a dream!
But supposing it is real—
I sink in despair at the thought.
How shameful I must look to others.

WIFE. I guessed that was why you hid.
But how can one know another's heart?
I wondered if, after you left me,
Like the dew vanishing with the dawn,
You took another wife,
"Man of Naniwa?"[13]

KUSAKA. The rush fires
You burn in your hut
Have blackened the walls with soot,

But your wife preserves her fresh beauty."
What woman except you, my wife,
Could I love, could I lie with?
"As I cut reeds without you,
I knew I had been wrong;
Life here by Naniwa Bay
Has grown so melancholy."[14]

WIFE. "You did no wrong.
'Fare thee well,' we said,
As our parting words:
Why should life by Naniwa Bay
Have grown so melancholy?"

KUSAKA. Now I know it is true—
Poetry, the art that began
With "Naniwa Harbor" and "Asaka Hill,"[15]
Has brought us together, man and wife![16]

CHORUS. I know I can't go on hiding forever,
Concealing my love in this hut where I live
As in a covered well: I push open the door.
  (He does so.)
But going out
  *(He comes out to stage
  center, beside the Wife.)*
I am so ashamed to be seen.
  (He looks at his sleeves.)

These three years that have passed,
Truly they are a dream.
But we meet in reality:
Let us rest beneath the trees
In this pine grove of Ō[17]
And talk of the past in Naniwa.
  (The Wife sits at the waki-*position. Kusaka sits at stage
  center.)*

CHIEF ATTENDANT. What greater happiness could come to a man?
Go with the lady, go with her to the Capital. *(To Kusaka.)*
But first, put on this nobleman's hat and robe. Then I will
offer a toast to your good fortune.
  (Kusaka retires to the kyōgen-*position where he attires him-
  self in a ceremonial hat and robe, and buckles on a sword.*

Meanwhile, the Villager enters and stands at the naming-place.)

VILLAGER. Excuse me, but is this gentleman the person you were asking about?

CHIEF ATTENDANT. That's right.

VILLAGER. Wonderful! Congratulations! I wondered who she could be looking for. To tell you the truth, we around here had always suspected he was no ordinary man. He knew simply everything. And now he turns out to be a gentleman of quality! It takes a long time to track down someone that way. Pure luck! Just because I happened along and said the lady should see the reed seller, and then I went and called him— that's why she got to meet him so quickly! It just shows what a reliable fellow I am. Are you going back to the Capital with Lord Saemon?

CHIEF ATTENDANT. Yes, I am.

VILLAGER. Then I'd like to go along too. Would that be all right?

CHIEF ATTENDANT. Certainly.

VILLAGER. That's wonderful!

CHIEF ATTENDANT. Would you please ask Lord Saemon to come out when he has finished dressing?

VILLAGER. At your service. I'll tell him. *(He goes to the* shite-*position.)* Excuse me, Lord Saemon, but I have a message for you. Would you come out just as soon as you've finished dressing? And please hurry.

(He exits. During the following passage for the Chorus, Kusaka comes forward and kneels at stage center.)

CHORUS. High as the mountains,
  Bottomless as the sea,
  Is the abiding love
  Between husband and wife.
  And this is the place
  Where this should most be true:
  Naniwa, between the mountains and sea.

KUSAKA. When a man regrets his prime,[18]
  "The past on Otoko Hill,"

CHORUS. When a woman sulks a moment,
  "A drooping lady-flower,"
  Poetry brings consolation,

Poetry, freighted with words of love,
Like autumn clover with the dew.
Our vow, that had all but perished,
With the dew is restored—
The life we found so hard to prolong.
KUSAKA. For I had fallen so
Into the forest of shame,
"The forest of Hazukashi,"[19]
But the trees blossomed into poems,
And the poems have been my strength.
CHORUS. "In Naniwa Harbor
The flowers have come to the trees;
They slept through the winter,
But now it is the spring—
See how the blossoms have opened!"[20]
So blossomed and flourished
The reign of Nintoku, the Emperor;
Men also knew him
As "Prince of Naniwa."
The poem on Asaka Hill
Tells of a girl of the court
And her bitterness when a noble
Refused the cup of wine she offered.
These two poems
Are the parents of all poetry.
They are the seeds
Of the poems of every generation,
The flowers of our language,
The first models of our people.
   (Kusaka rises and dances.)
So it is said that poetry
Soothes the invisible gods and demons;
It comforts the warrior's raging spirit
And reveals the love of husband and wife,[21]
As I now know from my own experience.
KUSAKA. "At Naniwa in Tsu
Spring seems like a passing dream;
CHORUS. Over the withered leaves of reeds
The winter wind blows."[22]
However waves may threaten

In the daily round of our lives,
We can never neglect poetry.
An entire beach of sand
Can be counted to the last grain,
But the delights of poetry
Are not to be numbered;[23]
Cherish them!
Here by Naniwa Bay, renowned in poetry,
We cast aside all our griefs
And take up again the pledge of the past,
Our hearts filled with joy.
    (Kusaka ends his dance and kneels.)

CHIEF ATTENDANT. Lord Saemon, please celebrate this happy occasion by dancing for us.

KUSAKA. Yes, I'll dance in celebration:
  My bitterness is lifted,
    (He rises.)

CHORUS. To the wave and the sound of the wave
  I dance, my sleeves waving high.
    (He lifts his sleeves and dances an otoko-mai, *a "male dance." When it has ended the Chorus begins again. Kusaka dances again as they sing.)*

CHORUS. I dance to forget the nights I slept alone,
  The sad nights at Naniwa on the bay,
  And to forget the moan of the waves,
  The sad nights at Naniwa on the bay,
  Where white waves submerge the young reeds.
  Here the moon still lingers,
  The plum flowers are in full blossom,
  In this province of Settsu.
  In the hut where I dwell
  "I slept through the winter,
  But now is the spring."[24]
  No longer alone,
  We are going back together
  To the skies of the Capital!
  I take a last look at the shore of Mitsu.
  How happy I am to return to the city,
  How happy I am to return to my wife!
    (He gives a final stamp at the shite-*pillar.)*

Notes

1. Naniwa was the capital during the reign of the Emperor Nintoku, whose traditional dates are 313 to 399. It was situated at about the same place as modern Ōsaka. Naniwa Bay is now called Ōsaka Bay.

2. Yodo was a river port near Kyoto where people boarded ship to go down the Yodo River to Ōsaka Bay.

3. From the famous poem by the Emperor Go-Toba, no. 36 in the *Shinkokinshū:* "When I look far out the mountain slopes are misty. Minase River—why did I think that only in autumn the nights could be lovely?"

4. Places near the mouth of the Yodo River.

5. A large island between Ōsaka and Shikoku.

6. There is a pun on the place-name Mitsu and *mitsu,* "has seen."

7. He is pleased because the reeds were well-known through poetry. The reeds were presumably used to weave hats or blinds.

8. "Reed" in Japanese is *ashi,* which also means "bad"; "rush" is *yoshi,* which also means "good." This occasions the play on words in the following passage and elsewhere: Is bad the same as good? (Or, are reeds the same as rushes?)

9. A poem by Naga Okimaro, no. 238 in the *Manyōshū.* See the translation by the Nippon Gakujutsu Shinkōkai, p. 61.

10. From a poem, no. 1086 in the *Goshūishū,* by the priest Nōin.

11. The passage that follows contains a series of plays on the word *mino* ("rain cloak") and *kasa* ("rain hat") mixed in with many poetical allusions.

12. An allusion to an anonymous poem, no. 1081 in the *Kokinshū:* "The hat which the *uguisu* is said to sew using green willow twigs as its thread is a hat of plum blossoms." This example of Japanese preciosity loses much in translation.

13. The words "Man of Naniwa" go both with what precedes (the Wife's reproach to her husband), and with what follows, a poem by Hitomaro included in the *Shūishū,* but ultimately from the *Manyōshū.*

14. This and the following poem are from *Yamato Monogatari.* Here the poems have a rather different meaning, however: They indicate the desire of husband and wife to come together again, and this leads to the eulogy of poetry that follows.

15. These two poems, extolled in the preface to the *Kokinshū* as "the mother and father" of all verse, reappear a little further on. The Naniwa poem is quoted in full, but the Asaka Hill poem is summarized.

16. The preface to the *Kokinshū* states that poetry "makes gentle the ties between men and women."

17. There is a play on *au* (pronounced *ō*), to meet, and Ō, the name of a pine forest. The location of the forest is unknown, and mention here may have been governed merely by the fondness for the play on words.

18. Everything between "When a man regrets . . ." and "consolation" is quoted from the *Kokinshū* preface. The two lines marked off by quotation marks are secondary meanings of the lines translated immediately above them. Otoko Hill is west of Kyoto.

19. The forest of Hazukashi was not far from Kyoto. The word *hazukashi* meant "ashamed."

20. This is the famous Naniwazu poem. See above, note 15.

21. The *Kokinshū* preface makes these three claims for poetry.

22. A celebrated poem by the poet Saigyō, no. 625 in the *Shinkokinshū*.

23. A reference to the *Kokinshū* preface.

24. An allusion to the Naniwazu poem.

Shōkun

TRANSLATED BY CARL SESAR

INTRODUCTION

Shōkun is classified as a play in the fifth category although the apparition at the end is not a true demon but the ghost of a foreign king. The play has been attributed to Zeami but seems to be considerably older. The importance of the mirror in the plot points to an earlier form of drama, and the categorization of the parts in the usual manner as *shite, waki,* and so on seems arbitrary. Possibly Zeami had a hand in reworking a text that was already archaic in his day.

The story of the play is originally found in the *Hou Han Shu,* or *History of the Later Han Dynasty,* in the section describing the Emperor Yüan Ti (r. 48–32 B.C.) Several accounts based on this source may be found in Japanese, an early one being in the collection *Konjaku Monogatari.* A barbarian tribe had reached the gates of the Han capital, and it was imperative to secure their withdrawal somehow. A minister suggested to the Emperor that he buy off the barbarian chieftain by offering him a court lady; the least favored one would do, since the barbarian would not know the difference. The Emperor agreed, and ordered painters to provide him with portraits of all the palace ladies, so that he might choose the least favored. The ladies were appalled at the thought of being sent to the barbarian chieftain, and bribed the painters to make their portraits beautiful. Only the most beautiful woman, Wang Chao-chün (Ō Shōkun in Japanese), was so confident of her beauty that she offered no bribe. The painter took his vengeance by defacing her portrait, and she was sent off with the barbarians.

Chao-chün became the subject of innumerable Chinese poems, some of them included in the collection *Wakan Rōei Shū*, and of the celebrated Yüan drama *Autumn in the Palace of Han* (translated in *Anthology of Chinese Literature*, edited by Cyril Birch). The Nō play gives the story a distinctively Japanese flavor, and the thematic material itself has elements with no counterpart in Chinese sources. The awkwardnesses in the play occasioned by the recasting into the form of a Nō—for example, the unconvincing way that Hakudō is made to disappear so that another *shite*, the barbarian king, may make his entrance—are more than compensated for by the beauty of the language and the effective use of the central theme.

Shōkun is performed by all schools of Nō.

167

SHŌKUN

(The Man enters and stands at the naming-place.)

MAN. I am a resident of the village of Kō in China. A couple
named Hakudō and Ōbo live here. They have an only
daughter named Shōkun whom the Emperor summoned and
favored with boundless affection. Because of certain events,
however, she was sent away to a barbarian land. This couple's
grief is heavier than any to be found in this world. Since I
have some business nearby, I think I shall go and call upon
them.

> *(He kneels at the waki-position. Ōbo, wearing the uba
> mask, enters and goes along the bridgeway to the first pine;
> Hakudō, wearing the akobujō mask, stops at the third pine.
> Both carry brooms.)*

TOGETHER. As we stand beneath this tree,

The scattered blossoms fall—

A snowfall unknown to the sky.

> *(Ōbo moves to stage center, Hakudō to the shite-position.
> They face front.)*

HAKUDŌ. We dwell in the villago of Kō, in China.[1]

TOGETHER. Hakudō and Ōbo are our names;

We are man and wife.

ŌBO. Humble as we are, we have a daughter

Renowned for her beauty.

> *(They face each other.)*

TOGETHER. We named her Shōkun.

But her features were so surpassingly lovely

169

That the Emperor summoned her.
Her name was changed to Bright Princess,
And she waited upon the Son of Heaven.
(They face front.)

HAKUDŌ. Blessed was her fortune, and yet,
 Perhaps by karma from a former existence,
 She was fated to leave his side
  (They face each other.)
TOGETHER. Chosen, of all the palace ladies,
 To be sent among a barbarian folk,
 Thousands of leagues away from the palace of Han,[2]
 To a distant land under unfamiliar skies.
 It grieves us to remember.
  (Weeping, they face front.)
HAKUDŌ. Even so, the attendants in her entourage
 Played many melodies on string and flute
 To ease the journey's hardships.
  (They face each other.)
TOGETHER. It is said that ever since,
 Men have played the lute on horseback.
 Suffering made her resemble her portrait:
 Shōkun's darkened eyebrows
 Were tinged with the willow-green of spring,
 But the spring has ended;
 The memory tangles our hearts in sorrow
 Like a willow in the wind.
 Beneath this tree, let us then
 Join with the wind and sweep the dust away.
  (They face front.)
HAKUDŌ. Let us sweep the garden clear.
 With these words
 The aged father takes up a broom.

ōBO. Once, in springtimes past,
  Our hearts were glad. Now we are old,
  Our lives a slender spider's thread,
  Drawn with sorrow,
  Our sleeves wet with tears
  For the memory of our child.

HAKUDŌ. I am ashamed to be seen like this.
  People will think me some mean fellow.

ōBO. The sun sinks behind the rim of hills,
  The evening bell tolls.

HAKUDŌ. Telling of our sorrow, the night wind

ōBO. Blows cold upon our sleeves; and yet,

HAKUDŌ. Remembering our child's fate,
    (They face each other.)

ōBO. We hardly feel the cold.

TOGETHER. Beneath this tree piled deep with fallen leaves,
  The storm winds so whirl up the dust
  They become dust themselves.
    (They mime sweeping.)

CHORUS. Beneath this tree piled deep with fallen leaves,
  The storm winds so whirl up the dust
  They become dust themselves.
  Alas, we too are as the dust;
  Our hearts clutch at the things
  Of a fleeting world of sorrow.
  We may sweep them away, but tears
  Still gather like dew upon our sleeves.
    (They look at their sleeves, weeping.)
  All such fallen leaves
  Scattered by the wind, adrift on the water,
  Will make our sleeves their resting place.
    *(They lower their heads so as to give their masks a sad
    expression.)*
  The moonlight glitters in our tears;
    *(They drop their brooms. Hakudō kneels at stage center;
    Ōbo kneels to his right.)*
  The moonlight glitters in our tears.
  Can it be she? I look, but no . . .
  I can barely hear the patter of hail

Falling upon the bamboo grass.

HAKUDŌ. We are overworn with grief. Let us rest.

(*The Man rises.*)

MAN. Excuse me. Is Hakudō at home?

HAKUDŌ. Who is it?

MAN. It is I. I have come to call.

HAKUDŌ. Please come in.

(*The Man kneels.*)

MAN. It is plain to see you are grieved over Shōkun.

HAKUDŌ. Thank you for visiting us in our sorrow.

MAN. May I ask why you remain beneath this willow tree, sweeping clean around it?

HAKUDŌ. When Shōkun was sent away to the barbarian land, she planted this willow. "If I should die in the barbarian land, this willow too will wither away." she told us. Look! Its branches are already withered.

(*He weeps.*)

MAN. Small wonder that you grieve. But why was Shōkun sent away to the barbarian land?

HAKUDŌ. Shōkun was banished to the barbarian land

CHORUS. To bring order to the empire;
That was how it first began.

HAKUDŌ. But the barbarian armies were strong;
There was no hope they would submit.

CHORUS. Hence a peace treaty was made,
With one condition, a royal promise
To give up a single beauty of the court.
The Emperor ordered that it be done,
But of the three thousand ladies he kept,
He could not decide whom to send away.
He ordered that portraits be painted
Of all the ladies at court,
Depicting their beauty and elegance
As on the sliding panels of the Immortals.[3]
If there were one less lovely than the rest,
She would be chosen to go to the barbarian king,
And so bring peace to the empire.
All the court ladies grieved; in despair
They spoke with the portrait artist,

Bribed him with presents,
And each struck a bargain with him,

HAKUDŌ. So that their painted features

CHORUS. Were beautiful, none less than the others:
Hair like the pliant willow in the wind,
Faces like the peach branch glittering with dew,
All lovely beyond comparison.
But of all, none could match the beauty of Shōkun,
Whom the Emperor loved deeply.
Whether she had rested her hopes in that,
Or whether due to her oversight,
Her likeness was poorer than all the others.
Though he loved her very deeply,
The Emperor could not go back on his word.
Thus, powerless to help her,
He sent Shōkun away to the barbarian land.
*(The stage assistant places a representation of a mirror near
the* shite-*pillar.)*

HAKUDŌ. In ancient times someone named Peach Leaf[4]
Exchanged solemn vows with a nymph.
After the nymph had passed away,
He held peach flowers before a mirror,
And the nymph's form became visible.
(He turns to Ōbo.)
So might it be with this willow.
Come, let us make Shōkun appear in the mirror.
(They both rise.)

ŌBO. It was a nymph who revealed herself.
How can that be compared to our case?

HAKUDŌ. No, it was not only that.
It was a loved one's reflection
That appeared in the mirror.

ŌBO. Showing the shapes of dreams

HAKUDŌ. There was the clear mirror of Shinyō.[5]

ŌBO. Seeing his native home in a mirror

HAKUDŌ. There was the traveler named Toketsu.[6]

ŌBO. But many years have passed since then,

HAKUDŌ. And the stream that mirrors the blossoms[7]

CHORUS. Is clouded, the blossoms scattered.

*(Ōbo kneels before the Chorus. Hakudō brings the mirror
to the front of the stage.)*

Even so, it may be that she will appear

In this mirror, clouded by our sorrow.

*(Hakudō looks in the mirror, quickly retreats a few steps,
kneels and weeps.)*

With these words,

They kneel weeping before the mirror;

They kneel weeping before the mirror.

*(The kyōgen interlude, omitted from the present transla-
tion, is performed at this point. At the Man's request the
kyōgen, a villager, accompanies Hakudō home. That is to
say, he sees Hakudō off down the bridgeway. After Hakudō
has exited, the villager retells Shōkun's story, then exits
himself. Shōkun then enters and stands at the first pine. As
her role is performed by a child actor, she is unmasked.)*

SHŌKUN. I am the ghost of Shōkun

Who was sent away to the land of the barbarians.

My parents, in grief over our parting,

Weep in grief beneath my spring willow.

(She weeps.)

I hasten now to the mirror,

That I may appear before them.

(She enters the stage.)

This spring night the moon is hidden in mist,

CHORUS. But even in the darkness they shall see me.

*(She sits on a stool before the flute player. Kokanya-zennu,
the barbarian king, rushes in and kneels at stage center,
facing the mirror. He wears the* kobeshimi *mask.)*

ŌBO. Oh, I am afraid! It is a demon!

Its body is covered with bristling hairs!

What sort of creature is it

That now appears in the mirror?

KOKANYA. I am the ghost of Kokanya-zennu,[8]

Chieftain of the barbarians.

ŌBO. Barbarians are at least men,

But you do not even look human.

I have never seen one, but from what I have heard

You resemble a demon out of hell.

You frighten me!

KOKANYA. Kokanya-zennu is also dead.

Therefore, like Shōkun, I have come
To stand before her parents.

ŌBO. You should not have come at all.

It frightens me just to look at you!

KOKANYA. But why should I frighten you so?

ŌBO. If you do not know,
Go to the mirror and look for yourself!

KOKANYA. Very well,
I shall make myself appear in the mirror.
(He rises.)
Truly a fearsome sight!
(He looks at his sleeves.)
As I go to the mirror and look,
(He looks in the mirror.)
I understand your fright.
(He backs away quickly, then begins to dance.)

CHORUS. Hair like a tangle of thorns,

Hair like a tangle of thorns

KOKANYA. Grows thickly over my body,

Standing straight up, pointing to the sky.

CHORUS. No paper cord could bind it,

KOKANYA. Only thick vines could tie it in place.

CHORUS. And the metal chains that dangle from my ears

KOKANYA. Make me look like a demon to you.

CHORUS. I am ashamed of my appearance!

I go before the mirror,
And whether I sit or stand,
I look like a demon, not a man.
Surely it is not myself I see.
Yet it is I. What a frightful visage!
It is too shameful!
He rises and departs.
*(He goes to kneel before the musicians, and throws his
sleeves over his head.)*
Yet Shōkun's beautiful eyebrows,
Are like the color of the willow.
The Jōwari mirror that reveals one's sins[9]

(He stands and spreads his arms wide before the mirror.)
Will not mar that beauty.
Like a flower she seems, seen dimly through
The clouded skies of their sorrow.
But it is her heart, clear as the crescent moon
Shining in the distance,
That is the mirror of her virtue.
  (He gives a final stamp of the foot near the shite-*pillar, then exits. Shōkun and Ōbo follow him.)*

Notes

1. The name Kō is given in Japanese *kana* only, and was presumably a Chinese-sounding name invented by the dramatist. The names of Shōkun's parents, Hakudō and Ōbo, were also apparently Japanese inventions.

2. From a poem by Ōe no Asatsuna, no. 702 in the *Wakan Rōei Shū:*
"A Tartar flute sounds in the frosty sky after I awake from dreams; My heart is torn by the moonlight ten thousand miles from the Han Palace."

3. A reference to the painting on the sliding-screen in the Shishinden Palace which depicted the thirty-two Chinese sages. The dramatist imagines that there was a similar painting in the Chinese palace of Shōkun's time.

4. The source of this story has not been found. Peach Leaf (Tōyō) may have been another invention of the dramatist.

5. Nothing is known about who Shinyō might have been.

6. Nothing is known about Toketsu.

7. The poem by Ise, no. 44 in the *Kokinshū,* is quoted, slightly paraphrased: "The water which for years has served as a mirror reflecting the blossoms is clouded over, now that the blossoms have scattered."

8. The Khan Hu-han-yeh, who appears also in the Yüan drama *Autumn in the Palace of Han.*

9. A mirror owned by the King of Hell which reflected all the good or evil deeds performed during his lifetime by the dead person who appears before the King.

The Shrine
in the Fields

(NONOMIYA)

TRANSLATED BY H. PAUL VARLEY

INTRODUCTION

The Shrine in the Fields, a play of the third category, has traditionally been ascribed to Zeami, but in recent years some scholars have expressed doubts about this attribution, largely for technical reasons of style. It is hard, however, to imagine who else but Zeami could have written so hauntingly evocative a work. Perhaps he wrote it in the last years of his life, a period not covered by the critical writings that are the firmest evidence for attribution; or perhaps, as Professor Konishi Jin'ichi has suggested, Zeami's second son, Motoyoshi, who is not credited with any plays in the repertory, may have written *The Shrine in the Fields, Yuya,* and various other masterpieces whose authorship is uncertain.

The play recalls the love affair between Prince Genji and Lady Rokujō, here called by her title, Miyasudokoro. Readers of *The Tale of Genji* will remember Rokujō mainly as the proud and elegant woman whose jealousy led to the death of Genji's wife, Aoi; this story is treated in the play *Aoi no Ue,* translated by Arthur Waley in *The Nō Plays of Japan.* In *The Shrine in the Fields,* however, Rokujō is treated with the utmost sympathy, and nothing suggests that her living ghost killed Aoi. The scenes from *The Tale of Genji* which provided material for the play include: Genji's visit to Rokujō; the humiliation of Rokujō when Aoi's carriage forced back her own at the Kamo Festival; and the visit to Nonomiya, the Shrine in the Fields, by Genji, when Rokujō's daughter, the new Virgin of the Ise Shrine, was in residence there.

The Emperor was always represented at Ise by a virgin of imperial blood. When a new virgin was appointed, before going to Ise she would reside for a considerable period just outside Kyoto at Nonomiya. (The word *miya* primarily means a shrine, but can also mean a palace.) Nonomiya was intimately associated with Ise, the chief shrine of the Sun Goddess. It served its main function only intermittently, however, and was therefore built like a temporary shrine with a *torii* of logs.

The season is the end of autumn and an air of melancholy and impermanence dominates the play.

The Shrine in the Fields is performed by all schools of Nō.

181

PERSONS   A TRAVELING PRIEST *(waki)*
A VILLAGE GIRL *(mae-jite)*
MIYASUDOKORO *(nochi-jite)*

PLACE   SAGANO IN YAMASHIRO PROVINCE

TIME   LATE AUTUMN, THE SEVENTH DAY OF THE
NINTH MONTH

THE SHRINE IN THE FIELDS
(NONOMIYA)

(The stage assistant places a torii *at the front of the stage. To either upright of the* torii *are attached short sections of fence made of brushwood twigs.*

The Priest enters. He carries a rosary in his hand. He stands at the naming-place.)

PRIEST. I am an itinerant priest. Recently I have been staying in the Capital, where I have visited all the famous sites and relics of the past. Autumn is nearing its close and Sagano will be lovely now. I think I shall go there for a visit. *(He turns towards the* torii, *indicating that he has already arrived in Sagano.)* When I asked people about this wood they told me it is the ancient site of the Shrine in the Fields. I would like to visit the place, though I am no more than a passing stranger. *(He advances to stage center, still facing the* torii.*)*
I enter the wood and I see
A rustic log *torii*
And a fence of brushwood twigs.
Surely nothing has changed from the past!
But why should time have spared this place?
Be that as it may, how lucky I am
To have come at this lovely time of year
And to be able to worship at such a place.
  (He kneels and presses his palms together.)
The Great Shrine at Ise
Makes no distinction
Between gods and Buddhas:
The teachings of the Buddhist Law
Have guided me straight along the path,
And I have arrived at the Shrine.
My heart is pure in the evening light,
Pure in the clear evening light!
  (The Girl enters. She wears the fukai *mask and carries a branch of* sakaki. *She stands at the* shite-*position and faces the musicians.)*

GIRL. Shrine in the Fields
    Where I have lived with flowers;
    Shrine in the Fields
    Where I have lived with flowers—
    What will be left when autumn has passed?
    (She faces front.)
    Now lonely autumn ends,
    But still my sleeves
    Wilt in a dew of tears;
    The dusk racks my body,
    And my heart of itself
    Takes on the fading colors
    Of the thousand flowers;
    It withers, as all things, with neglect.[1]

    Each year on this day,
    Unknown to anyone else,
    I return to the old remains.
    In the wood at the Shrine in the Fields
    Autumn has drawn to a close
    And the harsh winds blow;
    Autumn has drawn to a close
    And the harsh winds blow;
    Colors so brilliant
    They pierced the senses
    Have faded and vanished;
    What remains now to recall
    The memories of the past?[2]
    What use was it to come here?
    (She takes a few steps to her right, then faces front.)
    Ahh—how I loathe the attachment
    That makes me go back and forth,
    Again and again on my journey
    To this meaningless, fugitive world.
    (The Priest rises and faces her.)

PRIEST. As I was resting in the shade of the trees, thinking about
    the past and refreshing my mind, a charming young lady
    has suddenly appeared. Please tell me who you are.

GIRL. It would be more appropriate if I asked who you are. This

is Nonomiya, the Shrine in the Fields,
where in ancient days the virgin
designated as the Priestess of Ise was
temporarily lodged. The custom has
fallen into disuse, but today, the
seventh day of the ninth month, is
still a time for recalling the past. Each year, unknown to
anyone else, I come to sweep the shrine and to perform a
service. I do not know where you have come from, but your
presence here is an intrusion. Please leave at once.

(She takes two steps towards the Priest.)

PRIEST. No, no. There can be no objection to my being here. I
am only a wandering priest who has renounced the uncertain
world. But tell me, why should you return here, to these old
ruins, on this particular day each year in search of the past?

GIRL. This is the day when Genji the Shining One visited this
place, the seventh day of the ninth month. He brought with
him a twig of *sakaki* and pushed it through the sacred fence.
Miyasudokoro at once composed the poem:
"This sacred enclosure
Has no cypress to mark the spot;
By some error you have picked
A twig of *sakaki* wood."[3]
It happened on this day!

PRIEST. That was truly a worthy poem.
—And the *sakaki* branch
You hold in your hand
Is the same color it was in the past.

GIRL. The same color as in the past?
How clever to put it that way!
Only the *sakaki* stays green forever,
And in its unvarying shade,

PRIEST. On the pathways through the wood,
The autumn deepens

GIRL. And leaves turn crimson only to scatter.

PRIEST. In the weed-grown fields
(She goes to the torii *and places the* sakaki *branch there.
The Priest kneels.)*

CHORUS. The stalks and leaf tips wither;

Nonomiya, the Shrine in the Fields,
Stands amidst the desolation
Of withered stalks and leaves.
The seventh day of the ninth month
Has returned again today
To this place of memories.
   (She moves to stage center.)
How fragile it seemed at the time,
This little fence of brushwood twigs.
   (She gazes at the fence.)
And the house that looked so temporary
Has now become the guardian's hut.[4]
   (She turns towards the gazing-pillar.)
A dim glow shines from inside:
I wonder if the longing within me
Reveals itself outwardly?
How lonely a place is this shrine,
How lonely a place is this palace!
   (She gazes across the front of the stage.)
PRIEST. Please tell me more of the story of Miyasudokoro.
   (The Girl kneels at stage center.)
CHORUS. The lady known as Miyasudokoro
   Became the wife of the former Crown Prince,
   The brother of Kiritsubo's Emperor,[5]
   A man at the height of his glory;
   They were like the color and perfume
   Of the same flower, indissolubly bound.
GIRL. They knew, of course, the truth
   That those who meet must part—
CHORUS. Why should it have surprised them?
   But it came so soon—like a nightmare—
   His death that left her alone.
GIRL. She could not remain in that state,
   Helpless and given to tears;
CHORUS. Soon Genji the Shining One
   Imposed his love and began
   Their clandestine meetings.
GIRL. How did their love affair end?
CHORUS. And why, after they separated,

Did his love never turn to hate?
With customary tenderness
He made his way through the fields
To distant Nonomiya.
The autumn flowers had all withered,
The voices of insects were sparse.
Oh, the loneliness of that journey!
Even the wind echoing in the pines
Reminded him there is no end
To the sadness of autumn.
So the Prince visited her,
And with the deepest affection
Spoke his love in many ways;
How noble and sensitive a man!

GIRL. Later, by the Katsura River,
She performed the cleansing rite,

CHORUS. Setting the white-wrapped branches[6]
Adrift on the river waves;
Herself like a drifting weed,
No roots or destination,
She moved at the water's will.[7]
"Through the waves of the eighty rapids
Of Suzuka River to Ise,
Who will worry if the waves wet me or no?"[8]
She wrote this poem to describe her journey.
Never before had a mother
Escorted her daughter, the Virgin,
All the way to the Také Palace.[9]
Mother and daughter on the way
Felt only the bitterness of regret.

(for Priest)
Now that I have heard your tale,
I am sure you are no ordinary woman.
Please tell me your name.

GIRL. Revealing my name
Would serve no purpose;
In my helplessness
I am ashamed of myself.
Sooner or later

My name will be known,
It can't be helped;
But now say a prayer for one nameless,
And not of this world.

CHORUS *(for Priest).* Not of this world?
What strange words to hear!
Then, have you died and departed

GIRL. This world, long ago,
A name my only monument:

CHORUS. Miyasudokoro

GIRL. Is myself.

CHORUS. Autumn winds rise at dusk;
  (She stands.)
Through the forest branches
The evening moonlight shines
  (She goes to the shite-*position.)*
Dimly illuminating,
Under the trees,
  (She looks at the torii.)*
The rustic logs of the *torii.*
She passes between the two pillars
And vanishes without a trace;
She has vanished without a trace.

  (She slowly exits. A Villager then enters and performs the
  kyōgen *interlude, a lengthy recapitulation of Miyasudo-*
  koro's story. The Priest asks the Villager to tell what he
  knows, and then the two men agree that the Priest has just
  seen the ghost of Miyasudokoro. The Priest decides to stay
  and read the sutras and prayers for her. The Villager with-
  draws.)

PRIEST. Alone I lie on the forest moss,
A sleeve of my robe spread beneath me—
Under forest trees, a mossy robe:[10]
My mat is grass of the same color.
Unfolding my memories
I shall offer prayers all night long;
I shall pray for her repose.
  (The Girl, now revealed as Miyasudokoro, enters and
  stands at the shite-*position.)*

MIYASUDOKORO. In this carriage,
   Lovely as the autumn flowers
   At Nonomiya,
   I too have returned to the past,
   To long ago.
PRIEST. How strange!
   In the faint moonlight
   The soft sounds
   Of an approaching carriage,
   A courtly carriage
   With reed blinds hanging—
   A sight of unimagined beauty!
   It must be you, Miyasudokoro!
   But what is the carriage you ride in?

MIYASUDOKORO. You ask about my carriage?
   I remember now
   That scene of long ago—
   The Kamo Festival,
   The jostling carriages.
   No one could tell
   Who their owners were,
   But thick as dewdrops
PRIEST. The splendid ranks crowded the place.
MIYASUDOKORO. Pleasure carriages of every description,
   And one among them of special magnificence,
   The Princess Aoi's.
PRIEST. "Make way for Her Highness's carriage!"
   The servants cried, clearing the crowd,
   And in the confusion
MIYASUDOKORO. I answered, "My carriage is small,
   I have nowhere else to put it."
   I stood my ground,
PRIEST. But around the carriage
MIYASUDOKORO. Men suddenly swarmed.

   (Her gestures suggest the actions described.)
CHORUS. Grasping the shafts,
   They pushed my carriage back
   Into the ranks of the servants.
   My carriage had come for no purpose,

My pleasure was gone,
And I knew my helplessness.
I realized now
That all that happened
Was surely retribution
For the sins of former lives.
Even now I am in agony:
Like the wheels of my carriage
I return again and again—
How long must I still keep returning?
I beg you, dispel this delusion!
I beg you, dispel my suffering!
> *(She presses her palms together in supplication.)*

MIYASUDOKORO. Remembering the vanished days
I dance, waving at the moon
My flowerlike sleeves,

CHORUS. As if begging it to restore the past.
> *(She goes to the shite-position and begins to dance. As her dance ends, the text resumes.)*

MIYASUDOKORO. Even the moon
At the Shrine in the Fields
Must remember the past;

CHORUS. Its light forlornly trickles
Through the leaves to the forest dew.
Through the leaves to the forest dew.

MIYASUDOKORO. This place, once my refuge,
This garden, still lingers

CHORUS. Unchanged from long ago,

MIYASUDOKORO. A beauty nowhere else,

CHORUS. Though transient, insubstantial

MIYASUDOKORO. As this little wooden fence

CHORUS. From which he used to brush the dew.
> *(She brushes the fence with her fan.)*

I, whom he visited,
And he, my lover too,
The whole world turned to dreams,
To aging ruins;
Whom shall I pine for now?
The voices of pine-crickets

Trill *rin, rin,*
The wind howls:
   (She advances to stage front. She gazes at the torii.*)*
How I remember
Nights at the Shrine in the Fields!
   *(Weeping, she withdraws to the area before the musicians
   and starts to dance. The text resumes when her dance has
   ended.)*

CHORUS. At this shrine we have always worshiped
   The divine wind that blows from Ise,
      (She goes before the torii.*)*
   The Inner and Outer Shrines.
   As I pass to and fro through this *torii*
   I seem to wander on the path of delusion:
   I waver between life and death.
      (She passes back and forth through the torii.*)*
   The gods will surely reject me!
   Again she climbs in her carriage and rides out
   The gate of the Burning House,
   The gate of the Burning House.[11]

Notes

1. The passage above hints at the fading love of Genji for Miyasudokoro.

2. The verb *shinobu,* "to recall the past," leads into the noun *shinobu no kusagoromo,* a robe made of a kind of printed cloth, the design pressed from leaves. This cloth is mentioned effectively in *The Brocade Tree,* but here it seems an extraneous ornament and is hence omitted from the translation.

3. The poem is quoted from *The Tale of Genji,* where it seems to mean that the visitor has come without invitation, pretending he had been invited. The poem is an allusive variation on poem no. 982 of the *Kokinshū:* "My hut is at the foot of Mount Miwa. If you love me come and visit me; my gate is the one with the cedar by it."

4. Commentators disagree on the nature of the hut, some taking it as the place where the guardian lives, others as a place where sacred food is prepared. The meaning in either case is that buildings which, like everything else at the Shrine in the Fields, seemed highly perishable have miraculously survived.

5. Kiritsubo was Genji's mother.

6. Streamers of paper or mulberry bark were inscribed with prayers and attached to *sakaki* branches, then tossed into the stream.

7. There are allusions here to the famous poem by Ono no Komachi in which she compares herself to a floating waterweed. See *Komachi at Sekidera.*

8. A slightly modified version of the poem Miyasudokoro sent to Genji at Nonomiya. Being wetted by the waves has the additional meaning of having her sleeves wetted by tears. In other words, she is sure nobody will care whether she weeps with sorrow or not.

9. The Virgin resided at Ise in the Také Palace.

10. A priest's robe was frequently called *kokegoromo,* literally "moss robe." Here it has that meaning, but also refers to the moss on the ground. Because it is autumn the grass too is faded like the priest's robe.

11. The Burning House is a familiar image for this world, which an enlightened person should flee as eagerly as from a burning house.

The Iron Crown

(KANAWA)

TRANSLATED BY EILEEN KATO

INTRODUCTION

The Iron Crown belongs to the fourth category of Nō plays. It has been attributed, rather doubtfully, to Zeami. The play has an exceptionally tight dramatic structure and displays convincing strength in its portrayal of a woman's jealous fury. Clearly it points the way to a more realistic theatre than other Nō plays on the theme of jealousy, but for this very reason it lacks the magical qualities of such a work as *Dōjōji*. A description of the *kanawa onna* mask usually worn by the *shite* in the first part of the play would seem to fit the character: "She is not a supernatural woman but an ordinary one, and her jealousy is unrelieved by nobler sentiments." Nevertheless, *Kanawa* is considered to be one of the finest examples of a dramatic Nō.

The source for *The Iron Crown* is an account in the *Heike Monogatari*. Slightly simplified, it runs as follows: In the reign of Emperor Saga (809 to 823) a certain noblewoman was possessed by jealousy. For seven days she shut herself up at the Kibune Shrine and prayed to the god that he change her into a demon so that she might kill the woman who had occasioned her jealousy. The god was moved by her distress, and instructed her to bathe for thirty-seven days in the rapids of the Uji River. The

194

woman, pleased by the oracle, returned to the Capital. Secluding herself in a deserted spot, she divided her long hair into five bunches and fashioned these bunches into horns. She daubed her face with vermilion and her body with cinnabar, set on her head an iron tripod with burning brands attached to its legs, and held in her mouth another brand, burning at both ends. Then, late at night, she ran out on the Yamato Highway, her crown aflame, terrifying all who saw her so greatly "that none but swooned in fright and perished." She killed the woman, and the man who had left her, and also killed their families, both men and women, high and low. To kill men, she changed into a woman, and vice versa. The people of the Capital, terrorized, all locked themselves in their houses.

It is unusual for a play to be introduced by a *kyōgen* actor instead of the *waki*. The *waki* in this play violates his traditional role by participating in the action, rather than observing it. Hence, the play might be said to have no true *waki*. In the Kanze school, the *shite* wears the *deigan* mask in the first part, and not the *kanawa onna*.

The Iron Crown is performed by all schools except Komparu.

195

THE IRON CROWN (KANAWA)

(The Attendant comes onstage and stops at the naming-place.)

ATTENDANT. I am an attendant at the Kibune Shrine. Last night
I saw an extraordinary apparition in a dream. A woman,
from the Capital evidently, came in the middle of the night
to worship at the shrine, and the gods gave the oracle that
her prayer would be granted. They said she must put a tripod on her head, with torches attached to its legs, daub her
face with red and wear scarlet clothing. And she must let
her heart be consumed with anger. The oracle directed me
to make sure I gave her this answer. I shall go and inform her.

> *(He retires to the rear of the stage, which means he has
> exited. The Woman enters and stops at the* shite-*position
> facing the musicians. She wears the* kanawa onna *mask and
> a conical* kasa *hat.)*

WOMAN. As the days unfold and pass,
My love becomes a robe
Whose fastenings ever multiply
To hold and bind me.
I shall go to the shrine of Kibune.

> *(She faces front.)*

"Even were it possible to rope
A wild horse with a spider's web,
Still would it be impossible to trust
The fickle man whose heart is drawn two ways."[1]
I knew that poem well,
And thought I had heeded it.
But how could I foreknow
How far he would go in falseness?
Oh grief that we should ever have pledged our love!
But I have brought this on myself.
My anguish is too terrible to bear:
I am going to Kibune Shrine
To pray the gods to punish him—

And not in some future life! but in this world!
Here where life can hold no meaning for me now.
To the fast-flowing Kibune River
I shall hurry my steps.
       (She begins describing her journey.)
The course of love has reached a bitter end;
Just so the road ends I have often traveled
In the dead of night,
Along the river bank at Tadasu.
Plunged in the darkness of my troubled mind,
Heedlessly I go by deep and muddy pools,
Knowing no joy in life, sure that death
Will soon dissolve my weary body.
I make my way through deep and dew-drenched grasses
On the lonely moors of Ichiwarano.
The moon is late tonight.
       *(She takes a few steps to her right, then returns to her
       original position.)*
In darkness I go by Kurama River.
I cross the bridge, and soon
I have arrived at the shrine of Kibune,
I have arrived at Kibune Shrine.
       *(Her return to her original position signifies her arrival.
       She takes off her hat and faces front.)*

WOMAN. I have made haste, so I have already arrived at the shrine
of Kibune. Now, with a quiet heart, let me pay my homage
at the shrine.
       *(She sits on a stool before the musicians. The Attendant
       comes onstage and sees her.)*

ATTENDANT. Why, this must be the woman! I shall tell her of the
oracle. *(He kneels to the right of the Woman.)* I beg your
pardon. I have something to tell you about the nightly visits
you have made to offer prayers to the gods. They have heard
your prayers, and here is the oracle we have received. You
must put a tripod on your head, with torches attached to
its legs, daub your face with red and wear scarlet clothing,
and you must fill your heart with fury. This is what the
oracle directs. See that you obey.

WOMAN. What an extraordinary thing for you to say! But how

could it possibly concern *me?* You must have mistaken me
for someone else.

ATTENDANT. No, it most certainly refers to you. Even while I'm
talking, everything about her is beginning to look sinister!
What's happening? Her face has completely changed! I'm
scared!

   (He exits, running.)

WOMAN. That was indeed an extraordinary oracle. Now I shall go
home and do as it commands.

CHORUS. In less time than it takes to tell,
   Her looks are all altered;
   In less time than it takes to tell,
   Her whole appearance has changed.
   She was a beautiful lady,
   But now her raven hair stands on end;
   It bristles skyward!
   Black clouds bank up the sky,
   And rain spills down.
   To the wild howl of the wind,
   The thunder joins its roar.
   Torn asunder are the bonds of love
   That even the God of Thunder could not break.
   I am become a demon filled with hate.
   Ah! I'll show him!
   I'll teach that faithless man a lesson!
   (Her movements become demonic, and she
   exits furiously. A Man comes onstage to
   the naming-place. He wears the costume
   of a commoner and carries a short sword.)

MAN. I live in Shimogyō, the lower part of the
   Capital. Lately I have been troubled by re-
   peated nightmares. Today I am going to visit
   Seimei, the diviner, to ask what they mean.
   (He goes to the end of the bridgeway and
   looks up toward the curtain.) May I come in?
     (The Diviner comes through the curtain.
     He wears a court cap and an elaborate robe
     over his stiff white divided skirts.)

DIVINER. Who is it?

MAN. I live in the Lower City. Lately I have been troubled by continuous nightmares, so I have come to consult you.

DIVINER. I see. This is most unusual. But there is no need to resort to divination. You have fallen victim to the jealous hatred of a woman. Your life would appear to be in danger this very night. Might this be the case?

MAN. I have nothing to conceal. I divorced my first wife and married another woman. Do you think that could be it?

DIVINER. Yes, I believe it is. The woman you divorced has, by her repeated prayers to the gods and Buddhas, secured an end to your life this very night. All my incantations are powerless.

MAN. It is lucky I came here to see you. I beseech you! Pray for me! Pray to save me!

DIVINER. Your only hope at this point is to transfer to another person the doom that threatens you. Quickly! Get offerings ready!

MAN. At once.

(The Diviner exits. The Man sits in a relaxed posture before the musicians. The stage assistant brings on a two-tiered stand. On the upper shelf is a wig and a samurai's eboshi hat. These represent the Man and his new wife. On the lower shelf are gohei, paper offerings used in Shinto ceremonies. Five-colored gohei—red, blue, yellow, black, and white—are attached to the uprights at the four corners of the stand. A sacred shimenawa cord is strung between the uprights. The stage assistant sets the stand on a one-mat platform, about three by six feet.

The Diviner enters and mounts the platform. He carries gohei *in his hand.)*

DIVINER. And now I shall try to transfer the curse. *(He describes setting up the altar.)* I have fashioned two life-size straw effigies of the man and his new wife. I place their names inside. Next, I prepare a three-tiered stand. On it, I place five-colored *gohei* and other offerings. And now I pray with the  utmost fervor. *(He begins his prayer.)* I most humbly prostrate myself in worship. *(He waves a* gohei *over the altar he has made, to purify it.*) Since the very beginning of creation, when, upon the rock throne of Heaven, our Heavenly Ancestors, Izanagi and Izanami, celebrated their august marriage, men and women have been joined in wedlock; and yin and yang, the way of male and female, has come down from ancient times. Why, then, should evil spirits interfere and take a couple's lives before their allotted span has run its course?

CHORUS. And when thus he has prayed
    To all the greater gods and lesser gods,
    The gods of Heaven and the gods of Earth,
    To all the Buddhas and Bodhisattvas,
    To the mighty demon-quelling Deva Kings,
    And all the Angel Hosts of Heavenly Children,[2]
    And the nine Great Luminaries,
    The sun, the moon, and the seven bright stars,
    And to all the twenty-eight great constellations,
    To every kind of Deity and Power,
    What prodigy is this?
    The rains pour down,
    The storm winds blow,
    The thunder roars
    And flash on flash of lightning rends the air,
    While the *gohei* flap and rustle
    The hair of his body stands on end;
    His mien grows wild and terrible.

      (*He puts down his* gohei *and withdraws to a place before the Chorus where he kneels. The living ghost of the Woman enters and stops at the first pine. The tripod crown is on her head and she wears the* hashihime *mask. She carries a demon's mallet.*)

GHOST. The flowers that open to the slanting rains
    And to the soft, warm winds of spring,
    Must scatter in the selfsame winds
    At the season's close.
    The moon that rises in the eastern hills
    Is hidden soon behind the western peaks.
    So too constant change rules all things.
    Action and retribution

Are like the turning of a wheel.
It is right I take swift vengeance
On people who have wronged me so.
They say that those who, for love,
Throw themselves into the Kamo River,
Are doomed to sink and never rise again,
And turn to demons green as Kamo waters.
Not I! I am the burning firefly
Grazing the shallows of Kibune River.
And these three blazing firebrands
I wear on my tripod crown
Have made of me a flame-red demon.
  (She comes onstage.)
CHORUS. She now draws near
  The pillow where her husband lies.
    (She mounts the platform.)
  And how is my lord?
  We have not seen each other lately!
    (She glares at the hat on the shelf.)
GHOST. Ah! I am filled with hate!
  When I pledged to be your wife
  I thought that, like the jeweled camellia flower,
  Our love would last a thousand ages,
  As many years before it as a seedling pine.
  Why did you abandon me this way?
  Ah! How I hate the man!
  To think I have been rejected!
    (She weeps.)
CHORUS. Rejected, spurned for another!
  I sink in helpless tears of heartsick loss,
  The bitter torture of remembered love.
    (She descends from the platform.)
  I hate him!
    (She goes to the shite-*pillar.)*
GHOST. Railing against my husband,
CHORUS. Sometimes my love wells up again,
GHOST. Sometimes my hatred rages.
    (She glares at the altar.)
CHORUS. Awake or asleep, my memory

Gives no reprieve from sorrow.
Now retribution is at hand!
   (Her pose shows she is ready to kill.)
Now he will learn what retribution means.
Even as the snow melts and vanishes
Tonight his life must end!
Tonight he shall die!
But ah! I still feel pity for him!
   (Her mood softens. Her dance during the following passage
   suggests the tortured feelings expressed.)
CHORUS. "When least desired, discord burgeons,
   Like trees on a mountain peak."[3]
   If even devoted lovers must taste some pain,
   What then of me?
   As month piled on month and year on year,
   My heart sank deeper and deeper into grief.
   My hate fed on itself and grew—
   Small wonder I became a vengeful demon!
GHOST. Now, now I am going to kill them!
   (She stares at the altar.)
CHORUS. Yes, I will kill them now!
   Then, brandishing her scourge above her head

   (She leaps on the platform and
   brandishes her demon-mallet.)
   She coils her rival's hair about her hand
   (She twists the wig on the shelf.)
   Now I strike! she cries.
   (She strikes the wig with her mallet.)
   Oh this bitter world, where we know not
   What is real and what a dream!
   See the wheel of fate has come round
   To the hour of retribution.
   No doubt you're sorry now!
   Repent, and know your crime.
   (She strikes the wig again.)
GHOST. And you, I hate still more!
CHORUS. And you, I hate still more!
   (She steps down from the platform and goes to the shite-
   pillar.)

Faithless man! I'll snatch you off with me!
She draws near the pallet where he lies,
  (She goes beside the altar and brandishes her mallet.)
But when she looks, oh horror!
The thirty Guardian Deities stand arrayed
"Evil demons, by their presence here,
Defile a holy place. Begone, vile thing!"
So the gods rebuke her, and she rages!
  (She stamps in time to the music.)
She loses the man she loves, and worse—
She has incurred the wrath of all the gods.
Now her strength is ebbing fast,
Her demon powers are failing,
And like a carriage with a broken wheel
She shivers and stops.
  (She kneels and bows, touching both her hands to the ground in defeat.)

GHOST. The wheel has turned and I have lost;
I must wait until it comes full circle.
Then my turn may come again.
But now I must go back.
  (She stands.)

CHORUS. Only her voice is clearly heard;
The demon now is invisible.
She has passed beyond the sight of men,
An evil spirit beyond the sight of men.
  (She gives a final stamp at the shite-*pillar to indicate she has disappeared.)*

Notes

1. An old poem of unknown origin. See Kenkō, *Essays in Idleness,* translated by Donald Keene, p. 183, for another use of this poem.

2. The deities invoked in this passage were those associated with magical potency. The "heavenly children" were the form in which various other divinities appeared in the world of men. The nine "great luminaries" were the sun, moon and five planets plus two stars. The different categories were not mutually exclusive.

3. Reference to a poem by Izumi Shikibu in *Shikashū.*

Yōkihi

BY KOMPARU ZENCHIKU/TRANSLATED BY CARL SESAR

INTRODUCTION

Yōkihi belongs to the third category of plays. The author, Komparu Zenchiku (1405–1468), based it almost entirely on the famous *Song of Everlasting Sorrow* by Po Chü-i (772–846), and frequently quoted the original text in Japanese translation. Po Chü-i was no less popular in Japan than in China, and echoes of his poetry are found throughout classical Japanese literature.

Yōkihi (Yang Kuei-fei in Chinese) was the favorite mistress of the Emperor Hsüan Tsung (r. 713–756). He fell in love with her when he was over sixty, though she was the wife of his son. He forced the son, Prince Shou, to divorce Yang Kuei-fei and took her into his harem. His infatuation led him also to favor members of her family, including her adopted son, An Lu-shan, a Turk of obscure origins who nursed ambitions of seizing the throne for himself. In 755 An Lu-shan at length staged his rebellion, putting the troops of the Emperor to rout. The Emperor's troops insisted that Yang Kuei-fei be put to death, and he had no choice but to turn her over to an executioner.

The *Song of Everlasting Sorrow* describes how the Emperor

first discovered Yang Kuei-fei, how their love grew, and how she finally died. It goes on to relate how the Emperor resorted to a Taoist magician to search for her in the afterworld. The magician found her on the mythical island of P'eng-lai, and brought back mementoes and a message for the Emperor.

In this play the Chinese names all are given in Japanese pronunciations. Yang Kuei-fei becomes Yōkihi, the Emperor Hsüan Tsung becomes Gensō, and the village of Ma Wei, where Yang Kuei-fei was strangled, is known as Bagai. But the changes go far beyond differences in pronunciation. The play is imbued with a peculiarly Japanese sense of bittersweet nostalgia. Yōkihi is not the scheming, ruthless woman of history, nor the voluptuous charmer of Chinese poetry, but a wraith, a poignant ghost who reenacts long-departed hours of happiness. The imagery, largely Buddhist, is also typical of Japanese, rather than of Chinese poetry. The play embodies to a high degree the mysterious beauty known in Japanese as *yūgen*.

Yōkihi is performed by all schools of Nō.

PERSONS A SORCERER *(waki)*
A VILLAGER *(kyōgen)*
YŌKIHI *(shite)*

PLACE THE HŌRAI PALACE IN THE LAND OF IMMORTALITY

TIME THE REIGN OF EMPEROR GENSŌ; THE EIGHTH MONTH

YŌKIHI

(The stage assistant places a representation of the Palace, covered by a cloth, before the musicians. The Sorcerer enters and stands at the naming-place, facing the musicians.)

SORCERER. At break of day
    I seek a path
    To a world unknown.
       (He faces front.)

I am a sorcerer in the service of Gensō, Emperor of China. My lord ruled the land with justice and rectitude, but delighting in fleshly pleasures and abandoning himself to the charms of women, he came to possess a maiden of unmatched loveliness, daughter of the house of Yō, named Yōkihi. But certain events brought her to death on the Plain of Bagai. Overcome with grief, my lord charged me to go quickly forth and find the resting place of her spirit. Above I searched the blue empyrean of Heaven; below, the depths of the Yellow Springs, but nowhere did I learn her spirit's dwelling place. I have not yet been to the Palace of Hōrai; hence I journey in haste now to Hōrai, Island of Everlasting Youth.

    Be they intimations of darkness,
    Would the black arts of sorcery
    Bring tidings of the place her spirit dwells!
    My ship rides an endless track of sea.
    See! Faintly visible, far beyond her sails,
    (He takes a few steps to his right, then returns to his place.)
    An island mountain rises in the mists!
    I have reached the Land of Immortality.

    (His return indicates his arrival at Hōrai. He faces front.)
I have journeyed so fast that I have already come to Hōrai, Island of Everlasting Youth. Here I shall make careful inquiry.

    (He turns to look up the bridgeway.
    The Villager enters and stands at the first pine. He has a fan and a short sword.)

211

SORCERER. Are you a resident of this place?

VILLAGER. What business have you that you should ask me that?

SORCERER. Is there a person here named Yōkihi?

VILLAGER. There is no one here of that name, but there is a lady called the Jade Princess who speaks day and night of her yearning for the court of China and the world she left. Might she be the one of whom you speak?

SORCERER. Well, then, please direct me to the Jade Princess.

VILLAGER. Certainly. In the woods you see there you will find a building with a plaque inscribed Residence of Great Purity. Go there and inquire.

SORCERER. Thank you for your kind instructions. I will inquire at my leisure.

VILLAGER. If there is anything more I can do, please let me know.

SORCERER. I shall be most obliged for your help.

VILLAGER. Very well, sir.

(He exits. The Sorcerer comes to stage center.)

SORCERER. I have come following the man's instructions to the Palace of Hōrai; and now as I look about I see palace grounds vast beyond all limit, halls of such splendid magnificence they seem to be encrusted with the Seven Treasures. The mightiest palaces of China, even the Hall of Eternal Life or the Palace of Black Horse Mountain, are no match for such infinite grandeur! How lovely a place this is!

SORCERER. Yes, there, just as he said, I see within the palace grounds a mansion with a plaque inscribed Residence of Great Purity. But I shall first stroll about and learn more of this place.

(He kneels at the waki-*position. Yōkihi speaks from within the covered palace.)*

YŌKIHI. Once, long ago,

In the gardens of Black Horse Mountain,
Together we viewed the flowers of Spring.
Truly is it said,
"All is transient and must pass away."
Here, in the autumn valleys of Hōrai,
Even the reflection of the moon
At which all alone I gaze
Weeps for me and soaks my sleeve.
O, longed-for time of old!

SORCERER. I, a sorcerer, am come as imperial messenger of the Son
  of Heaven, ruler of China. Does the Jade Princess live here?

YŌKIHI. What did you say . . . a messenger of the Emperor of
  China? What brings you here?

  So saying,

  (describing her actions.)

  She parts the nine-fold flower curtains,

  And raising the jeweled blind, ·

  (The stage assistant removes the cloth.
  Yōkihi is wearing the waka-onna
  mask and is seated on a low stool.)

SORCERER. She reveals herself,

  (He bows to her.)

YŌKIHI. Her hair a cloud,

SORCERER. Her face a flower,

TOGETHER. Tears gather in her eyes,

  Full of all sorrowing . . .

CHORUS. O branch of pear blossom

  Glittering with rain!

  The crimson lotuses of Taieki,

  The green willows of Biyō Palace,

  Could they surpass such loveliness?

  Small wonder the painted palace ladies

  Paled before her beauty!

SORCERER. I must speak with you. Even while you still dwelt
  among the living within the inner palace our lord was ne-
  glectful of affairs of government and court. But how much
  worse has he become ever since you disappeared! He has
  given himself entirely to grief, until now his very life appears
  to be in danger. That is why, by my lord's command, I have
  journeyed here. Now that I have seen your beauty I realize
  why my lord's feelings lie so deep. More than ever do I pity
  him!

YŌKIHI. Yes, it is as you say. And it would seem a sign of his great
  affection that you have journeyed all this way in quest of the
  dwelling place of a person now vanished, a spirit intangible
  as the dew. But your visit only multiplies the pain. Aster
  flowers wither in an uncertain wind; so I too hate these fitful
  winds of tidings. I can no longer bear the tears of love;
  memories of the world I knew destroy my soul.

(She weeps.)

SORCERER. That must not be! I shall
return at once and inform his
Majesty. But please give me some
token of my visit.

(Yōkihi receives a jeweled
hairpin from the stage assistant.)

YŌKIHI. This shall be a token. So saying,
she removes her jeweled hairpin
and presents it to the sorcerer.

(She holds out the hairpin.
The Sorcerer takes it and
retreats a few steps.)

SORCERER. No, no! Such objects may be found in the mortal
world too—is it likely my lord would believe me? If there
were some pledge you and he exchanged, unknown to any
other, that would serve as proof.

(He bows.)

YŌKIHI. Of course, that is so. I remember now the words we offered the Two Stars as our vow that night in early autumn,
Seventh Night:

CHORUS. "In heaven may we be twin birds that share a wing;
On Earth may we be twin trees with branches intertwined."
Remind him of this privately.
See how I let fall among my tears
These words untold to any other!

(She weeps.)

Such was our vow,
But in the sad way of the world,
The everlasting wheel of Birth and Death,
My body was left on the fields of Bagai,
My soul has come to the Palace of Immortals.
The twin bird longs for her mate,
Alone, she tucks in her wing;
The twin tree's branches wither,
Swiftly their color fades.
But if our hearts still keep a single course
May we hope at least to meet again.
Tell him this.

SORCERER. I shall take my leave—

If only I could bring you with me on my return
How joyful I would be!
YŌKIHI. Wasted so thin for love
My sash binds thrice about my body,
I know not when we may meet again.
Wait, therefore, a little longer.
I shall reenact the pleasures
Of evenings long ago.
(She goes to the shite-*position.)*
CHORUS. Behold!
In the Palace of Black Horse Mountain,
A moonlit night's revelry!
Dance of the Robe of Feathers!
YŌKIHI. I danced with that pin in my hair.
*(The Sorcerer returns the hairpin to Yōkihi, moves back
and kneels.)*
CHORUS. Taking back her jeweled hairpin,
YŌKIHI. My dancing sleeve lifts it to my head!
CHORUS. Soyaya!
Dance of the Rainbow Skirt, of the Robe of Feathers!
Her tears fall without her knowing,
They drench her sleeves.
*(She retires to the stage assistant's position and puts
the pin in her hair. The Sorcerer kneels at
the* waki-*position.)*
YŌKIHI. All, all is a play of fantasy and dreams,
CHORUS. The dance of a swift-doomed butterfly.
(At the end of her dance, she stands before the musicians.)
YŌKIHI. When I think upon the far, far past gone long ago,
I cannot tell when these countless lives began.
CHORUS. Nor in the eternal round of incarnations yet to come
Is there an end to Birth and Death.
YŌKIHI. Yet of all the twenty-five existences,
Which escapes the unalterable principle
That he who is born must die?
CHORUS. Heavenly beings themselves fall victim
To the five-fold signs of death.
They that dwell within the Northern Continent,
Most blessed of all around Mount Shumi,

Live out a thousand years, then die.

YŌKIHI. How much more wretched the boundaries
　　Of uncertain fate!
　　　(She begins to dance.)

CHORUS. This is the greatest of all sorrows!
　　Once I too dwelt immortal in the upper world,
　　But by certain ancient ties of karma,
　　Briefly I came born to the world of men,
　　Reared carefully in the secluded chambers
　　Of the house of Yō, there unknown to any man
　　Until my lord heard of me. Swiftly
　　He summoned me to the palace and named me his empress.
　　"We shall grow old together and share a single grave,"
　　He promised me. How useless were his words!
　　The ties are broken.
　　Only one has reached this isle; I alone
　　Dwell here, helpless as the foam, the dew.
　　By rare chance we have met—
　　Please tell him gently of the sad days gone by.

YŌKIHI. And yet, how it rankles when I recall

CHORUS. The seventh night of the seventh moon,
　　My lord and I murmured a secret pledge:
　　"Twin birds that share a wing;
　　Twin trees whose branches intertwine."
　　These words, too, have come to nothing.
　　Parting is sad after one night's pledge of love,
　　How much worse, then, after many months and years
　　　together!
　　Were there no death-parting in the world,
　　I should have remained with him
　　A thousand years, ten thousand years.
　　There is no escape.
　　They say, "Those who meet must part."
　　We, too, have met and parted.
　　　(She finishes her dance, the kuse-mai, *and begins a* jono-
　　　mai *dance.)*

CHORUS. Dance of the Robe of Feathers!

YŌKIHI. Dance of the Robe of Feathers!
　　Rarely do I perform it. Yet a young girl's

CHORUS. Fluttering sleeves well express what is in her heart.

YŌKIHI. A tale of longed-for times of old

CHORUS. A tale of longed-for times of old!

(The stage assistant removes her hairpin and places it in her hand.)

Were one to exhaust its telling

Many months and many days should pass.

She changes step in her dance,

Offering once again her jeweled hairpin,

As token of the visit.

"I take my leave—farewell," the imperial envoy says,

And goes back to the Capital.

(He goes up the bridgeway. Yōkihi looks after him, from stage center.)

YŌKIHI. Wait, wait! There is more . . .

(They kneel facing each other. The Sorcerer is at the third pine.)

CHORUS. Never in life will I meet my lord again.

It was but a fleeting world of sorrow,

(They stand. The Sorcerer exits.)

But how I long for those days gone by!

O this hopeless parting!

(She kneels inside the palace and weeps.)

In the Tower of Eternal Life

She falls, weeping,

To remain forever.

(She comes out of the palace and stands there, weeping.)

The Priest and the Willow

(YUGYŌ YANAGI)

BY KANZE KOJIRŌ NOBUMITSU/TRANSLATED BY JANINE BEICHMAN

INTRODUCTION

The Priest and the Willow is classed in the third category, even though it contains no female characters, no doubt because it was difficult to fit this spirit play—which is not, however, a "god" play—into any other category. It was written by Kanze Kojirō Nobumitsu (1435–1516). One source for the play is the poem by Saigyō in the *Shinkokinshū:*

> By the side of a road
> Where a clear stream flowed
> In a willow's shade
> I thought I would pause a moment,
> But stood rooted to the spot.

A story similar to the play in plot was current in Nobumitsu's time. The *Fujisawa Chikan Oboegaki,* under the date 1471, tells of an errant priest who encountered an old man who proved to be the spirit of a willow tree. The willow spirit accepted a

220

prayer card from the priest, as he does in the play, and he and the priest exchanged poems. Then the spirit disappeared into his tree.

The errant priest of the play is a *yugyō shōnin,* a "wandering saint" of the *jishū,* the "perpetual sect" of Pure Land Buddhism. The *jishū* was so called because it advocated perpetual, twenty-four-hours-a-day recitation of the Nembutsu, the invocation to Amida Buddha. *Yugyō shōnin* wandered all over the country distributing prayer cards. The priest of the play is retracing the steps of Saigyō, the great wandering priest and poet of the late twelfth century.

In several other plays such as *Saigyō-zakura* or *Bashō,* the *shite* is the spirit of a tree, but *The Priest and the Willow* is perhaps the most successful example of this theme. It is performed by all schools of Nō.

221

PERSONS   AN ERRANT PRIEST *(waki)*
TWO COMPANIONS TO THE PRIEST *(wakizure)*
AN OLD MAN, LATER THE SPIRIT OF THE
WITHERED WILLOW *(shite)*
A VILLAGER *(kyōgen)*

PLACE   NEAR SHIRAKAWA IN IWAKI PROVINCE

TIME   AUTUMN, THE NINTH MONTH

THE PRIEST AND THE WILLOW (YUGYŌ YANAGI)

(The stage assistant places a representation of a grave mound before the musicians. It is surmounted by a tuft of leaves, and is covered on four sides by a cloth. The Priest and his Companions enter and face each other at stage center. They have fans and rosaries.)

PRIEST AND COMPANIONS. In traveling robes

> We go, not knowing
> When we shall return:
> In traveling robes
> We go, not knowing
> When we shall return.
> Our hearts hurry ahead
> To spread the Buddha's word.
> *(The Priest faces front.)*

PRIEST. I am an errant priest, a wanderer through the provinces. I follow the teachings of Ippen, the holy man, and spread the blessings of the errant teachings to the sixty provinces of the land. To all men far and wide I offer prayer cards,[1] testimony that salvation is certain for every believer. Lately I have been in the province of Kazusa, but now I turn my steps toward the north.

> *(He faces his Companions.)*

PRIEST AND COMPANIONS. We roam the provinces of Akitsusu[2]

> On the path of the Law;
> Through all the provinces
> On the path of the Law;
> The moon, unerring in its course,[3]
> Sheds its light deep into our hearts.
> They say this is Shirakawa Barrier
> Where the deep North begins
> Where autumn winds rise,
> And the evening mists spread.

223

(The Priest faces front, takes a few steps forward, then returns to his previous position as this passage ends.)

Where will we lodge tonight
In robes, cord-tied?
The tide of day
Has ebbed and turned to darkness,
The sun has set, and day
Has given way to evening dark.

(The Priest faces front.)

PRIEST. I have hurried on my way, and have already passed the famed barrier of Shirakawa. I see many roads here. I think I shall take the broad one.

COMPANIONS. By all means.

(They start toward the waki-*position. The Old Man enters, wearing the* akobujō *mask. He carries a rosary in his hand. He starts down the bridgeway.)*

OLD MAN. Excuse me! I have something to say to the companions of the holy wandering priest.

(The Companions kneel before the Chorus. The Priest stands at the waki-*position and faces the Old Man.)*

PRIEST. To me? Is it a prayer card you want? I know your legs are old, but do hurry a bit more.

OLD MAN. Oh, thank you. I'll be glad to receive a card. But first, I have something else to tell you. Years ago, another errant priest came here. But he took the other road, the abandoned one, saying that he preferred old ways. I have come here from a great distance, to show you the path he took.

PRIEST. How strange! An errant priest, one of my predecessors, traveled along this old path that is a path no longer!

OLD MAN. Yes, I assure you, for in the past this new road did not exist. The path he took followed the river bank, this side of the clump of trees you see over there. That is where the highway was.

A famous tree, known as
The Withered Willow, stands
There on the path;
If a saintly priest like you
Would pray before it, then
Even a tree or a blade of grass

Could achieve Buddhahood.

CHORUS. Please come this way, he says,
    I'm not the old horse of the story,[4]
    But I'll show you the way.
    Come quickly, travelers.
        (The Old Man comes onstage.)
    Truly the path looks forsaken,
    An old, abandoned road:
    All signs of man have faded
    From this waste of goose grass,
    Mugwort, tangled rush grass
    And low reeds, withered like
    My sleeves by the autumn frosts and dews
    I brush with my robes as I pass
    To find, on an old mound,
        (He turns to the mound.)
    Where the past lingers,
    A withered willow tree,
    Its branches desolate.
    The path its shadow treads
    Stretches on forever,
    And over it travels
    Only the wind;
    Through the endless landscape travels
    Only the wind.
        (He turns to the Priest.)

OLD MAN. This tree standing on the old mound is the Withered
    Willow. Examine it carefully!
        (The Priest turns toward the mound.)

PRIEST. Indeed, the tree on the mound really is the famous willow!
        Water runs no more
        Between the river's banks,
        And here by the dry bed
        Stands a withered willow,
        So overgrown with ivy
        And clinging creepers,
        It hardly can be seen.
        Green moss buries its branches;
        Its appearance truly bespeaks

Its years of stars and frosts.
How long has this famous tree been here?
Please tell me its full story.
(He turns to the Old Man.)

OLD MAN. Long ago, in the days of the Cloistered Emperor Toba, there was a palace guard named Satō Byōe Norikiyo who took priestly vows and became known as the poet Saigyō. Once he came to this province from the Capital. It was the middle of the sixth month, the "waterless month" as it is called. He stopped to rest a moment in the shade of this tree on the river bank, and, as he rested, he composed a poem.

PRIEST. Your story interests me. How did Saigyō's poem go?

OLD MAN. I am sure your ceaseless prayers through the days' six watches leave you no leisure, but have you never seen the collection in which it appears, the *Shinkokinshū?*

(The Priest sits.)

CHORUS. By the side of a road
Where a clear stream flowed,
In a willow's shade;
Where a clear stream flowed,
In a willow's shade,
(The Old Man goes toward the mound.)
I thought I would pause a moment
But stood rooted to the spot.
(He stands at stage center.)
These words of mine as I enjoyed the cool
(He kneels.)

Have been passed on
From generation to generation,
And linger like this old tree,
Evoking distant memories.
Thus the old man, blessed
(The Old Man and the Priest salute one another by pressing their palms together in respect.)
By ten invocations from the holy priest,[5]
Made as if to leave his presence.
(The Old Man rises.)
He approached, or so it seemed,
The old mound of the Withered Willow Tree

Only to disappear.
He approached the mound
And disappeared.

(He goes to the right of the mound, opens his arms wide toward the front of the stage, then enters the mound. The Villager, who wears a short sword at his side, enters and goes to the naming-place.)

VILLAGER. I live in this neighborhood. I thought I would amuse myself today by visiting the willow on the old mound. *(He sees the Priest.)* Oh, there's a priest I've never seen in these parts before. I'm surprised to see anyone resting here—where have you come from and where are you headed?

PRIEST. I am an errant priest and I am making a circuit of the provinces. Are you from this area?

VILLAGER. Yes, I certainly am.

PRIEST. Then won't you come a bit closer? I'd like to ask you something.

VILLAGER. With pleasure. *(He kneels at stage center.)* Well then, what would you like to ask me?

PRIEST. I know it is an odd request, but would you tell me what you know about the Withered Willow?

VILLAGER. That certainly *is* an odd request! It's true I live nearby, but I don't know much about such things. Still, it would be a shame if you ask me a question the very first time we ever meet and I tell you I don't know anything about the tree. So I'll tell you what I've heard.

PRIEST. I shall be much obliged.

VILLAGER. Well, then, this is the extent of what I have heard about the willow on the old mound. Satō Byōe Norikiyo, a palace guard in the service of the seventy-fourth emperor, the Cloistered Emperor Toba, was an eighth-generation descendant of Tawara no Tōta Hidesato, and the son of Lieutenant of the Outer Guards Yasukiyo. He became a priest in his middle years, and took the name Saigyō. He made a circuit of the provinces as a part of his religious austerities, and when he was on his way to Mutsu, he passed by this place. It was the middle of the sixth month, and when he saw a withered willow tree here by the river, he thought it might be a cool place. He came here and, as he expected, a cool breeze was blowing. That was why he turned to the willow and composed this poem:

By the side of a road
Where a clear stream flowed,
In a willow's shade
I thought I would pause a moment,
But stood rooted to the spot.

This is a rustic place, no doubt. But we speak of this tree with veneration and call it the Willow of the Old Mound, because it is the tree that inspired Saigyō's poem. I hear that this poem has even been included in the *Shinkokinshū*. I should tell you also that this road was not here in olden times. Saigyō took a path that came from the river bank, a little this side of the village you see over there. Other priests of the errant sect who had come north before him also took that path, they say. Anyway, that is as much as I have heard. Why should you ask about it? It's certainly puzzling.

PRIEST. How kind of you to tell me the story. I had no special reason for asking. But just now, as I was walking along the path over there, an old man suddenly came up and offered to guide me. He said this was the old path and he kindly told me the story of the Withered Willow, just as you did a moment ago. Then he disappeared by the mound.

VILLAGER. That is incredible! What an amazing thing to be told! There's no doubt about it, that must have been the spirit of the Withered Willow! And I'm sure you'll see another miracle if you stay here a little longer.

PRIEST. This has been such a remarkable experience that I shall indeed remain a while longer. I shall chant the blessed sutras, and await another miracle.

VILLAGER. If there is any way I can help you, please call on me again.

PRIEST. I shall.

VILLAGER. I am at your service.

(He exits.)

PRIEST. Unbelievable! The Withered Willow was talking to me!

PRIEST AND COMPANIONS. We have chanted sutras
To the telling of our beads
To the telling of our beads

We have called upon his name
Until the bell of evening
Joined its voice to ours.
Through this cloudless night
We will sleep under the moon,
Our sleeves spread out upon the dew
Our sleeves spread out upon the dew.

(The Spirit of the Willow speaks from inside the mound.)

SPIRIT. The Gensui River ripples[6]
Like silk and the swallows
Return from the sea
With spring, but you have gone
To Keitai, and only
A broken willow twig
Remains of our parting.
The willow tree that withered
In vain, has found its season;
Now it has encountered
The holy Law, the teaching
Of Amida, who guides
Even the crooked
Straight to Paradise.

CHORUS. Drawn by the blessed
Power of his vow:
"Let all beings call my name,
And they shall be reborn
Into my Pure Land"[7]—
Even trees and grasses
Can attain Enlightenment,
Even an ancient willow.
An old man, his white hair tangled
Like the slender willow twigs
Above him, is suddenly revealed.
His court hat is wrinkled
And his frame droops like a willow
Heavy with years.

*(The stage assistant removes the cloth from the mound,
and the Spirit is revealed. He wears the* shiwajō *mask and
a court hat. The Priest turns to him.)*

PRIEST. How perfectly amazing! A strange-looking old man has
shown himself from the roots of the Withered Willow, there
among the old mound's deep grasses. He wears a courtier's
hat and robe!

SPIRIT. Why are you so surprised? I have already appeared before
you. I was the old man who guided you at dusk.

PRIEST. Then the man who guided me
To the old path was the spirit
Of the Withered Willow Tree?

SPIRIT. Without the teachings
Of the holy Law,
Insentient trees and grasses
Could surely not gain Paradise.

PRIEST. That is true indeed.
One calling of his name,
Or ten, it matters not,

SPIRIT. A single invocation
Suffices for salvation.[8]

PRIEST. Amida's teaching

SPIRIT. Sinks into our hearts.

CHORUS. Each time a man
In this world
Calls upon his name,
(The Spirit leaves the mound.)
A new lotus is born
In his western realm;
And when, after a lifetime
Of unremitting devotion,
The man at last dies,
The flower comes
To this world to meet him,
And lead him up
To the highest empyrean.
Truly a joyful teaching!
*(He kneels to the right of the mound and bows to the
Priest with his palms pressed together.)*

SPIRIT. Shaka, the Buddha that was,
Has already perished;
Miroku, the Buddha to be,

Has not yet been born.
In this world between,
How can we reach Buddhahood,
Save by relying
On Amida's merciful Vow?
　(*He rises.*)

CHORUS. Amida on whom we rely with all our hearts,
　Cleanse us with the waters of your wisdom!
　We bow down to you in humble worship.
　In your Original Vow to save all creatures,
　No falsehood can be found; we trust our lives
　To your world-transcending mercy.
　In the vessel of your saving power
　We shall ride on the Way of the Law.
　(*He goes before the mound.*)

SPIRIT. And reach the Far Shore of Paradise!
　Leaflike is your boat
　But has it not that strength?

CHORUS. In the Yellow Emperor's time,[9]
　His minister, Kateki, heard
　The sighing of the autumn wind
　And noticed how a spider rode
　On a fallen willow leaf,
　Spinning out across the water;
　So he devised the first boat,
　Surely this too we owe to the willow!

SPIRIT. There were willows too
　In Gensō's Kasei Palace,[10]
　For an old poem describes

CHORUS. "The willows before the palace,
　The blossoms before the temple,"
　Famous trees which men
　Never tired of contemplating.
　(*The Spirit begins to dance to the Chorus' singing.*)
　In Rakuyō, long ago,[11]
　In the ancient days of
　The Temple of Pure Waters,
　Cascading waves appeared,
　Five-colored; one who climbed

To seek their source found there
A withered willow tree
That poured forth golden light,
And in that instant
Kannon of the Willows stood revealed.
Traces of the sacred presence
Have since lingered on;
It has become a holy place
To which men bend their steps
For the miracles worked there.
And when nobles played kickball
As cherries bloomed in the Capital,
The grounds were marked by four trees,
One a willow with trailing branches;
Underneath the tree at dusk,
You could hear the rapid echoes
Of their lacquered wooden shoes.

SPIRIT. Willow green and cherry pink
Mingled in the brocades
Adorning the players.
Through bamboo blinds, a scent
Wafted out on the breeze.
And out jumped a leashed cat,[12]
Parting the blinds to reveal
A girl's face, and drawing Kashiwagi
Down the leash-long path of love,
Helpless as the oak leaves
On the tree that bears his name.
But love's fruitless stories
Are nothing to me.
My robe, my hat are like the willow,
An old and faded green; my frail feet
Drift with the wind, unheeding.
An aged willow tree,
All my strength gone,

　　*(He retreats a little and holds onto the post on the right
　　side of the mound.)*
I feebly dance,
A figure in your dream,

Though to you I may seem real.
   (He ends his dance and faces the Priest.)
Joyfully I accept the teachings
And in the Way of the Law
CHORUS. I set out, confident,
   My companion the unerring moon.
   (Before the text resumes, he dances a stately jonomai
   dance.)
SPIRIT. The dance of the garden[13]
   Of willows and flowers
   Must have resembled this dance—
   Gentle as a green willow
   Swaying in the breeze raised
   By the wings of song thrushes
   Flying among its branches.
   I danced the Willow Dance,
   For I have become a Bodhisattva
   Of singing and dancing,
   Twirling my sleeves
   Over and over, I rejoice
   That I have received from you,
   O priest, the sacred teachings!
   (He half-kneels.)
   My dance of thanks has ended,
   And tears of farewell
   (He weeps.)

CHORUS. Are threaded like pearls
   On the spring willow's boughs.
SPIRIT. I take my leave.
   But as I speak, the cock crows
   At the bend of parting.
   (He rises.)
SPIRIT. I would offer you
   A willow twig bent
   Into a circle,[14]
CHORUS. But the twig should be broken
   From a pliant green willow,
SPIRIT. And I am an old tree
   With few branches.

CHORUS. Only this year is left,
        (He comes forward.)
    And I shall dread the wind.
    On uncertain feet,
    Faltering, frail,
        (He retreats unsteadily.)
    The willow shall fall.
    That we have met even
    A single night in your dream
        (He sits.)
    As you lie on the ground
    Is proof that in former lives
    We two were bound by ties
    That now have brought me
    From a saint the Holy Law.

        (He turns to the Priest and rises to a half-kneeling posi-
        tion.)
    The autumn winds
    Blow in from the west,
    Sweep through the dew
        (He stands and flutters his fan.)
    And the leaves on the trees,
    Scattering dew, scattering leaves;
    They leave nothing but
    A withered willow tree.
        (He opens his arms wide at the shite-*position, and gives*
        a final stamp of the foot.)

Notes

1. The text says literally that he offers cards to 600,000 people, but this number is clearly used simply as an indication of great crowds, and is influenced by mention of the "sixty provinces" in the previous statement. Ippen, the founder of the Jishū sect, is also reputed to have had a dream in which the words "six hundred thousand people" were each the first word of a quatrain. The cards distributed by the errant priests (*yugyōsō*) bore the inscription "Namu Amida Butsu: Kettei Ōjō Rokujūmannin," meaning, "Hail Amida Buddha: Salvation is Certain for 600,000 people."

2. Akitsusu or Akitsushima was a poetic old name for Japan.

3. For the believer in Amida Buddhism west was the most important direction because Amida's paradise was situated to the west; the moon, moving westward in the sky, therefore served as an inspiration.

4. A reference to the old story of how when Duke Hsüan of Chi and Kuan Chung were lost on the way an old horse guided them. The incident is related in the work *Han Fei Tzu*.

5. The Invocation is the calling on the name of Amida Buddha practiced by believers in Amidism. It was believed that if one could have a high-ranking priest say the Invocation ten times for one, and one joined in the recitation, it was possible to attain Buddhahood.

6. From a poem by Li Chün-yü found in the collection *San-t'i-shih;* the lines in question run: "The Yüan River (Gensui) is patterned with ripples like thin silk, the swallows return from the sea; you, still bitter over the sprig of willow broken as a parting pledge, go to Ching-tai."

7. This passage is quoted from the writings of Zendō (Shan-tao), a celebrated Chinese priest who propagated the Amidist teachings.

8. The Pure Land Buddhism taught by Hōnen emphasized the importance of reciting the Invocation as often as possible, but Shinran, Hōnen's disciple, insisted that calling Amida's name even once sufficed for salvation.

9. This story is related in other plays (e.g., *Jinen Koji*), but the source has not been found.

10. Reference is being made to the Hua-ch'ing Palace of the Emperor Hsüan Tsung. A poem by Wang Chien in the collection *San-t'i-shih* mentions the willows before the palace.

11. Rakuyō was the Japanese pronunciation for Lo-yang, long the capital of China. It was (and is still) used as a poetic name for Kyoto. The Temple of Pure Waters (Kiyomizu-dera) has for its chief divinity the Kannon of the Willow Branch. Even today ascetics purify themselves under the "pure water" that cascades down from the mountain.

12. This passage is difficult to fit smoothly into the translation. It is an extended reference to the first part of the "Wakana" chapter in *The Tale of Genji*. The mishap caused by a cat on a leash chasing after a small kitten leads to Kashiwagi's seeing Nyosan and falling in love with her on the spot, the disastrous beginning of their unhappy affair. The name Kashiwagi means literally "oak tree," giving rise to the statement a few lines farther on.

13. This was the name of a *gagaku* piece, presumably an elegant dance.

14. There was a custom of giving a sprig of willow bent round into a circle as a parting gift. References to this practice may be found in both Chinese and Japanese poetry.

Dōjōji

BY KANZE KOJIRŌ NOBUMITSU / TRANSLATED BY DONALD KEENE

INTRODUCTION

Dōjōji, a play of the fourth category, is now generally attributed to Kanze Kojirō Nobumitsu (1435–1516), although some scholars still accept the traditional view that it was written by Kan'ami and modified by Zeami. This highly dramatic story of a woman's jealousy creates a unique impression in performance, largely because of the hypnotic dance called *rambyōshi,* which is accompanied by the weird, almost animallike cries uttered by the player of the *kotsuzumi* drum. The actor's leap into the bell provides another unforgettable highlight.

The text as now performed seems to be a mangled version of a longer work. The play *Kanemaki,* now no longer performed by professional Nō actors though it survives in the countryside, is strikingly similar and perhaps a somewhat older version of the same theme. *Kanemaki* was no doubt abandoned when it became clear that *Dōjōji,* whatever its purely literary merits, was incomparably effective in the theatre.

The earliest suriviving source of the legend incorporated in the play is found in the *Honchō Hokke Reigenki,* a collection of Buddhist miracle stories compiled about 1040. In this account a lustful widow is attracted to a handsome young priest, and demands that he sleep with her. The priest is dismayed by her advances, but, in order to assuage her, promises that on his return from his pilgrimage he will spend the night with her. He however takes another road on his return, and the widow, realizing that she has been spurned despite her long, impatient waiting, gives herself to such intense wrath that she turns into a serpent. In this form she pursues the priest and, in the manner described in this play, eventually destroys him. In *Dōjōji*, on the other hand, the woman is a girl who has been led astray by her father's thoughtless joke. This difference allows us to feel sympathy for her, and thus intensifies the drama.

A remarkable feature of *Dōjōji* is the great bell, a stage property not found in any other Nō drama. At the start of a performance the servants, acting as stage assistants, make several attempts to thread the rope through the ring attached to a rafter over the stage before they finally succeed. This not only supplies a touch of informality but gives the roles of the servants an integral importance they rarely possess in Nō. The prop is used with powerful effect at the climax of the play when the actor leaps inside, a dangerous feat requiring perfect coordination if the actor is not to be injured by the leaden bell as it falls.

Dōjōji depends for its success less on the poetry than on the dramatic situation and the spectacle. It is easy to imagine why the play has often been adapted for use in less aristocratic theatres; the Kabuki version in particular is a perennial favorite.

The play is performed by all schools of Nō. The texts show an unusually large number of variants, chiefly in the prose passages. The present translation makes use of both the Kanze and Komparu texts in an attempt to provide the most effective version of the story.

239

PERSONS THE ABBOT OF DŌJŌJI *(waki)*
TWO PRIESTS OF THE TEMPLE *(wakizure)*
TWO TEMPLE SERVANTS *(kyōgen)*
A DANCER *(mae-jite)*
THE SERPENT DEMON *(nochi-jite)*

PLACE DŌJŌJI, A TEMPLE IN KII PROVINCE

TIME THE THIRD MONTH

DŌJŌJI

(As the opening flute is played the Abbot, the Two Priests, and the First Servant enter. The Priests and the Servant kneel on the bridgeway, but the Abbot continues on to the stage.)

ABBOT. I am the abbot of Dōjōji, a temple in the Province of Kii. For many years no bell has hung in the belfry tower of the temple, and for a good reason. I have decided lately to restore the ancient custom and at my order a new bell has been cast. In the calendar today is a day of good omen. I have ordered that the bell be raised into the tower and that there be a service of dedication.

(He calls towards the bridgeway.)

Servant!

FIRST SERVANT. Here I am, sir.

ABBOT. Today is marked in the calendar as a lucky day, and I want you to hoist the bell into the belfry.

FIRST SERVANT. Yes, certainly, sir.

(As the Servant stands the two Priests enter the stage from the bridgeway and sit at the waki-position behind the waki. The Servant leaves the bridgeway but returns shortly with another Servant. They carry between them on bamboo poles the prop, a huge bell. Two stage assistants help them.)

FIRST SERVANT. *Ei tō, ei tō.*

SECOND SERVANT. *Ei ya, ei ya.*

FIRST SERVANT. *Ei tō, ei tō.*

SECOND SERVANT. *Ei ya, ei ya.*

241

(Groaning under the strain, they lower the bell halfway down the bridgeway.)

FIRST SERVANT. Let's rest a while.

SECOND SERVANT. A good idea.

FIRST SERVANT. It's certainly a heavy bell.

SECOND SERVANT. Amazingly heavy.

FIRST SERVANT. Well, shall we lift it again?

SECOND SERVANT. All right.

(They lift the bell again.)

FIRST SERVANT. *Ei tō, ei tō.*

SECOND SERVANT. *Ei ya, ei ya.*

FIRST SERVANT. *Ei tō, ei tō.*

SECOND SERVANT. *Ei ya, ei ya.*

(They reach the middle of the stage.)

FIRST SERVANT. Let's put it down right here.

SECOND SERVANT. Right you are.

FIRST SERVANT. Everything under control?

SECOND SERVANT. Everything's going fine.

(With appropriate cries they set the bell down.)

FIRST SERVANT. Now for hoisting it into the belfry.

SECOND SERVANT. Right you are.

(The two Servants, helped by the stage assistants, use poles to thread the rope of the prop through the ring set in the ceiling. Then, with rhythmic shouts they hoist the prop to the appropriate height.)

FIRST SERVANT. It looks more impressive than ever, now that we've hoisted it up there.

SECOND SERVANT. That's right. It's certainly an impressive sight.

FIRST SERVANT. Let's waste no time in telling the Abbot about this.

(The First Servant goes before the gazing-pillar and addresses the Abbot.)

FIRST SERVANT. Excuse me, sir. We've raised the bell into the belfry.

ABBOT. You've raised it, you say?

FIRST SERVANT. Yes, that's just what I said, sir.

ABBOT. Then we will hold the dedication service today. For certain reasons best known to me, women are not to be admitted to the courtyard where the ceremonies are held. Make sure that everyone understands this.

FIRST SERVANT. Your orders shall be obeyed.

(He goes to the naming-place where he addresses people off-stage.)

Listen, you people! The new bell of the Dōjōji is to be dedicated today. All who wish to attend the ceremony are welcome. However, for reasons known only to himself, the Abbot has ordered that women are not to be allowed inside the courtyard where the service will take place. Take care you all obey his orders!

(He goes to kneel before the flute player. The Dancer enters. She wears the fukai *mask, a long wig, a brocade outer robe, an inner kimono with a fish-scale pattern, and a crested garment tied around her waist. She stands at the* shite-*position and faces the area before the musicians.)*

DANCER. My sin, my guilt, will melt away,

My sin, my guilt, will melt away,

I will go to the service for the bell.

(She faces forward).

I am a dancer who lives in a remote village of this Province of Kii. I have heard that a bell is to be dedicated at the Dōjōji, and so I am hurrying there now, in the hopes of improving my chances of salvation.

The moon will soon be sinking;

As I pass the groves of little pines

The rising tide weaves veils of mist around them.

But look—can it be my heart's impatience?—

(She takes a few steps to the right, then returns to her original position. This indicates she has reached the temple.)

Dusk has not yet fallen, the sun's still high,[1]

But I have already arrived:

I am here at the Temple of Dōjōji.

(She faces forward.)

My journey has been swift, and now I have reached the temple. I shall go at once to watch the ceremony.

(She moves towards the center of the stage. The First Servant rises.)

FIRST SERVANT. Stop! You can't go into the courtyard. Women aren't allowed.

DANCER. But I'm not like other women. I'm only a dancer. I live nearby and I am to perform a dance at the dedication of the bell. Please let me see the ceremony.

FIRST SERVANT *(to himself)*. A dancer? That's right, I suppose she doesn't count as an ordinary woman. *(to Dancer)* Very well, I'll let you into the courtyard on my own, but in return you must dance for me. *(He goes before flute player, picks up a tall court cap lying on the stage, and brings it to the Dancer.)* Here, take this hat. It just happened to be around. Put it on and let's see you dance.[2]

DANCER. With pleasure. I'll dance for you as best I can.

(She retires to stage assistant's position to alter her costume. The Servant returns to his original place and sits. The Dancer puts on the hat and goes to the first pine on the bridgeway. She looks beyond the pillar at the bell, then glides onto the stage to the suddenly stepped-up tempo of large drum. She stops just past the shite-*pillar.)*

DANCER. How happy you have made me! I will dance for you. *(She describes her actions.)* Borrowing for a moment a courtier's hat, she puts it on her head.

Her feet already stamp the rhythm.
Apart from cherry blossoms,
There are only the pines,
Apart from cherry blossoms,
There are only the pines.
When the darkness starts to fall
The temple bell will resound.

(She lifts the hem of her robe a little with her left hand, and dances the following passage as if she were climbing step by step up to the bell. This is the famous rambyōshi *dance, accompanied by the weird cries and pounding of the* ko-tsuzumi *drum.)*

Prince Michinari, at the imperial command,
First raised these sacred walls.
And because the temple was his work,
Tachibana no Michinari,
They called it Dōjōji.[3]

(The rhythm of the dance grows more rapid and intense.)

CHORUS *(for the Dancer)*. To a temple in the mountains

Now, on this evening in spring,
I have come, I have seen
CHORUS. The blossoms scattered with the evening bell,
The blossoms scatter, the blossoms fall.
DANCER. And all the while,
And all the while,
At temples everywhere across the land
The sinking moon strikes the bell.
The birds sing, and frost and snow fills the sky;
Soon the swelling tide will recede.
The peaceful fishers will show their lights
In villages along the river banks—
And if the watchers sleep when danger threatens
I'll not let my chances pass me by!

(The Servants have become hypnotized by the rhythm of the dance. The Dancer looks at the Abbot and the Priests. The Chorus describes her actions.)
CHORUS. Up to the bell she stealthily creeps
Pretending to go on with her dance.
(She holds her fan and looks at the bell.)
She starts to strike it!
(She swings the fan back and forth like a bell-hammer.)
This loathsome bell, now I remember it!
(She unfastens the cord of her hat, then strikes the hat from her hand with a blow of her fan. She stands under the bell.)
Placing her hand on the dragon-head boss,[4]
She seems to fly upward into the bell.
She wraps the bell around her,
She has disappeared.
(At the words, "Placing her hand," the Dancer rests her hand on the edge of the bell, then leaps up into it. At the same moment the stage assistant loosens the rope and drops the bell over her. The Servants, who have been drowsing, hypnotized by the dance, wake up, startled by the noise of the bell falling. The First Servant tumbles in confusion on the stage; the Second Servant falls on the bridgeway.)
BOTH SERVANTS *(variously)*. Ho! Hi! What was that frightful noise? That awful crashing racket? I'm so frightened I don't know what I'm doing!

FIRST SERVANT. That certainly was a terrible crash. I wonder where the other fellow went. *(He sees the Second Servant.)* Hey there, are you all right?

SECOND SERVANT. How about you?

FIRST SERVANT. I still don't know yet.

SECOND SERVANT. No wonder. We got so carried away by her dance we dozed off. Then came that awful bang. What do you think that was?

FIRST SERVANT. Do you suppose it was thunder? If it was thunder, there should have been some sort of warning—a little clap or two before the big one. Strange, very strange.

SECOND SERVANT. Yes, you're right. Whatever it was, the earth shook something terrible.

FIRST SERVANT. I don't think it was an earthquake. Look—come over here. *(He discovers the bell and claps his hands in recognition.)* Here's what made the noise.

SECOND SERVANT. You're right!

FIRST SERVANT. I hung it up very carefully, but the loop must've snapped. How else could it fall?

SECOND SERVANT. No. Look. The loop's all right. Nothing's broken. It's certainly a mystery. *(He touches the bell.)* Oww! This bell is scorching hot!

FIRST SERVANT. Why should falling make it hot? *(He too touches the bell.)* Oww! Boiling hot!

SECOND SERVANT. It's a problem, all right. What do you suppose it can mean? It's beyond me. Well, we'd better report what's happened. We can't leave things this way.

FIRST SERVANT. That's a good idea. Too bad if the Abbot heard about it from anyone but us! We've got to do something. But I don't think I should be the one to tell. You tell him.

SECOND SERVANT. Telling him is no problem, but it would look peculiar if I went. You tell him—you were left in charge.

FIRST SERVANT. That's what makes it so hard! You tell him, please.
(He pushes the Second Servant forward.)

SECOND SERVANT. No, it's not my business to tell him. *You* tell him. Hurry! *(He pushes the First Servant.)*

FIRST SERVANT. Please, I beg of you, as a favor. You tell him.

SECOND SERVANT. Why should I? You tell him. I don't know anything about it. *(The Second Servant leaves. The First Servant watches him go.)*

FIRST SERVANT. He's gone! Now I have no choice. I'll have to tell the Abbot, and it's going to get me into trouble. Well, I'll get it over with. *(He goes up to the Abbot.)* It fell down.

ABBOT. What fell down?

FIRST SERVANT. The bell. It fell from the belfry.

ABBOT. What? Our bell? From the belfry?

FIRST SERVANT. Yes, Master.

ABBOT. What caused it?

FIRST SERVANT. I fastened it very carefully, but all the same it fell down. Ah! That reminds me. There was a dancer here a little while ago. She said she lives nearby, and asked me to let her into the courtyard to see the dedication of the bell. Of course I told her that it wasn't allowed, but she said she wasn't an ordinary woman, and that she was going to offer a dance. So I let her in. I wonder if she had something to do with this?

ABBOT. You idiot! What a stupid thing to do! I knew this would happen. That's why I forbade you strictly to allow any women in here! You blundering fool!

FIRST SERVANT. Ahhhh. *(He bows to the ground.)*

ABBOT. I suppose I must go now and take a look.

FIRST SERVANT. Yes, Master. Please hurry. Help! Help! *(He exits, still crying for help.)*

ABBOT *(to the Priests)*. Priests, come with me. *(They stand and go to the bell.)* Do you know why I gave the order that no woman was to be permitted to enter the temple during the dedication of the bell?

PRIEST. No, Master. We have no idea.

ABBOT. Then I will tell you.

PRIESTS. Yes, please tell us the whole story.

ABBOT. Many years ago there lived in this region a man who was the steward of the manor of Manago, and he had an only daughter. In those days too there was a certain *yamabushi* priest who came here every year from the northern provinces

on his way to worship at the shrine of Kumano, and he would always stay with this same steward. The priest never forgot to bring charming little presents for the steward's daughter, and the steward, who doted on the girl, as a joke once told her, "Some day that priest will be your husband, and you will be his wife!" In her childish innocence the girl thought he was speaking the truth, and for months and years she waited.

Time passed and once again the priest came to the landlord's house. Late one night, after everyone else was asleep, the girl went to his bedroom and chided him: "Do you intend to leave me here forever? Claim me soon as your wife."

Amazed to hear these words, the priest turned the girl away with a joking answer. That night he crept out into the darkness and came to this temple, imploring us to hide him. But having nowhere else we could hide him, we lowered the bell and hid him inside. Soon the girl followed, swearing she would never let him go. At that time the River Hitaka was swollen to a furious flood and the girl could not cross over. She ran up and down the bank, wild with rage, until at last her jealous fury turned her into a venomous snake, and she easily swam across the river.

The serpent glided here, to the Temple of Dōjōji, and searched here and there until her suspicions were aroused by the lowered bell. Taking the metal loop between her teeth, she coiled herself around the bell in seven coils. Then, breathing smoke and flames, she lashed the bell with her tail. At once the bronze grew hot, boiling hot, and the monk, hidden inside, was roasted alive. *(to the Priests)* Isn't that a horrible story?

PRIEST. Unspeakable! The worst I have ever heard!

ABBOT. I have felt her jealous ghost about here, and I feared she might bring some harm to our new bell. All of our austerities and penances have been for strength in this moment. Pray with all your hearts. Let us try to raise the bell again.

PRIESTS. We will, Master. *(The Abbot and the Priests stand on either side of the bell, facing it.)*

ABBOT. Though the waters of Hitaka River seethe and dry up,
Though the sands of its shores run out,
Can the sacred strength of our holy order fail?

(They pray, their rosaries clasped in their hands.)

PRIESTS *(describing their actions).* All raise their voices together

ABBOT. To the East, the Guardian King, Conqueror of the Three Realms;[5]

PRIESTS. To the South, the Guardian King, Conqueror of the Demons;

ABBOT. To the West, the Guardian King, Conqueror of Evil Serpents and Dragons;

PRIESTS. To the North, the Guardian King, Conqueror of Frightful Monsters;

ABBOT. And you in the Center, Messenger of the Sun, All Holy Immovable One,

TOGETHER. Will you make the
    bell move?
Show us the power of your
    avenging noose!
Namaku Samanda Basarada
Senda Makaroshana Sowataya
Un Tarata Kamman
"I dedicate myself to the universal diamond,
May this raging fury be destroyed!"[6]
"He who hearkens to My Law shall gain enlightenment,
He who knows My Heart will be a Buddha in this flesh."[7]
Now that we have prayed
For the serpent's salvation,
What rancor could it bear us?
As the moon at daybreak

ABBOT. Strikes the hanging bell—

CHORUS. Look! Look! It moves!
Pray with all your hearts!
Pray to raise the bell!
    (They rub their rosaries frantically. The stage assistant lifts the bell a little and the Demon shakes it from within.)
Here the Priests, joining hands,
Invoke the sacred spell of the Thousand-Handed-One,
The Song of Salvation of the Guardian King,
The Immovable One, the Flaming One.
Black smoke rises from their frantic prayers.
And as they pray,
And as they pray,

Though no one strikes the bell, it sounds!
  (The Demon inside the bell strikes cymbals.)
Though no one tugs the rope, the bell begins to dance!
  (The stage assistant pulls the
  bell up farther, and the Demon
  shakes it.)
Soon it rises to the belfry tower,
Look! A serpent form emerges!

  (The stage assistant lifts the bell completely. The Dancer,
  now transformed into a Demon, wears the hannya *mask.*
  She has removed her outer brocade robe. When she is clear
  of the bell she takes up her mallet, then picks up her outer
  robe in both hands and wraps it around her waist. She
  stands and tries to drive the Abbot away. The Abbot and
  Priests pray, trying to subdue her. The Demon is driven
  onto the bridgeway where she drops her outer robe. Then
  she is forced back as far as the curtain, only to turn on the
  Abbot again, this time compelling him to withdraw. She
  stands with her back to the shite-*pillar, throws one arm*
  around it, pauses, and then invades the stage again. She
  tries to pull the bell down, but the Abbot forces her to the
  ground with the power of his rosary. The Demon rises
  again, and during the following passage sung by the
  Chorus, she and the Abbot struggle.)

CHORUS. Humbly we ask the help of the Green-bodied,
  The Green Dragon of the East;[8]
  Humbly we ask the help of the White-bodied,
  The White Dragon of the West;
  Humbly we ask the help of the Yellow-bodied,
  The Yellow Dragon of the Center,
  All ye countless Dragon Kings of the three thousand worlds:
  Have mercy, hear our prayers!
  If now you show your mercy, your benevolence,
  What refuge can the serpent find?
  And as we pray,
  Defeated by our prayers,
  Behold the serpent fall!
    (She staggers back under the pressure of the Abbot's prayers
    and drops to the ground.)

Again she springs to her feet,
The breath she vomits at the bell
Has turned to raging flames.
  (She rises and rushes to the bridgeway.)
Her body burns in her own fire.
She leaps into the river pool,
  (She rushes through the curtain.)
Into the waves of the River Hitaka,
And there she vanishes.
The Priests, their prayers granted,
Return to the temple,
Return to the temple.
  (The Abbot gives a final stamp of the foot near the shite-
pillar.)

Notes

1. There is a play here on the name of the River Hitaka ("sun high").

2. The tall courtier's hat was worn by the women dancers called *shirabyōshi* who flourished from the twelfth century. It became customary for professional dancers to wear such a hat when they performed.

3. The name Michinari is pronounced in the Sino-Japanese reading as Dōjō. Dōjōji would therefore mean the "temple of Michinari."

4. A metal ornament in the shape of a dragon's head on the bell.

5. The following passage is a prayer much favored by *yamabushi* priests for invoking the five *myōō* or *rajas*, the messengers of Vairocana's wrath against evil spirits.

6. This is a mantra of Fudō, the Immovable.

7. This is part of the Vow of Fudō.

8. The following is the invocation to the Five Dragon Kings, but the North and South have been omitted.

The Queen Mother
of the West

(SEIŌBO)

TRANSLATED BY CARL SESAR

INTRODUCTION

The Queen Mother of the West (Seiōbo), a play of the first category, has been attributed to Komparu Zenchiku, but there is little evidence concerning the authorship. It is a work of a stately and festive nature, suitably auspicious for the opening play in the traditional program of five plays. There is no dramatic conflict, portrayal of character, or suspense in the manner of a normal Western play, but this very simplicity has been praised by Japanese critics, and we can imagine that such a work would effectively establish the special mood for a day to be spent in the Nō theatre.

The work is based on a part of the vast body of Chinese legends concerning Hsi Wang Mu, the Queen Mother of the West. She is mentioned in *Shan hai ching* (Hill and Water Classic) as follows: "The Jade Mountain . . . is the abode of the Queen Mother of the West. Her appearance is that of a human being. She has a panther's tail and a dog's teeth, and can howl loudly. Her hair hangs loose, and she wears a coronet. She presides over the calamities and punishments sent by God." (From the translation by Herbert Giles.) King Mu of the Chou Dynasty was said to have visited Hsi Wang Mu, and for this reason the play was set during his reign.

But *Seiōbo* (the Japanese rendering of Hsi Wang Mu) is more closely based on the story of the Queen Mother's visit to the court of Han Wu-ti, told in *Han Wu-ti nei chuan*. Here she is depicted as a beautiful woman, rather than as a monster. According to this account, the Emperor was present in his palace in the fourth month of the first year of Yüan Feng (110 B.C.) when suddenly a maiden of striking beauty appeared to inform the Emperor that because of his virtue Hsi Wang Mu would soon pay a visit to his court. On the appointed day she indeed arrived, seated on a chariot of purple clouds drawn by many-colored dragons, accompanied by a lavish entourage of attendants mounted on fabulous creatures. She provided the Emperor with a feast prepared in the kitchens of heaven, including a dish of seven peaches from a tree in her garden which bore fruit once every three thousand years. Anyone who ate this fruit obtained immortality. After making this gift she soared back up to heaven. A version of this legend was recorded in *Kara Monogatari*, a collection of poem-tales on Chinese themes composed about 1250. Another Nō play, *Tōbōsaku* by Komparu Zempō, is based on the same story, but adds a strong Buddhist coloration.

The Queen Mother of the West is performed by all schools of Nō.

255

PERSONS A COURT OFFICIAL *(kyōgen)*
EMPEROR MU OF CHINA *(waki)*
A MINISTER *(wakizure)*
THE QUEEN MOTHER OF THE WEST *(shite)*
ATTENDANT TO QUEEN MOTHER *(tsure)*

PLACE CHINA

TIME THE CHOU DYNASTY; THE THIRD MONTH

THE QUEEN MOTHER OF THE WEST (SEIŌBO)

(The stage assistant places a low dais at the waki-*position, and sets upon it a prop representing the imperial palace. The Official comes onstage to the naming-place.)*

OFFICIAL. I am an official in the service of Emperor Mu of Chou. Because my lord is a wise and worthy king, the wind as it blows does not sound among the trees, nor do the people lock their doors. Truly, a most auspicious reign! He ordered eight swift steeds and journeyed to Mount Reiju in India,[1] where directly from Buddha's hand he received two verses of the Fumonbon.[2] Therefore, whatever he may wish shall come to pass.

Today the Emperor shall visit this palace, and there shall be all manner of royal entertainments. Let one and all attend!

(The Official exits. The Emperor, wearing a crown, enters and sits on the dais. The Minister follows him and kneels on the upstage side of the dais.)

MINISTER.* We are thankful!

From the Three Kings and the Five Emperors of old
Down to the present age,
Never has there been a sage lord such as this.

CHORUS. The light of his majesty
Is like the sun;
MINISTER. His heart, like the sea,
CHORUS. Is vast and plentiful;
His mercy
MINISTER. Shines in heaven and permeates the earth;
CHORUS. While like the numberless stars,

---

*The Kanze school text, translated here, has the *waki* (the Emperor) say these lines, but such self-praise, even from an Emperor, seems peculiar. Following the suggestion made by Sanari Kentarō in *Yōkyoku Taikan,* the speech is here assigned to a more likely person, the Minister.

257

While like the numberless stars
That fill all heaven,
Flocking toward the Northern Star
As they wheel across the skies,
The hundred officials, lords and ministers,
"Dwellers among the clouds" cluster around him.
Nobles of one thousand, ten thousand households,
Waving their pennants and lifting their shields,
Swarm about the gates of the four quarters.
Such is their brilliance,
Mingled with the shining city
Built of gold and silver and precious jewels,
That should night and day contend which is the brighter,
There would be no victor.
One may compare it to the Kikenjō,[3]
Such are the joys therein,
Such are the joys therein.

(The Queen appears, accompanied by an Attendant. She wears the zō mask while the Attendant wears the tsure mask. The Queen stands at the third pine, the Attendant at the first pine. Both carry sprays of peach blossoms over their shoulders.)

QUEEN AND ATTENDANT *(together)*. "The peach and the plum are mute,
Yet people make their way to them."
So it is with this capital;
Noble and base mingle together
With no distance between them.

(They come onstage. The Queen stands at the shite-position, the Attendant at stage center.)

QUEEN. O wondrous!
To this land,
Where in the four seasons' cycle,
Grasses and trees grow each in their appointed time,
The rich season of Buddha's flower has come,
The Flower of the Wonderful Law.
And now *this* flower, too,
That blossoms once in three thousand years,
Knowing that now is its season,

Shall also bloom, and be an adornment of the spring.

QUEEN AND ATTENDANT *(together).* We shall present it to your
    Majesty,

We shall present it to your Majesty.

Vast is the heart of the Son of Heaven,

Vast is the heart of the Son of Heaven.

Like a steed traversing endless distances,

Enlightened, he treads the Path of the Law,

The topmost Path, a thousand leagues and beyond;

Vast as Spirit Mountain,

The Meeting Place of the Law,

Vast as that vast teaching,

Is the sincerity of this sovereign;

He is a true king,

To whom all the world joyously submits.

*(The Queen and the Attendant change
places. The Queen faces the Emperor
and holds out her spray of peach
blossoms.)*

QUEEN. I wish to speak to the Emperor.

EMPEROR. Who is it desires to speak with me?

QUEEN. I have here the peach blossom whose seed blooms but once
    in three thousand years. Because of the splendid virtue of
    your Majesty, this flower has bloomed in the present age.
    Hence I have come to present it to you.

EMPEROR. You say a flower that blossoms
    Once in three thousand years?
    Can this be the fabled peach blossom
    From the gardens of the Queen Mother of the West?

QUEEN. Whether it is so or not
    I will not at present say.

EMPEROR. Then indeed, this is that famed flower.

QUEEN. "The peach and plum are mute,[4]

EMPEROR. While many springs for many years

QUEEN. Have come and gone."

EMPEROR. But this spring . . .

CHORUS. "This year,[5]
    The peach that blooms once in three thousand years,
    This year,

The peach that blooms once in three thousand years,
Has bloomed in spring."
It is because my lord's mercy extends
To the Four Quarters of the universe.
A seed of prosperity in the land
For myriad ages,
Such is the wonder of this peach blossom.
   (The Queen goes to the shite-*pillar and hands her peach
   blossoms to the stage assistant.)*
How strange!
Before our very eyes a heavenly lady appears!
How strange!
QUEEN. Do not wonder!
   Far above the clouds,
   Where moonlight glittering in the dew
   Seems to take shelter upon our sleeves,[6]
   His mercy reaches,
      (She looks up.)
   Shining down in infinite colors.
CHORUS. A fading thing is the flower
   Of the heart of man in this world. . . .[7]
QUEEN. I, amid heaven's
CHORUS. Pleasures,
   Greet the days, attend the dusk,
   While the years pass on,
   Yet the span of my life is endless.
   In truth, I am a manifestation of Seiōbo,
   Queen Mother of the West;
   I shall return in my true form
   To present you with the seed of this flower.
   So saying,
   She rises up to heaven,
   She rises up to heaven.

      (At the shite-*position, the Queen spreads her arms wide
      toward the front of the stage, then exits.*
         *The Official enters and retells the story just presented in
      plainer language. The play proper resumes after he exits.)*
EMPEROR AND MINISTER *(together).* With blended voices,
   Strings and flutes in the *ryo* and *ritsu* modes,
   With blended voices,

Strings and flutes in the *ryo* and *ritsu* modes
Make melodies.
The sounds of music carry across the heavens.
O sky winds!
Be considerate of her path upon the clouds!
> *(The Queen appears, wearing the zō mask and a "heavenly phoenix crown." She is dressed in purple and scarlet, and a sword hangs at her waist. Her Attendant is dressed as before, and carries a tray with a peach on it. The Queen stops at the first pine, the Attendant at the third pine.)*

CHORUS. O wonderful, wonderful!
The Queen of Heaven's Immortal Realm
Honors us with her presence;
> *(The Queen moves to the shite-position and the Attendant to the first pine.)*

Many peacocks, phoenixes, and birds of paradise
Fly about, singing in chorus.
> *(The Queen looks around the stage.)*

They begin to dance!
Their wings, like fluttering sleeves,
Become heavenly robes,
Become heavenly robes.

QUEEN. Here are all kinds of offerings,
> *(She faces the Emperor.)*

CHORUS. Here are all kinds of offerings,
Among them, most resplendently,
The figure of Seiōbo appears!
Her radiance fills the courtyard;
She wears a robe of scarlet brocade,
> *(She stands at stage center.)*

QUEEN. She keeps a sword at her waist,
> *(She looks at her sword.)*

CHORUS. She keeps a sword at her waist,
And wears a *shinnei* hat.[8]
> *(The Queen points to her hat with her fan.)*

From her waiting lady's hands
She takes the jeweled drinking cup that contains the peach,
And holds it aloft.

(She goes to the shite-*pillar and takes the tray with the peach on it from her Attendant. The Attendant goes to kneel before the Chorus.)*

QUEEN. I offer this peach seed to you.

(She kneels before the dais and places the tray upon it.)

CHORUS. He takes the drinking cup of flowers
And at once he becomes intoxicated.

(She rises and goes to the shite-*pillar, then performs a dance. As the text resumes, she continues to dance to the chanting of the Chorus.)*

CHORUS. The flowers, too are drunk,
The flowers in the cup are drunk.
Ah, the Feast of the Winding Stream,
Where one hinders the drifting winecups!
In the waters of the royal stream,
Gentle maidens sport merrily,
Their sleeves and skirts in fluttering disarray,
While the Flower Birds Amid the Clouds,[9]
Hovering in the spring breeze,
Take to their clouded paths.
The Queen Mother too, soars up in their company,
The Queen Mother too, soars up in their company!
Their whereabouts is lost in the track of sky.

(She stamps once at the shite-*position, then exits.)*

Notes

1. Reijuzan or Ryōjusen was the Japanese name for Vulture Peak (Sanskrit, Gṛdhrakūṭa), a mountain famous for vultures and caverns, inhabited by ascetics, where Shakyamuni taught the doctrines of the Lotus and many other sutras.

2. A *gāthā* from a section of the *Lotus Sutra* which runs: "He, who is provided with all merits, looks at creation with eyes of mercy; he brings happiness boundless as the sea, so let us offer thanks."

3. The palace of Shakra (Taishakuten) in the Trāyastriṃśāḥ (Tōri) heaven situated on the top of Mount Sumeru. The name Kikenjō means literally the Palace which is a Delight to Behold.

4. From a poem by Sugawara no Fumitoki, no. 548 in the *Wakan Rōei Shū:* "The peach and plum say nothing; how many springs have come to a close? The smoke and mist leave no traces; who lived here long ago?"

5. From the poem by Ōshikōchi no Mitsune in *Shūishū:* "I have, it would seem, been present this spring when the peach, which is said to bear fruit only once in three thousand years has burst into blossoms."

6. From the poem by Fujiwara no Masatsune, no. 436 in the *Shinkokinshū.* "The dew is so thick it is hard to brush it away; why should the moonlight have chosen to lodge on such a narrow sleeve?"

7. From the famous poem by Ono no Komachi, no. 797 in the *Kokinshū.* "That which fades without letting its color be seen is the flower of the heart of man in this world."

8. A kind of crown decorated with hawk feathers, reputedly worn by the Queen Mother of the West.

9. The name of a silk pattern, used for ceremonial robes, showing such regal birds as peacocks or phoenixes sporting amidst blossoms and clouds.

Kanehira

TRANSLATED BY STANLEIGH H. JONES, JR.

INTRODUCTION

Kanehira is a play belonging to the second category. It has traditionally been attributed to Zeami, but recent critics tend to dispute the attribution on stylistic grounds. The action described in the work is a dramatization of material from the *Heike Monogatari*, especially the sections "The Battle of Kawara" and "The Death of Kiso."

Kiso Yoshinaka (1154–1184) was a brilliant Minamoto general in the war against the Taira. In 1184 the Emperor named him Commanding General Subduing the Barbarians (*seii taishōgun*), the highest military honor. Soon afterwards, however, fighting broke out when he quarreled with his ally Minamoto Yoshitsune. Imai Kanehira, a friend of Yoshinaka's from their youngest days (they had the same wet-nurse), served as Yoshinaka's chief of staff

266

in the rebellion. The tragic deaths of Yoshinaka and Kanehira provided stirring theatrical material. The powerful descriptions of battle in the second part of *Kanehira* exemplify the spirit of the warrior plays, and provide a striking contrast to the calm nobility of the "god play" which preceded this play.

Kanehira is remarkable for the journey (*michiyuki*) which takes up the entire first part of the play. It is by far the longest travel description in Nō. Though not in itself dramatic, it builds up suspense for the narration to follow. A related play, *Tomoe*, recounts the death of Yoshinaka from the viewpoint of his mistress, Tomoe. Tomoe was also a warrior, and she became the only woman *shite* in a work of the second category.

Kanehira is performed by all schools of Nō.

PERSONS   A PRIEST FROM KISO PROVINCE *(waki)*
AN OLD BOATMAN, LATER REVEALED TO BE
KANEHIRA'S GHOST *(mae-jite)*
A FERRYMAN AT YABASE *(kyōgen)*
THE GHOST OF IMAI KANEHIRA *(nochi-jite)*

PLACE   PART I: A BOAT TRAVELING BETWEEN YABASE AND
AWAZU IN ŌMI PROVINCE
PART II: AWAZU PLAIN IN ŌMI

TIME   EARLY SUMMER, THE FOURTH MONTH

KANEHIRA

PART 1

(The Priest enters to the naming-place and faces the rear of the stage.)

PRIEST. I begin my journey from Shinano,
    I begin my journey from Shinano—
    I shall seek the grave of Lord Kiso.
    (He faces front.)
    I am a priest from the mountain village of Kiso. I have heard
that Lord Kiso met his death upon the Plain of Awazu in the
province of Ōmi. I shall go there to pray for his soul's repose.
And now I hasten on to Awazu Moor.
    Ah, the road through Shinano
    Famed for Kiso's hanging bridge.
    Famed for Kiso's swinging bridge.
    I will pray before his grave!
    Night after night in wayside fields,
      (He takes two or three steps
      to his right, then returns.)
    Brief hours of sleep under shading grass,
    Day after day I journey,
    And now before I know it
    I am on the road of Ōmi,
    I have reached the strand at Yabase,
    Reached Yabase shore.
      (His return signifies his arrival at Yabase. He kneels at the
      waki-*position. The stage attendant brings on a representa-*
      tion of the boat, and places it near the shite-*pillar. The*
      Boatman enters, wearing the asakurajō *mask and carrying*
      a bamboo pole.)

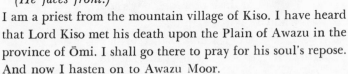

BOATMAN. I bear the weight
    Of years of fruitless labor,
    Piled high like the brushwood in my boat.
    But before these fagots kindle

My heart will char with flames of longing.

(The Priest rises and faces the Boatman.)

PRIEST. Ho there! Take me across in your boat.

BOATMAN. This is not the ferry between Yabase and Yamada. Look, the boat is loaded with brushwood. I cannot ferry you across.

PRIEST. I can see that you carry firewood in your boat, but there is no other boat at the crossing now. I am a priest—as a special favor, please ferry me across.

BOATMAN. True indeed, being a priest you are not the same as other men. Yes, it says in the *Sutra,* "like finding a ferry at a crossing."[1]

PRIEST. To wait at dusk of a long day's journey

And find at last a ship . . .

BOATMAN. How strange that chance brings us together.

TOGETHER. If this were the boat for Yabase

On the sea of Ōmi,[2]

It would be a traveler's ferry, nothing more.

CHORUS *(for the Boatman).* But this craft carries fagots

Across an inconstant world—

Hauling firewood, for a wretched living.

My sleeve is never dry, seasoned to my tears

As my bamboo pole to the water.

You are a stranger, yet a man of the Law.

How can I begrudge you passage?

(He beckons to the Priest.)

Hurry come aboard,

Hurry hurry come aboard.

(The Priest kneels in the boat. The Boatman makes poling motions.)

PRIEST. Boatman, I've something to ask you. These shores and mountains I see, surely they are all famous places. Please tell me their names.

BOATMAN. Yes, all are well-known places. Ask and I will tell you about them.

(The Priest looks upward.)

PRIEST. First of all, the great mountain over there—is that Mount Hiei?

(The Boatman looks up too.)

BOATMAN. Yes, that indeed is Mount Hiei.

    (He turns a little to his right.)

At the foot are the twenty-one shrines of Sannō. And on that peak so green with foliage is Hachiōji Shrine. You can see all the houses in Tozu-Sakamoto.

    (He turns to the Priest.)

PRIEST. Mount Hiei lies northeast of the Capital, does it not?

BOATMAN. You are right. Mount Hiei guards the demons' gateway into the Capital and wards off evil spirits. It is called the Pinnacle of the Highest Doctrine after the example of Vulture Peak[3]—you must have heard of it. It is known also as Mount Tendai because of its resemblance to the Cavern of the Four Lights in China.[4] The Great Teacher Dengyō, in common cause with the Emperor Kammu, founded his temple there in the Enryaku era. He wrote the lines, "Send down your divine grace upon these timbers that I raise."[5] You can see all the way to the Main Central Hall at the crest.

PRIEST. Is the place they call the Covered Bridge of Ōmiya also in Sakamoto?

BOATMAN. Yes, that rather thickly wooded spot at the foot of the mountain is the Ōmiya Covered Bridge.

PRIEST. I am grateful when I hear the Buddha's words, "All living creatures equally possess the Buddha nature," that even we, so humble, can hope for grace.

BOATMAN. So, the Buddha and all living things being one, there is no gulf between us, even a priest like you, and me.

PRIEST. From that peak of loftiest doctrine,

    Thick as branches on a tree,

    His teachings can be seen everywhere.

BOATMAN. And at its base, the sea of contemplation

    Overflows its banks,

PRIEST. Revealing to us the triple teachings:

    The holy rules, meditation, wisdom—

BOATMAN. The names we give the three pagodas.[6]

CHORUS *(for the Boatman).* In one thought three thousand worlds revealed;[7]

So here are placed three thousand priests.

This law of perfect harmony
Is cloudless as the moon above Yokawa.
(*The Boatman turns to the right.*)
At the mountain's foot, the little waves
(*He looks toward the bridgeway.*)
Lap at the single pine of Kara Cape in Shiga,
From where the sacred car will cross the water.[8]
(*He looks upward.*)
The ruffling waves, like ripples from the plying pole,
Roll in bubbles onto the opposite shore;
Distant Awazu forest now is near.
The little waves lick at the now more distant shore behind
 them.
And the mountain cherries, known from long ago,
Are green with leaves; no blossoms now remain
In mountains tressed with summer foliage.
The brushwood boat has crossed the blue-hued
 waters;
The priest, impatient for his destination,
Urges the boat across the last low waves.
Quickly they have reached Awazu beach,
Quickly they have reached Awazu.
(*The Priest gets out of the boat and goes to kneel at the
waki-position. The Boatman gets out too, and exits. The
stage assistant removes the boat. The Ferryman enters with
a pole over his shoulder.*)

INTERLUDE

FERRYMAN. I am the ferryman of Yabase Beach. I am on duty at
 the ferry today and I think I shall take the boat across. I am
 glad the weather is so fine.
 (*He sees the Priest.*)
 You there, sir, if you wish to cross over I will take you.
PRIEST. I have just come from the other side.
FERRYMAN. That cannot be. Our regulations say I cannot put my
 boat out on another's day of duty. He cannot interfere on
 days when I am on duty: Today is my turn, so no one could
 have ferried you across. Are you telling me the truth?

PRIEST. I do not lie. But come here, I want to ask you more.

(The Ferryman puts down his pole at stage center, and kneels.)

FERRYMAN. Yes, sir. What do you want to ask?

PRIEST. Something unusual. I would like you to tell me how Lord Kiso and Kanehira died.

FERRYMAN. Strange indeed! I do not know the details. I will try and tell you what I have heard.

PRIEST. Please do.

FERRYMAN. First, as to how Lord Yoshinaka died and what then happened to Imai no Shirō Kanehira: Lord Kiso, victorious in the battle with the Taira in the north, took advantage of his triumph and marched to the capital at Kyoto. He was astonished to learn that more than sixty thousand troops were coming from Kamakura to attack him, all because of his arrogance and tyranny in the Capital. At once he set about to defend Uji and Seta, and since Seta was his main defense point he sent Kanehira there. To Uji he ordered Tate no Rokurō, Nunoi no Ōyata, Nishina, Takanashi and Yamada no Jirō. Coming from the eastern provinces, Noriyori and Yoshitsune divided their troops into two forces. With Noriyori in command, over thirty thousand made for Seta and camped at Seta Bridge. Toward Uji twenty thousand troops led by Yoshitsune crossed through Iga and arrived at Uji Bridge. At both Uji and Seta the bridges had been torn down. Is was past the twentieth of the first month, and the snow on the lofty peak of Mount Hiei had melted. The waters of the rivers were high and it seemed unlikely that the force at Uji would be able to cross. But Kajiwara Genta and Sasaki no Shirō took the lead and the whole force plunged shouting into Uji River and crossed over. The approaches to Uji thus attacked and destroyed, Lord Kiso's soldiers fled to Mount Kobata, to Fushimi and Daigo. At Seta, Inage no Saburō also devised a means of crossing and the main defenses there were breached. Lord Kiso wished to see Kanehira again, and to his delight, while he was retreating toward Seta they came upon each other on the beach of Uchide at Ōtsu. Then Kanehira raised aloft his banner and some three hundred of their fleeing allies saw it and gathered round them. Deciding that with this force they could make one last valiant stand, furiously they fought. Then when only these two, lord and vassal, were left Kanehira said to Lord Kiso: "Make your way to that grove of pine over there and take your life." Kanehira remained behind and fought, but as soon as he heard the cry that Lord Kiso had been slain, he killed himself right then, they say. Lord Kiso, while heading for the pine grove, had been killed by Ishida no Jirō. That is the story as I have heard it. But what had you in mind when you asked me?

PRIEST. Thank you for telling me these things. I am a priest from the mountain village of Kiso. I have come here to pray for the repose of the spirits of Lord Kiso and Kanehira. Before I met you an old man who looked like a ferryman came by. I asked him to carry me across, which he did, and on the way he told me about all the famous places we passed. The boat came to this place, but when I turned to look for him again he had vanished from sight.

FERRYMAN. I think the ghost of Kanehira appeared to you and has brought you to this beach. Stay here awhile. I think you should pray for Kanehira's repose.

PRIEST. Yes. I will stay here awhile, recite the blessed scriptures, and pray for his spirit's peace.

FERRYMAN. If you need anything from me, please call on me again.

PRIEST. I will.

FERRYMAN. I am at your service.

(He exits.)

PART II

(The scene is now the Plain of Awazu.)

PRIEST. I lie upon a dew-laden mat of grass,
    I lie upon a dew-laden mat of grass.
    Day darkens and night has come
    And for that body, that dead soul,
    Departed from this bitter world
    Upon Awazu Moor,
    Now I offer up my litany,
    For Kanehira's remains
    I now shall pray.

(The ghost of Kanehira enters, wearing the heita *mask and a long sword. He stands at the* shite-*position.)*

KANEHIRA. Horror of naked blades
    Smashing on bone,
    Scenes of eyes gouged out,
    And shields floating on crimson waves
    Like scattered blossoms
    Breaking against a weir.
      (He turns to the right.)
    In the morning wind of Awazu
    Fleeting as a cloud, as foam,

CHORUS *(for Kanehira).* A swelling chorus of war cries,

KANEHIRA. And in those shouting voices
    The din of Hell's own crossroads.
      (He stamps in place. The Priest turns to him.)

PRIEST. What sort of man are you
    Who, girded in armor, comes beside
    My pillow of grass upon Awazu Field?

KANEHIRA. You talk like a fool!
    Was it not your wish to pray for my remains
    That brought you here?
    Kanehira stands before you!

PRIEST. No longer, then, of this world,
    Imai no Shirō Kanehira.
    Can this be a dream?

KANEHIRA. You think that what you see now is a dream? You have
    already seen me in reality. Have you forgotten we met and
    talked in my boat?

PRIEST. Then he whom I saw in that boat,
    The boatman at Yabase beach . . .

KANEHIRA. I am that boatman—that was my true form.

PRIEST. Yes, from the first word
    I thought your manner strange.
    And that boatman yesterday . . .

KANEHIRA. No boatman he.

PRIEST. A fisherman then . . .

KANEHIRA. Certainly not!

CHORUS *(for Kanehira).* The warrior who appeared before you
    Looking like the boatman of Yabase strand,
    The boatman at the bay of Yabase—

None other than myself!
Oh, make of this boat
A vessel of the Law
And bear me to that far shore![9]
   (He takes two steps toward the Priest.)
CHORUS. How quickly we come and go
   Along the crossroads of life and death.
   It is not always true
   That old men die before the young:
   Dreams, fantasies, bubbles, shadows—
   Which one last the longest?
      *(During the above lines Kanehira moves to stage center
      and sits on a stool.)*
KANEHIRA. Brief is our glory
   As the one-day blossom of the rose of Sharon.
CHORUS *(for Kanehira)*. With scarcely seven soldiers left
   Of all those born to warrior's blood,
   In the moon's thin trickle of light
   Away went Lord Kiso,
   Down this road through Ōmi.
KANEHIRA. And I, Kanehira, found him
   As I was coming from Seta.
CHORUS *(for Kanehira)*. We became more than three hundred
      strong.
KANEHIRA. Then the fighting began.
   We battled, we struggled,
   Till at last, all but two,
   Lord and vassal, had perished.
CHORUS. Now there is no chance.
   "Make for the pine grove and take your life there,"
   Kanehira says; with sad hearts they ride hard,
   Fleeing, lord and liege,
   To the stand of pine on Awazu Moor.
   Then shouts Kanehira:
   "The enemy is coming with many men.
   I will hold them off with my arrows."
   But as he grasps the reins and wheels his mount about,
   Lord Kiso stops him: "I fled the enemy
   Only because I hoped to be with you."

He too turns his steed.
Kanehira speaks proudly.
"It breaks my heart to hear you say these words;
What disgrace to ages yet unborn
Should Lord Kiso die at another's hands!
I beg you, by your own hand take your life.
I will presently be with you."
Shamed thus by Kanehira,
Again Kiso veers his horse and rides away.
Dejected and alone, he rides
Across Awazu Heath to the copse of pine.
        (*He looks toward the bridgeway.*)

KANEHIRA. It is now the end of the first month.
CHORUS. Spring is in the air,
        (*He sweeps his gaze across the front of the stage.*)
Still, though, the wind bites in the misty chill.
The sky grows dark, and aimless clouds
Are blown by mountain winds of Hiei.
Lord Kiso, uncertain of his way along the road,
Plunges his horse into a quagmire
Thinly sheeted with frost.
        (*He looks down and stamps his feet.*)
Though he pulls, the horse will not rise up,
Though he beats it the horse cannot move.
        (*He makes beating motions behind himself with his fan.*)
It sinks into the mire
Till he cannot see its head.
"What shall I do now? I am finished!
All is hopeless!"—in despair
He decides to end his life on the spot.
He puts his hand upon his sword.
But still, he thinks of Kanehira—where is he?
He looks behind him, far in the distance . . .
        (*He looks toward the bridgeway.*)

KANEHIRA. But just then . . . from where can it have come?
CHORUS. Suddenly a lethal shaft,
        A single arrow winging from a bow,
        Drives into his helmet—
        A mortal wound, unbearable the pain.

Down from his mount he topples, dead,
And mingles with the earth of this faraway land.
  (He strikes his knee and kneels.)
KANEHIRA. This is the spot.
  (He stands and turns to the priest.)
First, in my place,
Pray for my lord's repose.

CHORUS *(for the Priest).* Truly a painful story.
Then, tell me, how did Kanehira die?
KANEHIRA. Kanehira knows nothing of what has happened.
One thought alone possesses his mind
Even at moments when he is not fighting—
To attend his lord's last moments.
  (From here on, Kanehira mimes the actions described.)
CHORUS. Quite suddenly,
From the enemy ranks a voice rings out:
KANEHIRA. "Lord Kiso has been slain!"
CHORUS. When Kanehira hears this voice
KANEHIRA. He thinks, "What is there left to hope for?"
CHORUS. Kanehira, his mind resolved,
KANEHIRA. Prepares to issue his final roar of defiance.
CHORUS. Setting his feet in the stirrups,
KANEHIRA. He cries out in a great voice:
"I am Imai no Shirō Kanehira,
Vassal by birth to the house of Lord Kiso!"
  *(He draws his sword and strikes
  a defiant posture.)*
CHORUS. Thus shouting out his name,
He hews his way through the horde
Displaying the secret art
Of one man against the strength of a thousand.
He drives them down to the beach of Awazu;
There, in the endless pounding of the surf
He slashes, amuck, with rolling stroke and crosswise cut.
Driving in, he hacks in all directions.
He shouts:
"Now I will show you how a man should take his life!"
Thrusting his great blade between his teeth,
Headlong he falls to the ground.

(He drops his sword and gives a final stamp of the foot to indicate he has disappeared.)
Running himself through
He perishes.
A spectacle to stop speech,
A sight astounding to the eyes
Was Kanehira's death.

Notes

1. From a passage in the *Lotus Sutra* which describes the Buddha's merciful compassion as being "like a child who has a mother, like having a ferry at a crossing, like having a doctor in time of illness, like having a lamp in darkness."

2. Lake Biwa, northeast of Kyoto. Because of its size (Japan's largest lake) it is often referred to in literature as the Sea of Ōmi.

3. Mountain in central India sacred because Shakyamuni preached his doctrines there.

4. Referring to Mount T'ien T'ai in China which was supposed to have a cave on its peak with openings in the four directions, thus being illuminated by the sun and moon.

5. Line from a poem by Saichō, no. 1921 in the *Shinkokinshū:* "All you Buddhas, Bodhisattvas, supreme in your universal wisdom! / Send down your divine grace upon these timbers that I raise." It was written at the time Saichō founded the Enryaku Monastery on Mount Hiei in 805, the beginning of the Tendai Sect of Buddhism in Japan. The era name Enryaku corresponds to the years of Emperor Kammu's reign, 782–806.

6. The Eastern Tower, the Western Tower, and Yokawa Tower, three towers said to have been built as symbols of these three teachings.

7. The Buddhist teaching of the Tendai sect that in one concentrated prayer one can comprehend the three thousand manifestations of the Buddhist Law.

8. Reference to the festival of the Hiyoshi Shrine at the foot of Mount Hiei during which the god's palanquin (*mikoshi*) is taken across Lake Biwa from Kara Cape.

9. Paradise is likened to a distant shore *(higan).*

The Imperial Visit to Ohara

(OHARA GOKŌ)

TRANSLATED BY CAROL HOCHSTEDLER

INTRODUCTION

The Imperial Visit to Ohara, a play belonging to the third category, is of unknown authorship, though it has been attributed
by various authorities to Zeami. It is drawn from the concluding
sections of *Heike Monogatari* ("The Tale of the Heike"), and
many passages in the play are quoted word for word from the
source.

In 1185 the Taira clan was destroyed by the Minamoto forces
at the battle of Dan-no-ura, referred to in the play as "Hayatomo
in Nagato." The Taira, a naval rather than a land power, had
carried off the Emperor Antoku, then seven years old, and when
defeat appeared inevitable, Lady Nii, the mother of Kenreimon-in
and grandmother of Antoku, jumped into the sea with the boy
emperor in her arms. Kenreimon-in tried to drown herself too,
but she was pulled from the water by a Minamoto soldier. She
soon afterwards retired to the Jakkō-in, a convent in the hills
north of Kyoto. The Retired Emperor Go-Shirakawa visited her

there in 1186, the year after the Taira defeat, and this visit is the subject of the play. The Retired Emperor, like Kenreimon-in, had taken Buddhist orders, but unlike her he continued to live in the Capital, taking an active part in political and other mundane affairs.

The play has extremely little action. Kenreimon-in's movements are almost entirely restricted to her entrances and exits; there is not even the final dance found in another static work, *Komachi at Sekidera*. The play is nevertheless filled with an unusual poignance, not only because of the beauty of the language but because of the situation: an empress, now dressed in the severe habit of a nun, recalls the death of her son and the destruction of her family.

The Imperial Visit to Ohara is performed by all schools of Nō, except Komparu.

PERSONS   A COURTIER IN THE SERVICE OF THE EMPEROR
(wakizure)
ATTENDANT OF THE COURTIER *(kyōgen)*
KENREIMON-IN, THE FORMER EMPRESS *(shite)*
AWA NO NAIJI, HER ATTENDANT *(tsure)*
DAINAGON NO TSUBONE, ANOTHER ATTENDANT *(tsure)*
THE RETIRED EMPEROR GO-SHIRAKAWA *(nochi-zure)*
THE COUNCILLOR MADENOKŌJI *(nochi-waki)*
PALANQUIN BEARERS *(wakizure)*

PLACE   THE JAKKŌ-IN, A CONVENT IN OHARA,
NORTH OF KYOTO

TIME   EARLY SUMMER, THE FOURTH MONTH OF
BUNJI 2 (1186)

THE IMPERIAL VISIT
TO OHARA (OHARA GOKŌ)

(The stage assistant places a representation of Kenreimon-in's retreat before the musicians. It is covered on all sides by a cloth. The Courtier, followed by his Attendant, enters and stands at the naming-place.)

COURTIER. I am a courtier in the service of the Retired Emperor Go-Shirakawa. Not long ago the Former Emperor, Lady Nii and the entire Taira clan met their end in the sea off Hayatomo in Nagato. The Former Empress hurled herself into the sea as well, but she was rescued and the life saved that she no longer thought was worth living. Noriyori, the Lord of Mikawa, and his brother Yoshitsune, the Lieutenant of the Guards, took her with them and restored the Three Imperial Treasures to the Capital. But she has chosen to pray for the salvation of Antoku, the Former Emperor, and of Lady Nii, and she has shrunk from the world to dwell at Ohara in the Jakkō-in, the Cloister of Quiet Radiance. The Retired Emperor recently announced his intention of visiting her. I shall order that the road to the mountains be prepared for his journey. *(He turns towards the Attendant.)* Is anyone there?

ATTENDANT. I am at your service.

COURTIER. His Majesty intends to visit Ohara. Prepare the road for his journey and have it purified.

ATTENDANT. Yes, sir. *(He goes to the naming-place as the Courtier exits.)* Give me your attention, everyone. It has been proclaimed that the Retired Emperor will visit Ohara. The way must be prepared for him. Please see to it that this is done.

(He exits. The stage assistant removes the cloth from Kenreimon-in's hut, to reveal Kenreimon-in sitting inside. She wears the waka-onna *mask. Tsubone and Naiji, both of whom wear* tsure *masks, kneel on either side of her. All three are dressed in dark nun's robes with soft white hoods that extend to drop over their shoulders. They carry rosaries. A basket rests before Tsubone.)*

285

KENREIMON-IN. "A mountain village
        Is loneliness itself,
        But better a brushwood hut
        Than the torments of this world."[1]
THREE WOMEN. A door of plaited branches,
        A gaping fence, the posts far apart
        As news from the Capital,
        Bamboo pillars thickly knotted
        As the griefs that have come our way:
        Everything in our daily round of life
        Becomes a source of sad reflections,
        Yet what peace we find,
        Living far from others' eyes!
        Some sounds at times come our way,
        Though not intended for our ears—
        The crack of a woodsman's axe,
        The crack of a woodsman's axe,
        The sighing of wind through branches,
        The crying of monkey voices;
        Except for these,
        Rare are the visitors who push their way
        Through hanging vines and twining grasses.
        "On Gannen's path the grass grows thick,"[2]
        Closing the way to my crowded thoughts.
        "Genken's door was sodden with rain."[3]
        Sodden too my sleeves with tears,
        Sodden too my sleeves with tears.
KENREIMON-IN. Dainagon no Tsubone, I think I shall go up the
        hill behind our temple and pick star anise.
TSUBONE. I shall go with you, and gather firewood and fern shoots
        for the kitchen.
KENREIMON-IN. Though it is sacrilege
        To make the comparison,
        Prince Siddhartha too[4]
        Left the capital
        Of King Shuddhodana
        And scaled the steep slopes
        Of Mount Dantaloka
        To pick herbs, draw water
        And gather firewood;

CHORUS. Practicing great austerities,
  He served the holy hermits,
  And at last he reached
  Complete illumination.
  I too would serve the Buddha.
    *(During the next three lines Kenreimon-in leaves her hut
    with Tsubone. At stage center, Tsubone hands her basket
    to Kenreimon-in, and they exit together. Naiji remains
    seated.)*
  She takes her flower basket
  And goes deep into the mountains,
  Deep into the mountains.

    *(The Retired Emperor Go-
    Shirakawa enters, accompanied
    by two Palanquin Bearers who
    hold a canopy over him. He
    carries a rosary. The Councillor
    Madenokōji, who wears a
    short sword, follows him.)*

COUNCILLOR AND BEARERS. The blossoms of the Capital have fallen,
  And in search of the lingering spring
  We follow the young green leaves
  Along the road to the mountains.
  We push through grasses deep in dew,
  Through dewy peonies,[5] to Ohara
  Hidden in the deep, damp grasses;
  Let us speed His Majesty on his way.
    *(Go-Shirakawa stops at the first pine. The Councillor goes
    to the naming-place, faces him and bows.)*

COUNCILLOR. Your Majesty has made such good time that already
  we have reached Ohara. *(He faces front.)*
  The procession has arrived in Ohara,
  And I let my eyes wander
  Over the Cloister of Quiet Radiance.
  The dew-laden garden
  Is thick with summer grasses;
  Willow boughs entwine
  Their tender green threads;
  The waterweeds on the pond,
  Trembling with the ripples,

Might be fine brocade
Spread out in the sun.
On the bank, the kerria roses
Flower in golden profusion;
Through a break in the towering,
Many-layered clouds
Floats a single cuckoo's call:
Each sight and sound seems to anticipate
Your Majesty's approach.

(He bows to Go-Shirakawa.)
GO-SHIRAKAWA. The Retired Emperor lets his gaze fall
On the margin of the pond.
"From the cherry on the bank
Blossoms scatter into the water;
Now the flowers on the waves
Have reached their fullest glory."[6]
CHORUS. From a break in the ancient rocks
Water falls, and its splashing
(Retired Emperor and Councillor look around them, as if admiring the scenery.)
From a break in the ancient rocks
Water falls, and its splashing
Seems to speak a history.
The fence twined with green ivy,
The distant mountains blue with haze—
No painter or poet could capture the scene.
A single temple hall stands here.
"The roof tiles are broken and entering mists
Seem a burning of eternal incense."[7]
Was it such a place the poem describes?

A place so ruined and desolate,
So lonely and bleak?
   (The Councillor turns to the hut.)

COUNCILLOR. This seems to be the retreat of the Former Empress.
   Ivy and morning glory
   Creep along the eaves,
   And the rank goosefoot weed
   Has choked the door.
   The picture of desolation!
      Excuse me! Is anyone inside the hermitage?
NAIJI. Who is there?
COUNCILLOR. I am the Middle Councillor Madenokōji.
NAIJI. Is it possible? What has brought you to these mountains
   where so few ever come?
COUNCILLOR. The Retired Emperor has journeyed here to visit the
   Former Empress in her retreat.
NAIJI. The Former Empress is not here. She has gone up the hill
   above to pick flowers.
      (The Councillor goes to Go-Shirakawa and bows.)
COUNCILLOR. I announced your visit, and was informed that the
   Former Empress is not here. She has climbed the hill up
   there to pick flowers. Please be seated and wait for her return.
      *(Go-Shirakawa comes onstage and sits on a stool at the
      waki-position. The Councillor sits before the Chorus, while
      the Bearers sit unobtrusively in place at the first pine. Naiji
      leaves the hut and starts towards the bridgeway as if in-
      tending to meet the Former Empress. Go-Shirakawa turns
      to her.)*
GO-SHIRAKAWA. Tell me, nun, who are you?
      (Naiji kneels at the shite-position.)

NAIJI. It is not surprising that
you fail to recognize me. I
am the daughter of late
Shinzei, the shadow of the
Awa no Naiji you once
knew. But I am not in the
least offended that you have
forgotten me, for though my appearance has become so ugly,
I am now indifferent even to the possibility of a tomorrow.

GO-SHIRAKAWA. Where has the Former Empress gone?

NAIJI. She has climbed the hill above here to pick flowers.

GO-SHIRAKAWA. Who went with her?

NAIJI. Dainagon no Tsubone. Please wait a few moments longer.
She should return soon.

> *(Kenreimon-in enters. She carries a basket of leaves and
> stops at the second pine. Tsubone, carrying twigs and ferns,
> stops at the third pine.)*

KENREIMON-IN. Yesterday has passed,
Today too will close in emptiness,
And I know nothing of tomorrow.
Such is my fate.
But never for a moment can I forget
The face of the Former Emperor.
> *(She presses her palms together in prayer.)*
For those whose sins lie heavy,
There is no other way
Than to call Amida's name
And be reborn in Paradise.
May our late Sovereign,
May Lady Nii,
And all our family

Achieve perfect awakening,
Blessed Lord Amida,
Namu Amida Butsu.

(She looks towards the stage.) I hear voices near my hut!

TSUBONE. Please rest here a moment.

> *(Kenreimon-in sits on a stool. Tsubone kneels. Naiji looks up the bridgeway, then turns to Go-Shirakawa.)*

NAIJI. The Former Empress is coming back now along the steep path.

GO-SHIRAKAWA. Which is the Former Empress, and which is Dainagon no Tsubone?

NAIJI. The Former Empress carries a flower basket over her arm. The other, with the firewood and sprigs of fern is Dainagon no Tsubone. *(She goes to the first pine, where she kneels facing Kenreimon-in.)* Madam, the Retired Emperor has come to visit you.

KENREIMON-IN. It is hard to forget
This world of delusion
And the attachment it still holds:
If gossip again stains my name,[8]
My tears will spill to stain these sleeves
So shabby I blush lest he see them.

> *(She weeps.)*

CHORUS *(for Kenreimon-in).* Yet he follows the Law,
The same path as myself;
To talk with him will bring comfort.
Before the window
I have called Amida's name;

> *(Naiji, carrying Kenreimon-in's basket, comes onto the stage and places the basket in the hut. She kneels before the flute player.)*

Before the window

I have called his Name,
In single-minded expectation
Of the light of his coming;
And by this brushwood door
I have offered ten-fold prayers
Awaiting the welcoming throng[9]
Of his holy Company;
But I never anticipated
This visit at dusk.
Has the past returned
To renew my tears?

> *(Kenreimon-in rises and goes to the first pine, Tsubone to the second pine.)*

KENREIMON-IN. Truly I am grateful
That my Lord has extended his kindness,
Even to Ohara, this lonely place,
Taking the narrow Seryō road in the mist,
And passing the clear spring of Oboro,
Where a radiance, not of the moon
But of his presence, now lingers.

CHORUS. How shall I describe the season
Favored by an imperial visit?

KENREIMON-IN. Spring has turned to early summer;
It is time for the Northern Festival.[10]
Young leaves still sprinkle the summer groves,
A last memento of the spring.

CHORUS. Are the white clouds hanging
Above the distant mountains

KENREIMON-IN. A keepsake to remind us
Of blossoms now scattered?

CHORUS. He has made his way through the fields
Covered so thickly with summer grasses
He could hardly know the way,
At last to reach his destination

KENREIMON-IN. Here at the Jakkō-in,
The Cloister of Quiet Radiance—
Let us treasure the peace and the light!

CHORUS. The sunlight sparkles like jewels
On lovely pine boughs blossoming

KENREIMON-IN. With waves of wisteria over the pond
   Which stretch their vines towards summer.
CHORUS. They too for the imperial visit
KENREIMON-IN. Have been waiting.
CHORUS. Late-flowering cherries

   Hidden in new leaves
   Have a loveliness rarer
   Than the year's first blossoms.
   Perhaps this unusual sight
   May move His Majesty.
     (Kenreimon-in and Tsubone come onstage.)
   But to show him this place
   Fills me with dread.
   His visit is more than I deserve.
   Is it proper that he tarry
   At my brushwood door?
   Is this a proper place
   For him to linger?
     (Kenreimon-in sits at stage center. Tsubone sits beside the
     Councillor.)
KENREIMON-IN. "I never dreamt
   That, dwelling deep in the hills,
   I should ever look
   As a stranger on the moon
   Shining on the Capital."[11]
   That is how I felt. Yet your visit to this mountain village has
   filled me with the profoundest gratitude.
GO-SHIRAKAWA. Not long ago
   someone told me you had seen
   with your own eyes the natures
   of the Six Realms. This

   puzzled me, for these should
   not be visible until one has
   become a Buddha or a
   Bodhisattva.
KENREIMON-IN. Your Majesty is quite correct, but when I think
   carefully over my past . . .
   I see what I am:
   A plant uprooted

From the brow of the shore;
CHORUS. When I survey my life,
    I see an unmoored boat on the river.
KENREIMON-IN. Yes, I knew the pleasures of Paradise,
    But they proved short-lived,
    Like crystals of dew on trailing vines,
    Not destined to long endure.
CHORUS. Before many years had passed,
    The five wasting ailments set in,
KENREIMON-IN. Yet I could not melt away
    When my decline had come,
CHORUS. But wandered in delusion
    At the crossroads of the Six Realms.[12]
    First, my whole clan
    Was tossed on the waves
    Of the Western Sea,
    Living all the time on ships,
    With never a safe harbor.
    We gazed at the sea, but it was salt,
    And useless to quench our thirst:
    I knew the Realm of Hungry Ghosts.
    Sometimes too we were gripped with fear
    As high inshore swells
    Threatened to capsize us
    Against the rocky coast.
    Then from the massed ships
    Rose shrieks and lamentation:
    I wondered in horror
    If this was how sinners howl
    In the Hell of Piercing Cries.
KENREIMON-IN. When we fought on land
CHORUS. I saw with my own eyes
    The Realm of the Ashuras
    And its terrifying wars.
    Then I heard the pounding hoofs
    Of numberless galloping horses,
    A sight and sound no different
    From the Realm of Beasts.
    Yet I suffered all these torments

In the Realm of Men.
What deeper sadness than this end
To a life that has turned all pain?

GO-SHIRAKAWA. That was indeed an incredible experience. But please tell me about the last moments of the Former Emperor.

KENREIMON-IN. What bitterness to relate what happened then! We were in Nagato Province, at the place called, I think, Hayatomo. The entire clan had agreed to withdraw for the time to Tsukushi, but Ogata no Saburō had a change of heart and betrayed us. We decided to attempt to reach Satsuma Bay, but the tide was against us. When it seemed that we were powerless to resist any further, Noritsune, the Lord of Noto, threw one arm around Tarō of Aki, and one arm around Tarō's brother. He gave a shout of, "Die with me!" and leapt into the sea.

The Middle Councillor Tomomori pulled up the anchor of his ship riding in the offing, and set it on his helmet. Then he and Ienaga, who had shared with him the same wet-nurse, grasped each other's bow and together plunged into the sea.[13]

At this moment the Lady Nii,
Dressed in double robes of leaden grey,
Tucked up her skirts of glossy silk,
And cried, "I am only a woman,
But I'll never fall in enemy hands!
I shall take our Sovereign with me!"
She took the Emperor Antoku's hand
And led him to the side of the ship.
"Where are we going?" he asked.
"This country is full of traitors,
A vile and odious place,
But the Realm of Supreme Bliss,
A wonderful place, lies beneath the waves;
We will go there together."
So she spoke to the Emperor,
Her voice choking with tears.
He said, "I understand,"
And, turning to the east,
Bade farewell to the Shining One,
Amaterasu, the Great Goddess.

CHORUS. Then he faced the west
    To call ten times the name
    Of Amida Buddha.
KENREIMON-IN. "Now at last I know
CHORUS. In the Mimosuso River,
    Deep beneath the waves,
    There lies another Capital."[14]
    This was his last poem;
    Then they plunged a thousand feet down.
    I myself followed them and sank,
    But a Genji warrior pulled me out,
    Adding unwelcome days
    To a worthless life.

    Now that I have seen your face once more
    My sleeves are damp with unwitting tears.
    How ashamed I am!
    How could these memories be exhausted?
    But already his men urge the Emperor
    To start on the homeward journey.

        (*The Councillor bows to Go-Shirakawa, who rises. The
        Bearers hold the canopy over him, and they start up the
        bridgeway, preceded by the Councillor. Kenreimon-in rises
        too and watches them leave, her hand resting on a pillar
        of her hut.*)
    To start on the homeward journey
    Soon the palanquin is ready,
    And they set out on the long road
    Leading away from the Jakkō-in.
KENREIMON-IN. The Former Empress
    From her door of plaited branches
CHORUS. Gazes after him for a while,
    Then turns again to her hut,
    She turns again to her hut.
        (*Go-Shirakawa's party exits. Kenreimon-in remains by the
        hut, weeping.*)

Notes

1. An anonymous poem, no. 944, in the *Kokinshū*.

2. A verse from poem no. 437 in the *Wakan Rōei Shū* by Tachibana Naomoto.

3. Another verse from the poem cited in note 2.

4. Siddhartha was the name by which Shakyamuni Buddha was known while still a layman.

5. *Fukamigusa* was a poetic name for the peony. It is used here as a pivot-word, the other meaning being "deep" (of the dew and grasses). It is not clear whether or not the meaning of "peony" is desired, or if it is merely decorative language.

6. This poem is included in the collection *Senzaishū* as the work of Go-shirakawa.

7. This quotation is derived from the *Heike Monogatari*, but the original source has not been discovered.

8. That is, she fears that receiving a visit from the Retired Emperor will give rise to gossip.

9. The worshipers of Amida Buddha believed that at the moment of death a host of bodhisattvas would come to welcome them to Amida's Western Paradise.

10. A reference to the Aoi Festival of the Kamo Shrine.

11. Quoted with a minor change from *Heike Monogatari*, where it is given as a poem by Kenreimon-in.

12. It was believed that after death one went to one of six realms, depending on one's actions on earth. In the following passages five of these realms are described. The sixth, Paradise, has already been mentioned.

13. There is some difference of interpretation on this line. Some commentators think the two men exchanged bows, but others think that the men held each other's bow to make sure they sank together.

14. This poem is derived not from the *Heike Monogatari*, the source of most of the material in the play, but from a work covering the same events, the *Gempei Seisui Ki*.

The Bird-scaring Boat

(TORIOI-BUNE)

BY KONGŌ YAGORŌ/TRANSLATED BY ROYALL TYLER

INTRODUCTION

The Bird-scaring Boat belongs to the fourth category of plays. It is attributed to Kongō Yagorō, who is also credited with the play *Genjō* but otherwise is passed over in silence by historians of Nō. There can be little question, however, but that *The Bird-scaring Boat* is, by Nō standards, a late work, probably of the sixteenth century.

The play combines two themes: the dishonor offered by a steward to his absent lord's wife and son, and the wife's longing for her husband. The circumstances of the alleged dishonor may seem unconvincing to us. Although the persons in the play consider that the scaring of birds from the crops is a most demeaning activity, degrading to the son and wife of a nobleman, the descriptions suggest a pleasant and even poetic manner of spending a day. We should not forget, however, that in the hieratically organized society of Japan the distinctions between proper and improper activities for a person of a particular station were absolute, and it was as distasteful to a young noble to scare birds as to wash laundry or sweep the kitchen. The play contains effective passages, but it is marred by some awkward transitions, and occasionally borders on melodrama. Both in the situation described and the treatment of the material it clearly belongs to a transitional period in Nō when the appeal had become theatrical rather than poetic. In this sense it foreshadows the popular theatre of the seventeenth century.

The sources of the plot have not been discovered. This is the only Nō play in which a retainer obliges his superior to perform menial labor. The treatment of the wife is also remarkable, for women are seldom credited in Nō with the kind of generosity the wife here displays. Again, in a Nō play of the classic period the role of the *wakizure*, generally no more than an attendant, would surely not have been permitted to overshadow that of the *waki*, nor would either *waki* or *wakizure* participate so actively in the plot. The *wakizure* (the Steward) serves as an antagonist to the *shite* (the Wife), rather than as merely a shadow or commentator.

Bird-scaring is still important to Japanese rice farmers. In this play many kinds of noisemakers are described. The prop used is a rather elaborate boat with attached noisemakers.

The play is performed by all schools of Nō.

301

PERSONS SAKO NO JŌ, STEWARD TO LORD HIGURASHI
  (wakizure)
  HIGURASHI'S WIFE *(shite)*
  HANAWAKA, HIGURASHI'S SON *(kokata)*
  LORD HIGURASHI *(waki)*
  SERVANT TO HIGURASHI *(kyōgen)*

PLACE HIGURASHI VILLAGE IN SATSUMA PROVINCE, KYUSHU

TIME AUTUMN, THE NINTH MONTH

THE BIRD-SCARING BOAT
(TORIOI-BUNE)

(Hanawaka and the Wife enter and kneel before the chorus. The Wife wears the fukai *mask. The Steward comes down to the first pine.)*

STEWARD. I am Sako the Steward. I serve Lord
　　Higurashi of Satsuma in Kyushu. A wide river
　　flows by Higurashi Village, and it empties
　　into a lake. Flocks of birds fly off the lake and
　　ravage the fields along its shores. So each year
　　we rig bird-scaring boats to frighten them
　　away. I should also tell you that Lord
　　Higurashi is away in the Capital, pleading
　　his own lawsuit. He has left his wife and his
　　young son, Hanawaka, behind. This year I have no servant to
　　scare off the birds. I have decided to ask Master Hanawaka to
　　perform this task for me.

　　　*(He comes onstage and stands at the naming-place, facing
　　the Wife.)* I am sorry to disturb you. Sako the Steward stands
　　before you.

　　　(He kneels at stage center. The Wife faces him.)

WIFE. Why are you here?

STEWARD. I beg to inform you
　　that my lord is expected
　　back from the Capital some
　　time this autumn.

WIFE. How happy Hanawaka will be
　　to hear it!

STEWARD. There is also something else. This year I have absolutely
　　no one to man my bird-scaring boat. I thought it might
　　amuse Master Hanawaka to come along and scare off the
　　birds. That is all I had to say.

WIFE. You mean you are proposing that Hanawaka frighten birds
　　from the fields? Hanawaka may only be a boy, but have you
　　forgotten that he is still your lord? I have never heard of

303

such callousness, Steward, asking your own lord to perform such demeaning work!

STEWARD. You call me callous? Calm down, I beg you, before you make such accusations, and listen to me. It often happens that a master is away for months, or even a year at the most. But my lord has already been away for ten years, and during all this time I have served you. And you still call me callous! But I will be brief for, as they say, much talk is a sign of ill-breeding. If you refuse to permit Hanawaka to go bird-scaring you will have to leave this house and go elsewhere.

WIFE. I admit that there is some truth in what you say. But Hana-waka is so young! Let me go. I'll frighten off the birds myself.

STEWARD. Certainly not! Master Hanawaka is only a child. No one will take it amiss if he goes. But if a noble lady like you is seen out on the marshes! Do you want to give me a bad reputation?

WIFE. I cannot bear to let Hanawaka go by himself. We will go together.

STEWARD. All right. Do as you wish. Tomorrow my boat will be ready and waiting for you. *(He goes to the* shite-*pillar.)* You mustn't be late, Master Hanawaka. Be there on time. *(He exits.)*

WIFE. Surely no child has ever known
　　Such misfortune as befalls my son!
　　We reared him with tender hopes,
　　And gave him the name Hanawaka,
　　"Flower of eternal spring,"[1]
　　All in vain! How shamefully
　　He has fallen into servitude!
　　(She turns toward Hanawaka.)

CHORUS. Down to the marshes we will go together,
　　Amidst the din of the peasants' clappers.

We will board the bird-scaring boat.
   (She describes their actions.)
Tears shed by mother and son
Fall thick as heavy dew.
   (The Wife and Hanawaka start towards the bridgeway.)
From the thick fields of rice
We will frighten the birds, she cries,
And from their lonely cottage,
Mother and son set forth,
Mother and son set forth.
   *(They start up the bridgeway, make the gesture of weeping,
   then exit.*
      Higurashi enters. He wears a short sword and a kasa
   *hat. He is followed by his Servant, who also wears a short
   sword. They stop at the naming-place and face toward the
   musicians.)*
HIGURASHI. This is my native place,
Where even autumn is untouched by melancholy,
Where even autumn is untouched by melancholy.
How happy I am to be home!
   (He removes his hat and faces front.)
I am from Higurashi in Kyushu.
For over ten years I have been in
the Capital, pleading in person an
important lawsuit. I have been
successful on every point, and
now I return in triumph to my
village. *(He turns to the Servant.)*
Is that you there?
SERVANT. I am at your service.
HIGURASHI. What is the meaning of those flutes and drums I hear
   coming from over there? Go and find out what is going on.
SERVANT. Yes, sir.
      (Higurashi kneels at the waki-*position. The Servant goes
   to the end of the bridgeway and addresses imaginary people
   offstage.)*
SERVANT. Hey! What's going on over there? Why all the flutes and
   drums? What? Bird-scaring boats, you say? *(to himself)* I'll
   tell him what they said. *(to Higurashi)* I asked them, and they

said it's the bird-scaring boats. It seems the boats are quite
a sight this year.

HIGURASHI. Of course! I remember the bird-scaring boats. They're
one of the sights of Kyushu. I'll wait here and have a look
at them. Please go ahead and tell people I am coming.

SERVANT. As you command, sir.

*(He withdraws to the rear of the stage. The stage assistant
brings on a prop representing a bird-scaring boat. Bells,
clappers, and a drum hang from a frame over the middle.*

*Hanawaka, the Wife, and the Steward enter. Hanawaka
and the Wife have changed their outer robes, and the Wife
now wears a kasa hat. The Steward's robe is off one shoulder to suggest he is engaged in strenuous work. He carries
a boating pole. They board the boat and the Steward mimes
poling.)*

STEWARD. A delightful day!
    Yesterday's spring shoots have turned[2]
    Before we knew it into heads of grain
    Rippling in the autumn wind; now we row out
    To chase the birds from the harvest fields.

WIFE AND HANAWAKA. Grieving we wait, uncertain as waterfowl,
    On waves that toss us about,
    And doubts cluster round us, countless.

STEWARD. Look at all the birds! Let's scatter them!
    (describes their actions)
    Forsaking all pride,
    Aboard a derelict boat,
    We will beat the drum.

WIFE AND HANAWAKA. We have built a guard hut in the marshes,

WIFE. And hang our boat with clappers;

ALL THREE. We glide out with the ebbing tide.

CHORUS. Birds fly up with raucous cries!

(The Wife looks up at the sky to her right.)

WIFE. In such a dream world,
Where even birds take fright,
Our labors are fruitless indeed.
    (She weeps.)

CHORUS. Truly, in this world of dreams
Each perception tells the truth,
Each perception tells the truth
That we ourselves are bubbles,
Froth dissolving on the waves
Where sea birds rock in sleep—
How curiously they rise and sink
    (She lets her gaze wander across the stage.)

With each wave of ripened grain
Billowing in the autumn fields!
Of late I've thought the rains would never clear;
The grassy banks look sodden as our boat approaches.
Oh, if I could sail, even for one night a year
Across the River of Heaven,
And again see my husband!
    *(The Steward lays down his pole and retires to the rear of
    the stage. The Wife removes her hat.)*
Alas! My prayers are empty dreams,
They do not reach so high as heaven.

WIFE. The steward said my lord would
return this autumn, but that was
only talk. Autumn is gone, and
the future holds no hope for me.
But I do not care for myself. It is
only Hanawaka's misfortune that
fills me with grief. *(She weeps.)*

HANAWAKA *(turning to the Wife).* I understand now why they say
the fallen flower has feelings but man has none.³ My father,
it is true, has stayed an unusually long time in the Capital,
as litigants must, worrying about us all the while. But if
Sako had any human decency he would never ruin his own
reputation and make my mother so unhappy. I hate him!
I wish my father were here! I would tell him.

WIFE. Even if your father lost his suit, we'd have
been spared this dreadful humiliation as long
as he were here with us.

CHORUS. How long must we drift so sadly,
How long are helpless tears to wet our sleeves
Like feathers of birds in the water?

(The Steward comes forward and faces the Wife.)

STEWARD. What are you blubbering about? If you've got something to cry about, wait till you get home. Look! The birds
are all out of the neighbors' fields, but they're still thick
on mine. Why do you think I brought you here?

(He boards the boat. Hanawaka stands.)

HANAWAKA. See how we cringe even before a servant!
Who knows what our end will be,
We who are as frail as the dew?

(The Wife steps out of the boat.)

WIFE. In the fields the late-ripening rice
Awaits the harvest, and the full autumn color
Draws the flocks of birds.

HANAWAKA. They scatter before our boats.
We row ahead to frighten them away,

WIFE. Sounding bells and clappers,
Noise makers of every kind!

HANAWAKA. Look! Look over there!

WIFE. On the other boats too

CHORUS. They're pounding drums,

(The Steward kneels.)

They're pounding drums
That shake the skies,

They rattle clappers
To scatter sparrow clouds.
To the shouts of pursuit
Are joined the constant roll of drums,
   (The Wife gestures with her fan to suggest driving off
   birds.)
And the rushing wind
Lashes the waves to whitecaps.
   (The Wife mimes beating the drum.)
Hanawaka, unhappy boy!
Chase away your griefs
As you drive off the waterfowl!
   (The Wife looks at Hanawaka, then faces front.)
When my yearning becomes unbearable
I turn my nightclothes inside out,[4]
Hoping to dream of him,
Only to wake, after fitful sleep,
To the dull thud of the fulling block,[5]
In the chill of night.
   (She comes forward.)
WIFE. My bitterness has grown each day,
   But no one even pities me.
   My tears increase in number,
   My troubled heart beats wildly,
   Wildly as this drum I pound.
   Others will hear this tuneless thumping—
   What will they think? How shaming!
   (The Wife beats the drum.)
   My bitter longing has never lifted

CHORUS. In all the months since he went away;[6]
   Even the full moon with its piercing light
   Cannot dispel the darkness in my heart.
   (She turns to her right.)
WIFE. See how the flocks of birds,
   See how the flocks of birds
   Start up from the rice leaves

Winging towards the clouds.
  (She looks into the distance.)
When shall we see them again?
Their voices tell us of parting
Like cockcrows at break of day;
They tell of separation.
Beat the little drum, the big drum,
Beat them both together—
Drive off the birds, every one!

  (The Wife boards the boat. The Steward rises.)

STEWARD. That's fine! The birds have all left my fields. Why don't you rest now?
  (They all sit. Higurashi rises and faces front.)

HIGURASHI. I have been so interested in watching the bird-scaring boats that I quite forgot I should be hurrying home. There are many boats here, but the ones with the big drums and clappers are the most picturesque. I'll ask that one over there to come closer. *(He turns towards the boat.)* Ahoy there! You—the boat with the big drum and clappers! Come in here!

STEWARD. That's strange! Who around here would dare order about Sako the Steward's boat in such a brusque way? *(He sees Higurashi.)* The man looks like a traveler. I can't imagine who he can be.

HIGURASHI. Come in close here, I said!

STEWARD. This is really incredible!
  (He describes his own actions.) I pole
  my bird-scaring boat up closer.
  (He mimes the action.) I take a careful
  look. *(He drops the pole.)*
  It's Lord Higurashi!
  *(He goes to stage center and bows
  to Higurashi.)*

HIGURASHI. What a surprise! Sako the Steward!
  Is that your boy?

HANAWAKA. No, I am Lord Higurashi's son.

HIGURASHI *(to Hanawaka)*. And is that your mother?

HANAWAKA. Yes. The lady is my mother.

HIGURASHI. Why are you doing this menial work?

HANAWAKA. My father's been in the Capital for years, but we still have no news of him. We thought we could trust Sako the Steward, but he said we had to scare the birds from the fields, or my mother and I would be turned out of our house. He made us so afraid that we got into this terrible boat, and I've been beating the drum. We're not used to working like this. Our luck seems to have run out like the tide. We've really gone down in the world.

(He weeps.)

HIGURASHI. This is unspeakable! They say a warrior's son re-sponds to his mother's wishes even in the womb, and by the time he is six he is ready to kill her enemies.[7] And you, my son, are over ten! How humiliated you must have felt! But I needn't go on. Everything happened because I spent so long in the Capital. I can hardly hold my head up before you. I intend to waste no time in killing this steward. I'll leave his body in the fields to rot. Get off the boat.

(Hanawaka and the Wife leave the boat and sit before the chorus. The stage assistant removes the boat. Higurashi grasps his sword in his hand and takes a few steps towards the Steward. The latter bows deeply.)

HIGURASHI. Well, Steward, that wasn't very prudent of you. When I appointed you my son's guardian I felt sure you would watch over him faithfully, and all the time I was in the Capital I kept wondering how I could reward you adequately. It seems I was wrong. Instead of looking after him, you drove your lord out of his house and employed him as a common laborer. Have you anything to say for yourself? Why are you silent?

(Higurashi draws his sword and takes a few steps. The Steward retreats to the shite-position, and from there bows towards Higurashi. The Wife comes forward and tugs at Higurashi's sleeve.)

WIFE. It is not his fault. The fault lies entirely with Hanawaka's
father, for having abandoned us so long.

> *(She steps back and faces Higurashi, who sits facing her.)*

Once someone strayed
Into a hermit's hut,
And thought he stayed half a day.
But when he returned home
He met his grandchildren
In the seventh generation.[8]
Ten long years of days and months went by,
Then just today you happen to return
And witness our humiliation—
An unlucky turn of events.

CHORUS. I shall speak no more of resentment,
I pray only that for our sakes
You will forgive Sako the Steward!

> *(The Wife and Hanawaka press their hands together in
> supplication before Higurashi.)*

HIGURASHI. How could I refuse such a plea?
The rice is threshed,
And now that autumn has ended
The watchman's work is done.
I forgive you, my steward.

> *(He beckons to the Steward and hands him his sword. The
> Steward goes to stage center and bows to Higurashi.)*

CHORUS. The tale is over, but in later years,

> *(All stand.)*

Hanawaka would inherit
All his lordship's domains.
Like a cherry tree in flower,

> *(Higurashi, the Wife, and Hanawaka exit up the bridge-
> way.)*

And famed beyond his tiny village,
He became a virtuous warrior;
And his line lived on for ages to come,
His line lived on forever.

> *(The Steward remains behind on the stage with Higurashi's
> sword over his shoulder.)*

Notes

1. The name *Hanawaka* may be divided into *hana,* flower, and *waka,* young.

2. From an anonymous poem, no. 172 in the *Kokinshū:* "Just yesterday I plucked the seedlings, but before I knew it the leaves of the rice-plants are rustling and the autumn wind blows."

3. This curious statement, apparently derived from the lines by Po Chü-i quoted in the *Wakan Rōei Shū* no. 126, means that although fallen blossoms obey the natural laws, man's heart is unnatural. The original lines by Po Chü-i, however, have a quite different meaning and background. They were written in grief when Po Chü-i visited the house of his intimate friend Yüan Chen who had just died: "The falling flowers drop from the tree wordlessly, to no purpose; the flowing water, with no intelligence, naturally flows into the pond." In other words, the poem was a complaint over the indifference of the flowers and stream to the human tragedy.

4. It was believed that a person who slept with his nightclothes turned inside out would dream of his absent lover.

5. The dull sound of the fulling block, struck at the end of autumn when clothes were to be changed for the winter, had peculiarly melancholy associations.

6. These lines are apparently derived from a poem by Sugawara no Michizane.

7. These extraordinary abilities of a warrior's son are reported in such works as the *Soga Monogatari.*

8. From poem no. 545 in the *Wakan Rōei Shū* by Ōe no Asatsuna. The poem refers to the woodsman who watches two children playing chess, and after what he thought was half a day the handle of his axe rots away, for hundreds of years have passed while he watched the game.

The Valley Rite

(TANIKŌ)

TRANSLATED BY ROYALL TYLER

INTRODUCTION

This anonymous play has been assigned to the fifth category, but it is certainly not a typical demon play. A boy's love for his mother and his loyalty towards his teacher are miraculously rewarded in the final scene. But what stands out in the reader's mind is the strangeness of the setting for this unexceptionable theme, and especially the barbaric quality of the climax. There is no other scene like it in the present Nō repertory. Although the play is apparently not an early one, it seems to portray an alien place and time, far more remote than the world of the other plays, when even a child's life counted as nothing against the fierce demands of ritual purity. No extant document attests the practice of ritual stoning among the *yamabushi* priests, and the sources of the play are unknown.

The *yamabushi* themselves are ascetics who combine esoteric Buddhism with Shinto practices and mountain worship. In Japanese tradition they are credited with possessing magical powers, and in many Nō plays they are summoned to quell

316

demons. Their founder was En no Gyōja (En the Ascetic), a seventh-century figure of whom little is known. The *yamabushi* are still active today. Their fire ceremonies can be seen in Kyoto; and Ōmine, a peak south of Nara which was the center of En no Gyōja's activities, is still the site of *yamabushi* pilgrimages and rituals. Mount Kazuraki, today called Katsuragi, lies west of Ōmine, and retains its importance to the *yamabushi*.

The structure of the play is unusual. In the version translated, that performed by the Hōshō school, the first part has no *shite*, and the *shite* of the second part does not utter a word. The action instead is centered on the *kokata* and on the *waki*. In other versions the mother in the first part is designated as the *shite* and the character En no Gyōja does not appear at all. Obviously the text has been much mutilated.

The play is in the repertories of all five schools, but is rarely performed, no doubt because the *shite* part is so insignificant.

317

THE VALLEY RITE (TANIKŌ)

(Before the music starts Matsuwaka and his Mother enter. She kneels before the waki-*position, and he before the chorus. The Mother wears the* fukai *mask.*

With the introductory flute Sotsu no Ajari, the Leader, comes down the bridgeway to the first pine. He is dressed in yamabushi *costume and hat and carries a rosary.)*

LEADER. I am a *yamabushi.* I live in the Capital at Imagumano in the Eastern Hills. I have a young disciple named Matsuwaka, a boy whose father is dead and who has no one but his mother. She feels so tenderly towards the unfortunate boy that she keeps him with her all the time. Tomorrow I shall be making my pilgrimage into the mountains. Before I go I shall visit Matsuwaka and say goodbye.

> *(He proceeds to the end of the bridgeway and faces the Mother.)*

Is anyone at home?

> *(Matsuwaka rises and goes to stage center.)*

MATSUWAKA. Who's there? Oh! My Master has come to see us!

LEADER. Well, Matsuwaka! Why have you failed to come to the temple for such a long time?

MATSUWAKA. My mother has not been feeling well, and I haven't been able to leave the house.

LEADER. I am sorry to hear that. Why didn't you let me know? Please tell her I have come.

> *(Matsuwaka stands before the Mother.)*

MATSUWAKA. Mother! My Master has come to see us!

MOTHER. Ask him to come in.

319

MATSUWAKA *(to the Leader).* Please come in.

> *(The Leader kneels at stage center and faces the Mother. Matsuwaka returns to her side.)*

LEADER. I'm sorry not to have visited you for such a long time. Matsuwaka tells me you are ill. How are you feeling?

MOTHER. Oh, much better! Please
don't worry about me.

LEADER. I'm greatly relieved. I've
come here today to tell you
I shall be going up the mountain
and to say goodbye.

MOTHER. I've heard that going up the mountain is an especially arduous act of austerity. Will you take Matsuwaka with you?

LEADER. No, no. Going into the mountains is an act of penance and self-mortification, quite out of the question for a young person.

MOTHER. Well, come back soon, safe and sound.

LEADER. Thank you. I'll be back soon. Matsuwaka, I want you to stay with your mother and take good care of her. I'll be leaving now.

> *(The Leader moves towards the* shite-*pillar. Matsuwaka rises, goes to stage center, and faces the Leader.)*

MATSUWAKA. I have something to tell you, Master.

> *(The Leader stops and faces Matsuwaka.)*

LEADER. What is it?

MATSUWAKA. I would like to go with you up the mountain.

LEADER. Oh, no. I've just told your mother, this pilgrimage involves difficult and exhausting observances. I couldn't think of it. Besides you shouldn't leave your mother when she's ill. It's quite out of the question.

MATSUWAKA. But it's just because my mother is ill that I want to go. I want to pray for her.

LEADER. I see. Filial piety is another matter. Let me ask her.

> *(The Leader kneels at stage center facing the Mother. Matsuwaka returns to sit beside her.)*

LEADER. I was about to leave when Matsuwaka told me he wants to go up the mountain with me. I reminded him that you are ill and that the pilgrimage is much too strenuous for a young person. I refused to take him. But he insists on going so that he can pray for you. What shall I do?

MOTHER. It's just as Matsuwaka told you. There's nothing he
longs to do more than go into the mountains with his
teacher.

(*to Matsuwaka*)

But since the day your father died
You, my only child, have been my life.
Even though we live together,
The moment you are out of sight
I think of you and nothing else.
Show consideration for my love:
Give up this plan. Please do not go.

MATSUWAKA. I know, Mother, but I am determined
To subject myself to hardships
So I may pray for your health in this life.

CHORUS. In face of such resolution
Master and Mother together
Weep at the depth of his love.

MOTHER. Very well then, I cannot keep you.
Go off with your master. But hurry,
Hurry home to me again.

MATSUWAKA. With eager steps I hurry off,
Anticipating my return.
A wearisome road lies ahead—
How far it is to Yamato!

MOTHER. For offerings lovingly tendered

MATSUWAKA. I will rip the sleeves of my priestly robe.[1]

(*During the following passage sung by the Chorus, the
Leader and Matsuwaka move towards the* shite-*pillar. The
Mother rises, takes two or three steps, and watches them
go.*)

CHORUS (*for the Mother*). Even as we part, I know the places
Where you will go. Now, no longer
Shall they be strange to me.
Clouds shall cling to the peaks
Of Takama and Kazuraki,[2]
Never clearing, like your mother's
Tears for her beloved son.
How to bear this pain of parting?

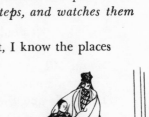

How to bear this pain?

*(The Leader and Matsuwaka exit, followed by the Mother.
The stage assistant places a platform about three by six
feet at stage right. A sapling is set into either end.*

*Enter Matsuwaka, the Leader, the Deputy, and Pil-
grims. All are dressed as* yamabushi *and carry rosaries.
The Leader also wears a short sword. They traverse the
bridgeway and come onto the stage.)*

LEADER. Here is the boy,

Unexpectedly among us,

Dressed to ascend the mountain,

In the cap and stole and mossy robe

Of a *yamabushi* priest.

(They face each other in two rows.)

LEADER AND PILGRIMS *(initially speaking
for Matsuwaka).*

Today at last I set out on the journey,

Today at last I set out on the journey.

My guidance on the Way ahead

Will be my deep resolve,

The strength of my love for my mother.

"There were horses at Kowata

But I came instead on foot."[3]

For whose sake?

For whom do I grieve at Uji Village?[4]

Today, our third day from the Capital,

We come to Spring River and the Moor of Jars.

The river wind is chill, and the plovers cry.

Their voices mark the dusk of day

Their voices mark the dusk of day.

We make out dimly from afar,

We make out dimly from afar

Mount Mikasa in Kasuga;

And now we have passed it by.

Though tempted to pause, we leave behind

The holy cypress grove of Furu;

Nor will we rest beneath Mount Miwa.

Who chose this place for our shelter

At the crest, among mossy rocks?

(The Leader takes a few steps forward, then returns to his former position, indicating they have arrived.)

Weary, we spread our priestly robes
Upon the fresh dew at Kazuraki.
Here we settle for a moment's rest,
Here we settle for a moment's rest.

(The Leader faces front.)

LEADER. We have come so fast that we have already reached the first cave. Let us rest here quietly for a while.

(All move from the waki-*position to a place before the musicians and kneel in a crescent.)*

MATSUWAKA *(to the Leader).* There's something I must tell you, Master.

LEADER. What is it?

MATSUWAKA. I began to feel sick on the way here.

LEADER. Hush! You mustn't say such a thing on this pilgrimage. You are only tired because you are not accustomed to traveling. All you need is a good rest.

(Matsuwaka removes his cap and outer garment, and lies down with his head in the Leader's lap.

The Deputy rises and addresses the Leader.)

DEPUTY. I have something to ask you, sir.

LEADER. What is it?

DEPUTY. I have just been told that the journey is making Master Matsuwaka ill. What is the trouble?

LEADER. He is a child and not accustomed to climbing. He's tired, that's all. There's nothing to worry about.

DEPUTY. I see. I am much relieved. *(He goes to the group of Pilgrims.)*

FIRST PILGRIM. We have just heard that Master Matsuwaka has fallen ill on the way. Why don't we look into this?

DEPUTY. I just asked the Leader. He says that the boy is not ill, only tired.

FIRST PILGRIM. No, the Leader is only making excuses. The boy
is seriously ill. You must inform the Leader that it is our
duty to hurl the boy into the valley, as our Rule requires.

DEPUTY. You are quite right. I shall urge this on our Leader.
(to the Leader) Just now when I asked about Master Matsuwaka you told me that the journey had tired him. But he's
already looking seriously ill. I hesitate to mention it, but our
Rule has prevailed since ancient times. All of us are agreed
that the Valley Rite must be performed.

LEADER. I am well aware of our Rule, but I felt so sorry for the
boy that I chose to overlook it. But there is no helping it. I
will patiently explain our Rule to him. Please give me a few
moments.

DEPUTY. Yes, of course. *(He returns to the group of Pilgrims.)*

LEADER. Now, Matsuwaka, listen carefully to me. Anyone who
falls ill upon this pilgrimage must at once be put to death.
That is what we call the Valley Rite. It is an inflexible rule
that we have observed from ancient times.
If only I could take your place,
How gladly would I yield my life!
But nothing I can do will help.

MATSUWAKA. I understand. I could ask for nothing better than to
give up my life upon this pilgrimage
But I know how much my mother will grieve,

And this fills me with terrible sorrow.
And you, fellow pilgrims, my friends
For so short a time, in former lives
You must have been my companions:
How sad I am to part with you!
CHORUS. The pilgrims, unable to speak,
    Cry aloud, they choke with their tears;
    Their hearts are filled with agony.
    (The Leader looks down in grief.)
PILGRIMS. Each of us is stricken with sorrow;
    Such is the way of an unhappy world.
    But our Rule is a solemn duty,
    And the gods watching from their realms,
    Will not permit us to transgress.
    We must hurl him into the valley.
    (All rise and stare at Matsuwaka.)

LEADER. He and I were sworn to each other
    As master and disciple, but now
    My mouth can find no words of comfort,
    My eyes grow dim with blinding tears.
    (The Leader weeps.)
CHORUS. He neither can restrain the tears
    Nor contravene the sacred Rule.
    He would join the boy if he could
    But even this is forbidden.
    Of all the sad things of this world
    The saddest is this separation:
    He must live and the boy must die.
    If he could die and the boy live
    The pain would surely not be so great.
    (now speaking for the Leader)
"All things shift with the changing world,
Like dreams and wraiths, foam, light and shade,
Like dew or the lightning flash.
Every man must know this truth."[5]
But have I failed to understand it?
Even the rigors of this pilgrimage
Bring no escape from the Burning House;[6]

Still I am assailed by sorrow
No different from a father's love:
The tormenting ties of the Three Worlds.[7]

DEPUTY. Time slips by even as we talk.

CHORUS. Each pilgrim musters up his courage
And cuts through the bonds of attachment
Though anguish sunders their breasts;
They hurl the boy into the ravine
And after him they fling stones and slates
And clods of earth to bury him.
Their hearts are torn and all cry aloud
In bitterest weeping,
In bitterest weeping.

> *(Two Pilgrims take Matsuwaka to the platform and put him on it. They push the platform to the gazing-pillar, then return to their places before the musicians, where they weep.*
>
> *The stage assistant covers Matsuwaka with a robe.)*

DEPUTY *(to the Leader)*. The dawn has broken. We must be on our way at once.

LEADER. I will not go on.

DEPUTY. If you, our Leader, refuse to go on, what will the rest of us do? I beg you, you must leave this place.

LEADER. Calm yourself and listen to me. What am I to say to the boy's mother when I return to the Capital? This grief of mine is no different from the boy's sickness. Throw me into the valley after him.

DEPUTY. How you must be suffering! I shall tell the others. Pilgrims! Our Leader says that grief and sickness are the same thing, and that we must throw him into the valley too. What are we to do?

FIRST PILGRIM. Of course we can understand the Master's feelings. But surely our long years of journeys into the moun-

tains and our painful austerities have been for just such a
moment. Let us pray to our Founder, En the Ascetic, and
to Fudō, the Guardian King, imploring them to bring
Master Matsuwaka back to life.

DEPUTY. An excellent suggestion. *(to the Leader)* Sir, we are all
agreed that the merit obtained through our long years of
ascetic practices has been for this very moment. We will
pray to our Founder, En the Upāsaka,[8] and ask Fudō, the
Guardian King, to use his cord to pull Master Matsuwaka
back to life.

LEADER. I hoped you would be of that mind. I will pray, with
heart and soul. All of you, join your strength with mine!
*(The Pilgrims throw their hanging sleeves over their
shoulders in preparation for the effort of prayer.)*

PILGRIMS. Such grief is more than justified;
To see and hear our Leader suffer
Makes our hearts feel one with his.
(All rise and face front.)

LEADER. Mighty Fudō, Holy Guardian King,
On whose might we have relied for years,

PILGRIMS. Mountain gods and Noble Beings,
Protectors of the Buddhist Law,

LEADER. And above all, our Founder,
En the Upāsaka:

PILGRIMS. Have compassion! Hear our plea!

CHORUS. Aid us! Send us here your envoy,
The god who dances *gigaku!*[9]

*(All vigorously rub their rosary beads and pray, then kneel
in a crescent as before.*

*En the Ascetic enters to the playing of a flute. He wears
a long white wig, a* koakujō *mask, and a Chinese hat, and
carries a pilgrim's staff.)*

EN THE ASCETIC. Through long and painful discipline,
  Through climbing steep mountain paths,
  The Three Poisons are purged away,[10]
  And the dark of delusion dispelled.
  On the seat of the man whose efforts
  Have piled up merit and virtue
  The moon of enlightenment is brilliant,
  It leaves no spot unillumined.

  In the silence where no voice is heard
  If a man reads this holy writing
  The Buddha will reveal his presence,
  In the form of pure and radiant light.[11]
  I pray you all, hearken to my words!
  The child displayed a nature
  Of peerless filial devotion,
  And for that reason I forthwith
  Will restore the boy to life!
  One and all, there is nothing to fear!
LEADER. Oh, awe-inspiring prodigy!
  But what manner of Ascetic are you
  Whose words of comfort we have heard?
EN. You recognize me as an Ascetic. Now I shall reveal myself,
  old and heavy with years.
LEADER. Side-locks and beard turned to snow,
EN. Hair like plaited strands of fiber,
CHORUS. The famed Upāsaka of Mount Kazuraki.
  The famed Upāsaka of Mount Kazuraki
  En the Ascetic, moved by this child,
  Has shown himself before your eyes.
  Oh, awe-inspiring prodigy!
  It is true of all living creatures,
  It is true of all living creatures,

That a parent dotes on its young,
Especially an only child;
Now I shall display to what degree
Buddha's mercy responds to man.
Wait! In a moment you will see!
I summon my messenger,
The demon Gigaku Ginyo.
Appear at my command, appear!
   (The god enters to the rapid playing of
   the flute and stops at the first pine.
   He wears the kobeshimi *mask and a red*
   wig, and carries an axe.)

CHORUS. The *gigaku* god comes flying,
   The *gigaku* god comes flying!
      (The god enters the stage.)
   He kneels before the Ascetic.
      (He kneels before En the Ascetic.)
   He bows his head to receive commands,
      (He rises and bows to En.)
   He soars above to the place of the stoning,
      (He jumps on the platform.)
   He lifts the clods, logs, boulders, and rocks
   Heaped on the boy, and clears them away.
      (He cuts down the two saplings with his axe and sweeps
      them aside.)
   Tenderly, gently, he parts the soil
      (He grasps Matsuwaka's robe.)

   And lifts the boy up, unhurt, in his arms,
      (He puts his arms around Matsuwaka.)
   Then carries him to the Ascetic.
      (They stand before En the Ascetic.)
   The face of the Ascetic shines with joy.
   He strokes the boy's hair with his hand,
      (En touches Matsuwaka's head with his rosary.)
   Compassionately, and speaks to him:
   "Most excellent, most admirable child!
   I marvel at your loving, filial heart!"
   He gives the boy to his master,
   Then turns to make his departure.

(The Ascetic starts down the bridgeway. The god rises and faces upstage.)

As he goes, the god of *gigaku*
Clears the way ahead of him.
They cleave and wind the ascending path,
The steep path of Takama peak:
Up to the clouds and mists they ride,
And, though no one can see from Kazuraki,
In truth they cross the Bridge of Crags
To Ōmine, far, far away.

(The god starts down the bridgeway.)

To Ōmine, far, far away.
They stride out over the void
And disappear from sight.

(As the Chorus stops singing the god stamps in place before the curtain.)

Notes

1. Strips of cloth or paper make a common form of votive offering. The word "sleeve" leads to mention of parting, from the familiar expression *sode no wakare.*

2. Takama is the name of the highest peak of the cluster of mountains known as Kazuraki.

3. Quoted from a poem by Hitomaro included in the collection *Shūishū:* "There were horses at Kowata in Yamashina but I came on foot, for love of you."

4. The name Uji often is used as a pun for *ushi,* meaning sad.

5. A familiar quotation from the *Avatamsaka Sūtra.*

6. A Buddhist metaphor for this mundane world, which should be fled from as if it were a burning house.

7. The three realms of rebirth: the realm of desire, the realm of form, and the realm of formlessness.

8. The term, *ubasoku* in Japanese, is used to describe laymen who, without abandoning their families, wish to lead a religious life.

9. *Gigaku* was an ancient court entertainment, originally from India or Central Asia. It is not clear why En no Gyōja is associated with a deity who performs this dance.

10. The Three Poisons *(sandoku)* are greed, anger, and folly.

11. A quotation from the *Lotus Sutra (Hokkekyō).*

NOTES ON TEXTS CONSULTED
IN MAKING THE TRANSLATIONS

The most reliable and helpful texts are in the two volumes *Yōkyoku Shū* edited by Yokomichi Mario and Omote Akira in the series Nihon Koten Bungaku Taikei. This work is cited below as NKBT. The texts given are the oldest known.

The seven-volume collection *Yōkyoku Taikan* edited by Sanari Kentarō is indispensable, but its notes are not as good or as detailed as those in NKBT and the translations into modern Japanese, though helpful, are often too free to give more than a general idea of the meaning. The work is cited below as YT. The texts used are of the Kanze School in almost all instances.

The three-volume collection *Yōkyoku Shū* edited by Tanaka Makoto in the Nihon Koten Zensho series has good notes and is often helpful in making translations. However, the texts used are of the Komparu School, and the prose parts of the plays often differ considerably from either NKBT or YT. Cited below as NKZ.

The six-volume collection *Yōkyoku Zenshū* edited by Nogami Toyoi-chirō has inadequate notes but is occasionally helpful. The texts used are of different schools.

Nogami Toyoichirō, *Yōkyoku Senshū* in Iwanami Bunko series, no. 1171–73, gives texts of the plays "for reading." There are no notes, but the clear division of parts sometimes makes the book useful.

In addition to the above each school of Nō publishes its own singing texts *(utai-bon)*. These are rarely of help in making translations except if one is particularly interested in the text of a school other than Kanze.

MATSUKAZE. (1) NKBT, Vol. I. (2) YT, Vol. V. (3) Toshi Nosé, "The Noh Play *Matsukaze*," in *Bulletin of the Faculty of Letters, Oka-yama University*, No. 14, May 1960. The Kita School text with a word-for-word translation. (4) Translation in *Japanese Noh Drama*, Vol. III, published by the Nippon Gakujutsu Shinkōkai, 1960. (5) Translation into modern Japanese by Tanaka Makoto in *Yōkyoku* in *Gendaigo-yaku Nihon Koten Bungaku Zenshū*, abbreviated GNKBZ.

MOTOMEZUKA. (1) NKBT, Vol. I. (2) YT, Vol. V. (3) Translation in *Japanese Noh Drama*, Vol. II, 1959.

333

KAYOI KOMACHI. (1) NKBT, Vol. I. (2) YT, Vol. II. (3) Translation by Roy E. Teele in *The Texas Quarterly*, Vol. VII, No. 2 (1964), Teele's translation is cast into lines with the same number of syllables as the original, and can be sung to the original music. (4) NKZ, Vol. II.

SEKIDERA KOMACHI. (1) NKBT, Vol. II. (2) YT, Vol. III. (3) NKZ, Vol. I.

NISHIKIGI. (1) YT, Vol. IV. (2) There is a paraphrase-translation by Ernest Fenollosa and Ezra Pound in *"Noh" or Accomplishment*. (3) NKZ, Vol. II. The present translation was originally published in *Drama Survey*, Summer 1965.

SEMIMARU. (1) YT, Vol. III. (2) Translation by Beatrice Lane Suzuki in *Nôgaku, Japanese Nô Plays*. (3) NKZ, Vol. III.

OBASUTE. (1) YT, Vol. V. (2) NKZ, Vol. I. The present translation was originally published in *Monumenta Nipponica*, Vol. XVIII, 1–4.

HANJO. (1) YT, Vol. IV. (2) NKBT, Vol. I. (3) NKZ, Vol. II. (4) Translation into modern Japanese by Tanaka Makoto in *Yôkyoku* (GNKBZ).

ASHIKARI. (1) NKBT, Vol. I. (2) YT, Vol. I. (3) NKZ, Vol. II.

SHŌKUN. (1) NKBT, Vol. I. (2) YT. Vol. III.

NONOMIYA. (1) NKBT, Vol. II. (2) YT, Vol. IV. (3) GNKBZ. (4) NKZ, Vol. I.

KANAWA. (1) NKBT, Vol. II. (2) YT, Vol. I. (3) NKZ, Vol. II.

YŌKIHI. (1) YT, Vol. V. (2) NKZ, Vol. II. The present translation was originally published in *Malahat Review*, No. 6.

YUGYŌ YANAGI. (1) NKBT, Vol. II. (2) YT, Vol. V. (3) NKZ, Vol. II.

DŌJŌJI. (1) NKBT, Vol. II. (2) YT, Vol. III. (3) GNKBZ. (4) Nogami, *Yôkyoku Senshû*, gives text performed by Komparu School with *kyôgen* of Ōkura School.

SEIŌBO. (1) YT, Vol. III. (2) NKZ, Vol. I.

KANEHIRA. (1) YT, Vol. I. (2) NKZ, Vol. I. The present translation was originally published in *Monumenta Nipponica*, Vol. XVIII, 1–4.

OHARA GOKŌ. (1) YT, Vol. I. (2) NKZ, Vol. I. (2) Translation into French by Noël Peri in *Le Nô*.

TORIOI-BUNE. (1) YT, Vol. IV. (2) Nogami, *Yôkyoku Zenshû*, Vol. IV.

TANIKŌ. (1) *Hôshô Ryū Utai-bon*. The text of the Hōshō School. (2) Nogami, *Yôkyoku Zenshû*, Vol. V. (3) YT, Vol. III. The Kanze text. (4) Waley, *The Nô Plays of Japan*, gives a much-abridged translation of the first part of the play.

SHORT BIBLIOGRAPHY

NOTE: An extensive list of translations of Nō plays into European languages can be found in *Japanese Literature in European Languages* compiled by the Japan P.E.N. Club in 1961 and supplemented by the same organization in 1964. The bibliography on all aspects of the Japanese theatre compiled by René Sieffert under the title *Bibliographie du théâtre japonais* is excellent, but it appeared in 1953, before much important work was published in Japan. The bibliography in *Nō, the Classical Theatre of Japan* by Donald Keene includes both Japanese and Western works.

Araki, James T. *The Ballad-Drama of Medieval Japan.* Berkeley, the University of California Press, 1964.

Fenollosa, Ernest, and Ezra Pound. *The Classic Noh Theatre of Japan.* New York, New Directions, 1959.

Hisamatsu Sen'ichi *et al. Shin Kokin Waka Shū* in Nihon Koten Bungaku Taikei Series. Tokyo, Iwanami, 1958.

Hōshō Kurō (publisher). *Hōshō Ryū Utai-bon.* Tokyo, Wanya Shoten, 1965.

Kawaguchi Hisao and Shida Nobuyoshi. *Wakan Rōei Shū Ryōjin Hishō* in Nihon Koten Bungaku Taikei series. Tokyo, Iwanami, 1965.

Keene, Donald. *Essays in Idleness: the Tsurezuregusa of Kenkō.* New York, Columbia University Press, 1967.

——. *Nō, the Classical Theatre of Japan.* Tokyo and Palo Alto, Kodansha International, 1966.

The Manyōshū. The Nippon Gakujutsu Shinkōkai Translation. New York, Columbia University Press, 1965.

Morris, Ivan. *The Pillow Book of Sei Shōnagon.* 2 vols. New York, Columbia University Press, 1967.

Nippon Gakujutsu Shinkōkai. *Japanese Noh Drama.* 3 vols. Tokyo, 1955–60.

Nogami Toyoichirō. *Yōkyoku Senshū* in Iwanami Bunko series. Tokyo, 1935.

——. *Yōkyoku Zenshū.* 6 vols. Tokyo, Chūō Kōron Sha, 1935–36.

O'Neill, P. G. *Early Nō Drama.* London, Lund Humphries, 1958.

Peri, Noël. *Le Nô.* Tokyo, Maison Franco-Japonaise, 1944.

Renondeau, Gaston. *Le Bouddhisme dans les Nô*. Tokyo, Maison Franco-Japonaise, 1950.

——. *Nô*. 2 vols. Tokyo, Maison Franco-Japonaise, 1954.

Saeki Umetomo. *Kokin Waka Shū* in Nihon Koten Bungaku Taikei series. Tokyo, 1958.

Sanari Kentarō. *Yōkyoku Taikan*. 2d ed. 7 vols. Tokyo, Meiji Shoin, 1954.

Sieffert, René. "Bibliographie du théâtre japonais" in *Bulletin de la Maison Franco-Japonaise*, Nouvelle Série, Tome II, 1953.

——. *La Tradition secrète du Nô*. Paris, Gallimard, 1960.

Tanaka Makoto. *Yōkyoku* in Gendaigo-yaku Nihon Koten Bungaku Zenshū series. Tokyo, Kawade, 1954.

——. *Yōkyoku Shū* in Nihon Koten Zensho series. 3 vols. Tokyo, Asahi Shimbun Sha, 1949–57.

Ueda, Makoto. *The Old Pine Tree and Other Noh Plays*. Lincoln, The University of Nebraska Press, 1962.

Waley, Arthur. *The Nō Plays of Japan*. London, Allen and Unwin, 1921.

Yokomichi Mario and Omote Akira. *Yōkyoku Shū* in Nihon Koten Bungaku Taikei series 2 vols. Tokyo, Iwanami Shoten, 1960–63.